Race, Class, and Affirmative Action

Race, Class, and Affirmative Action

College Admissions in a New Era

JULIE J. PARK

HARVARD EDUCATION PRESS
CAMBRIDGE, MASSACHUSETTS

Paperback ISBN 9798895570456

Library of Congress Cataloging-in-Publication Data

Names: Park, Julie J., 1982– author.
Title: Race, class, and affirmative action : college admissions in a new era / Julie J. Park.
Description: Cambridge, Massachusetts : Harvard Education Press, [2026] | Includes bibliographical references and index.
Identifiers: LCCN 2025024331 | ISBN 9798895570456 paperback
Subjects: LCSH: Universities and colleges—United States—Admission | Affirmative action programs in education—Law and legislation—United States | Education and state—United States | College environment—United States | College applications—United States | Educational equalization—United States
Classification: LCC LB2351.2 .P3735 2026
LC record available at https://lccn.loc.gov/2025024331

Published by Harvard Education Press,
an imprint of the Harvard Education Publishing Group

Harvard Education Press
8 Story Street
Cambridge, MA 02138

Cover Design: Patrick Ciano
Cover Image: tellmemore000 via iStock

The typefaces in this book are Minion Pro and ITC Stone Sans.

Contents

Foreword

In the landscape of higher education, selective college admissions processes have long been scrutinized and debated, and understandably so. Where you go to college significantly shapes future opportunities. Selective colleges and universities offer vast resources to support students' educational journeys, provide access to prestigious networks, and open pathways to positions of power and influence in our society. Graduates have improved career prospects and higher earnings, particularly if they are students of color, low-income students, or members of other historically underserved groups. Yet, individuals from these groups remain severely underrepresented at these institutions. Expanding access to these institutions for historically underserved populations helps ensure that race, ethnicity, immigrant status, sex, gender, and other markers of historically marginalized identities do not determine educational, health, and other life outcomes. These goals serve our mutual interest and that of a just, multiracial democracy.

Yet, the higher education sector faces unprecedented challenges for addressing the racialized and socioeconomic barriers that hinder access to educational opportunities. Evolving legislative and policy pressures have rolled backed equity-promoting and diversity-related programs, and this trend is intensifying with the second Trump administration. Indeed, for decades, the promise of higher education and that of selective and competitive colleges in promoting equal access and opportunity has faced resistance, misunderstanding, and entrenched inequities. The societal benefits of expanding access and opportunity for underserved populations are overlooked. Access to higher education and selective colleges is primarily experienced as an individual benefit, viewed through a zero-sum mentality where one person's gain is perceived as another's loss. And legal and policy debates around selective college admissions, including those around legacy admissions and affirmative action, fuel and intensify this individualistic zero-sum mentality.

In this book, Julie Park meticulously delves into the complexities and inequalities of this system, offering a comprehensive and timely analysis. She examines the broader context of college admissions, including the historical and ongoing exclusion of underrepresented populations. The book highlights how our education system has systematically marginalized certain groups, from the era of segregation to the present day. Racism and inequality in education are persistent issues that continue to shape students' experiences. Through personal narratives, empirical research, and policy analysis, Park disentangles these complexities and inequities in the college admissions process. The stories of students navigating admissions, coupled with rigorous data analysis, provide a compelling and humanizing account of the system's challenges and inequities.

Race, Class, and Affirmative Action: College Admissions in a New Era challenges us to confront these and other uncomfortable truths about our education system. Park's analysis leads us through the everyday policies and practices that colleges engage in, such as legacy preferences, nonresident recruitment, and early decision policies, that exacerbate racial, ethnic, and socioeconomic inequities. These practices, often defended as meritocratic, disproportionately benefit affluent and White students. The book calls for a reevaluation of these policies, advocating for a more inclusive and just approach. Park leads us to envision a future where access to higher education is truly equitable. And she provides a comprehensive analysis of the possibilities for change, ranging from actionable tools for a more equitable review of applicants, to broader strategies for enacting incremental and transformative change in college admissions. The insights and recommendations in these pages are practical steps toward creating a more fair and just educational landscape.

This book is incredibly timely given the Supreme Court's ruling in *Students for Fair Admissions v. Harvard* (2023), which altered the landscape of race-conscious admissions policies. For decades, colleges implemented race-conscious admissions processes to realize the educational and societal benefits of a diverse student body. The Court's ruling in *SFFA* forces institutions to rethink how race is considered in admissions, but not to the extent that opponents of the practice have claimed. It does not prohibit considering race altogether. It allows for an individualized review of how race relates to an applicant's lived experience. This book provides an accessible overview for educators trying to make sense of this complicated ruling within a sociopolitical climate where actors like Ed Blum, who orchestrated the lawsuit, threaten colleges with ongoing lawsuits, generating fear that can lead education professionals to abandon essential policies and practices that remain lawful. Park offers thoughtful and multifaceted strategies for educators to resist these pressures.

The book also highlights the urgency of reassessing current approaches to admissions in the aftermath of the *SFFA* ruling and to do so despite the substantial headwinds facing the higher education sector. Park urges us to rethink the values and practices underpinning college admissions and to strive for a fair, inclusive, and just system. She is both a researcher and a participant in the work she writes about. She is sympathetic to the challenges facing educators and an unflinching critic of the policies and practices that institutions enact to contribute to structural inequities. Her analysis is a challenge and a path forward for educators, administrators, policymakers, and advocates committed to transforming the landscape of higher education for the better.

As a researcher and legal scholar who is deeply invested in realizing the promise of our multiracial democracy, I hope that one day, policies and practices in the legal, policy, and education arenas will serve to expand rather than to restrict access and opportunity for underserved populations. The systematic exclusion of students of color, low-income students, and other historically marginalized groups at selective and competitive colleges harms us all. Colleges and universities, through their admissions policies and practices, can transform what they consider meritorious and deserving of admission to serve their important role in sustaining a just, multiracial democracy. Educational, health, and other life outcomes should not be contingent on race, ethnicity, income, or any other marker of a marginalized identity. Park's examination of the flaws and inequities in the college admission process is both a call to action and an informative roadmap to realize this transformative future. As we move forward in an era of increasing scrutiny and reform in higher education and we grapple with the complexities of college admissions, Julie Park provides a guiding light, illuminating the path toward a more just and inclusive society.

Liliana M. Garces
Ken McIntyre Professor for Excellence in School Leadership
University of Texas at Austin

Introduction

In June 2023, the Supreme Court of the United States (SCOTUS) ruled to restrict race-conscious admissions in the landmark cases *Students for Fair Admissions* (SFFA) *v. Harvard* and *SFFA v. the University of North Carolina* (UNC), *Chapel Hill*. Although anticipated by many, the ruling has sparked a nationwide crisis for the higher education community as institutions grapple with the aftermath of the Court's decision. Many grieved the decision, recognizing that it represented a major rollback of efforts to advance civil rights. Institutions are still trying to understand the fallout from the decision. In Fall 2024, the first press releases documenting the damage rolled out. First, MIT (Massachusetts Institute of Technology) announced that underrepresented racially minoritized (URM) student enrollment plunged from a typical 25 percent of the first-year class to 16 percent.[1] Black student enrollment dropped from 11 to 3 percent of the first-year class at Amherst College, from 13.8 percent to 5.7 percent at Johns Hopkins University, and 7.3 percent to 4.7 percent at Tufts University.[2] Latinx enrollment rose at some institutions but dropped at others, such as Johns Hopkins (20.8 percent to 10.7 percent) and Amherst (12 percent to 8 percent).[3] Certain schools even chose not to report numbers for specific groups.[4] While some schools managed to dodge major drops in diversity, assessing the system-wide impact has been challenging due to shifts in how institutions report data.[5] Still, the negative impact of the ruling was clear at numerous institutions.

Race-conscious admissions, while never perfect, has been a pivotal tool in the history of higher education, enabling the demographic transformation of numerous historically White institutions. Despite the racialized stereotype of the so-called affirmative action baby being Black or Brown, White women and Asian Americans have benefited significantly from such policies over the years, both as direct beneficiaries and then also from being able to experience more diverse campus environments.[6] Still, over the decades, both groups have participated in campaigns to eradicate race-conscious admissions. White women were the face of the lawsuits that preceded the *SFFA* cases at the Supreme Court: *Grutter v. Bollinger*, *Gratz v. Bollinger*, *Fisher I v. University of Texas, Austin*, and *Fisher II v. University of Texas, Austin*. These cases were unsuccessful in dismantling race-conscious admissions. They also did little to shift public opinion against race-conscious policies. The traditional camps of who supported or opposed race-conscious admissions stayed fairly stable. To more meaningfully destabilize race-conscious admissions would take a different strategy.

So Edward Blum, the organizer of the Fisher cases, decided to change tactics. "I needed Asian plaintiffs," he admitted bluntly in a 2015 talk.[7] So much for not judging anyone due to skin color. In this day and age, efforts to court a new anti–affirmative action Cinderella meant setting up a web site with a studious looking Asian American student, with the headline "Were You Denied Admission to Harvard? It May Be Because You're the Wrong Race," and "Harvard University NOT FAIR" blaring in large letters.[8] His timing was fortuitous, coinciding with a period when selective college admissions was becoming even more competitive. Much of this dynamic was due to population growth and external forces; there were simply more students graduating from high school. Additionally, places like Harvard still gave considerable bumps to legacies and recruited athletes, groups that are heavily White.[9] Still, some Asian Americans worried that they were being rejected due to race, and not because of preferences for lacrosse players. Public misconceptions about what race-conscious admissions even was proliferated. Some falsely assumed that schools had quotas against Asian Americans, or that other people of color were being admitted solely because of their race. With all the confusion, race-conscious admissions policies were an easy target to blame.

The rest is history. In 2014, SFFA filed suit in the US District Court for the District of Massachusetts, with whispers that an eventual audience before SCOTUS was the goal. Blum's group also sued UNC in a companion case that did not focus specifically on Asian American plaintiffs, but argued against race-conscious admissions at UNC. Both the district and appellate courts upheld Harvard and UNC's ability to consider, in a limited fashion, race/ethnicity in admissions. However, with its conservative majority, SCOTUS was less sympathetic and ruled that the programs used at both institutions were unconstitutional.

As the higher education community deals with the blow of the SCOTUS decision, confusion persists about what exactly happened with *SFFA v. Harvard*, as well as how to deal with the decision itself.[10] Was race-conscious admissions in higher education totally eliminated, or was it restricted? Can institutions still consider how race shapes applicants' lives? Did SCOTUS rule that Asian Americans were systematically discriminated against by Harvard, or did it sidestep the question? Are there still legal options on the table? (Preview: Yes!) Are race-neutral approaches to pursuing diversity still okay? (Yes!) If universities have to rely increasingly on class-based affirmative action, what do such practices look like, and will they be enough? (Spoiler: Generally not!) What sorts of policies are needed to maximize equity in a new landscape, and what practices should be scrutinized for perpetuating inequality? What about the future of standardized tests, and other parts of the application like the essay and letters of recommendation? How will the ruling affect everyday campus life, and what sorts of programs and initiatives can universities still use to foster inclusive environments?

If you're still trying to make sense of the ruling, you've come to the right place. In *Race, Class and Affirmative Action: College Admissions in a New Era*, I'll walk readers through these thorny questions, helping you understand the implications of the ruling for admissions and campus life. I'll draw on the most relevant research to address questions that institutions are wrestling with after the ruling. Overall, I'll argue that higher education cannot stay content with a system that maintains the status quo. Too many institutions have yet to let go of practices that undermine systemic, transformative change. Still, change is possible, and I'll outline options. I'll also argue for a shift in how we understand selective college attendance. Instead of admissions magically identifying the "best and brightest," going to an "elite" school is very much a "pay to play," racialized system, where admission and attendance often reflect a student's ability to pay for opportunities.

We'll talk about the unique roles of race and class throughout the book. Yes, race and racial inequality have not gone away. Race-conscious admissions is restricted, but it's not totally dead. I'll introduce you to arguments that say *SFFA* is not a particularly colorblind ruling, and explain how institutions still have leeway to consider applicants' experiences related to race. I'll encourage some institutions to consider remaining legal options for defending a more direct, conventional form of holistic race-conscious admissions, such as addressing institution-specific discrimination and institutional obligations under Title VI.[11] These options feel far-fetched in the current political climate, but we never know how the tables might turn. Regardless, the higher education landscape is in dire need of institutions that will explore paths that have yet to be taken. So far, institutions have mainly responded to the *SFFA* ruling with initiatives that are based on socioeconomic status (SES). These efforts are important, but they often are not enough to stem major regressions in racial diversity, given that race and class are not interchangeable in admissions.[12] We cannot abandon the dream of racial equity, even with the ongoing attacks on diversity, equity, and inclusion. In a post-*SFFA* landscape, I'll remind universities of their responsibility to prepare students for our country's racially and economically diverse democracy, while highlighting options that can help advance diversity, equity, and inclusion in these turbulent times.

I won't lie—I'm worried about things. I was worried in 2023, and I'm even more worried in 2025. That said, writing this book has made me surprisingly hopeful. Hearing about transformation at the University of California, Davis School of Medicine makes me hopeful. Seeing so many schools stick with test-optional and witnessing the success of test-free admissions in California makes me hopeful. Reading commentary on how *SFFA* is not a particularly colorblind ruling, and Justice Roberts' words on how institutions can recognize the role of race in students' lives, makes me hopeful.[13] Learning about Supreme Court precedent in *City of Richmond v. J. A. Croson* makes me hopeful. I know more about these things now that I've written an entire book on admissions post-*SFFA*, and I'd like to share them with you. Yes, there's no shortage of things to worry about, but we can't let go of hope. Over the years, so many people have fought and sacrificed so people of all races/ethnicities could pursue education in this country. Remembering their acts of courage and perseverance makes me hopeful.

SOME THINGS TO KEEP IN MIND

A heads-up. The admissions landscape is constantly changing, with updates constantly rolling out about the demographic makeup of student bodies and policies being used by institutions. Over the course of writing this book, I redrafted entire chapters because so many things changed in a very short period of time. As I wrap the book up in early/mid-2025, the country is grappling with the reelection of Donald Trump and the ripple effects for universities. While most of the information in this book should stay relevant, some of the ins and outs of different issues may change due to shifts in policy, political dynamics, litigation, or new research.

Things were already glum for the higher education community following June 2023. Things got even worse in 2025 following President Trump's attacks on everything from academic freedom to diversity, equity, and inclusion. At first, I tried to update this book to address all the executive orders and demands that came out after January 2025. Each declaration felt so surreal; it felt like there couldn't be more rolling down the pipeline. Boy, was I wrong. In the midst of swirling chaos, the book's purpose has taken on a new meaning to me. Yes, it's still a book about what happened in *SFFA v. Harvard* and the implications thereof. However, it's also a book about what *should* be happening due to the Supreme Court 2023 ruling in *SFFA*, versus how things are playing out due to the political chaos of Trump 2.0. The Trump administration has made many suspect claims about what is illegal due to *SFFA*. No doubt, these statements are having a massive chilling effect on the country, as institutions hope to avoid scrutiny. Amidst the confusion, I hope to bring some clarity about what the ruling actually says, and options for institutions moving forward.

Let's not forget that political administrations can and will change. Some of the ideas that I'm bringing up in this book, like the idea of using untested legal defenses for race-conscious admissions, seem far-fetched in the current legal environment. That said, we never know what the future will bring. We can't let the current climate of "repressive legalism" squash our ability to imagine a better future.[14] In this book, I'll stake out some positions, such as my sense that moving back to required standardized testing isn't helpful for racial/ethnic diversity at many institutions. However, I'm open to being proven wrong, and only time will tell how things shake out on the ground. Finally, while I'm covering a lot in this book, there's so much to say about the SCOTUS decision and race-conscious admissions that I don't address due to space and my own limitations. For example, I don't do a deep dive into the details of *SFFA v. UNC*, nor do I spend a lot of time unpacking the dissenting opinions filed in *SFFA*. I don't go into detail on the implications of *SFFA* for Native American and other Indigenous populations, among other topics. Whole other books could be written on those topics, and I do hope that future authors will give them the space that they deserve.

Another heads-up: Throughout the book, I am going to use the term *conventional race-conscious admissions* to refer to holistic, race-conscious admissions as it was practiced at most selective colleges and universities prior to the *SFFA* ruling. The practice of giving students points for being from a particular racial/ethnic group was struck down in the SCOTUS ruling in *Gratz v. Bollinger* in 2003, leaving schools with non–points based, holistic, race-conscious admissions, a.k.a. "conventional" race-conscious admissions. Such policies had been used at Harvard even before the *Bakke* case in 1978, where students were evaluated in a holistic fashion, versus associating race/ethnicity with points or some sort of automatic bump. In conventional race-conscious admissions, an admissions reader could view a student's self-identified racial/ethnic identification as listed on the application. However, one's race/ethnicity did not provide the applicant with any sort of automatic advantage in the admissions process. Instead, the reader had direct knowledge of the student's race/ethnicity and could use it to contextualize a student's experiences, enhancing understanding of how a student might contribute to the diversity of a student body. Contrary to popular opinion, being a URM student did not result in automatic admissions. In the Harvard case, expert David Card estimated that the boost associated with coming from a URM background in general was quite small, smaller than the effect associated with one's intended major, intended career, or neighborhood/school context.[15] In short, race was not operating in a formulaic, determinative way.

To note, disagreement exists over whether holistic race-conscious admissions even is affirmative action, although the two terms are often used interchangeably.[16] Just knowing an applicant's race and taking it into context does not mean that an institution will act affirmatively in anyone's favor. That said, race-conscious admissions opens the door for institutions to act affirmatively if they choose to, and it has been the primary vehicle for affirmative action–related efforts in admissions for decades. I actually would have preferred using "race-conscious admissions" in the book title, but nothing sells a book like alliteration (or let's hope). For the most part, in this book, we're going to be discussing the specific issue of race-conscious admissions as the issue addressed by SCOTUS in *SFFA*.

In full disclosure, I served as a consulting expert in *SFFA v. Harvard* on the side of Harvard, and all opinions here are my own. Tracking the case closely, I learned a lot about the role of social science in the legal arena. A huge part of the Harvard case was the "Battle of the Statistics," where experts David Card and Peter Arcidiacono each filed mammoth reports analyzing Harvard's data and of course, came to different conclusions. The reports are a great example of all the microlevel decisions that go into an analysis, which in turn can influence the outcome of a study. For example, Card observed how Arcidiacono omitted certain variables from his models, such as private school attendance, parental occupation, and intended career.[17] Arcidiacono excluded the athletes, legacies, donor-related children, and children of faculty/staff (ALDC) from his baseline sample, even though these students make up almost 30 percent of accepted students.[18] He also excluded early action applicants from the baseline sample, which struck me as odd.[19] Arcidiacono argued that even if he made the changes that Card argued for, his conclusion that Harvard discriminated against Asian Americans would remain the same. Still, key differences existed between the models.

The dueling expert reports remind us how research doesn't just fall down from the sky from stone tablets—it's constructed by ordinary people who bring their own worldviews and perspectives to the table. The different reports showcase the myriad of choices that go into constructing an analysis *and* interpreting its findings. We'll come back to the issue of interpretation a lot, especially in our conversations around standardized testing in chapter 4. There's research, and then there's what you think should happen due to the findings. Oftentimes, there isn't a single obvious path forward, and it's important to consider all the potential options and trade-offs in policy decisions. Hopefully, this book will help you think through the options that exist based on the research that's out there.

COMING ATTRACTIONS: WHAT WE'RE GOING TO COVER

The book is organized into three main sections. The first two chapters will address the current context surrounding selective college admissions and the SCOTUS ruling itself. Chapter 1, "Selective College Admissions: A Broken System, Even Before the Supreme Court Ruling," will explain problems with college admissions that existed prior to the SCOTUS ruling. I'll talk about forces that have worked to "push out" racially minoritized students (and in particular, URM students), as well as those that work to "pull in" other students. Given these forces, race-conscious admissions was, and still is, a much-needed intervention in a landscape of entrenched inequality. While far too many students face notable barriers to college attendance, others experience individual and structural-level privilege that advantages in them the process, from paying $5,000 to "publish" a research paper to paying thousands of dollars a year to play travel/club sports.[20] Institutions reward this behavior, with even public, taxpayer supported land-grant institutions deploying practices that privilege the wealthy.[21] Altogether, I'll explain how contemporary selective college admissions is a relentless rat race: a perfect storm where scarcity, both real and perceived, has been met with unprecedented high demand in a system of widening inequality. The result is a system of perverse incentives, where high levels of stress are all too common. In the end, no one is very happy, and almost everyone loses, whether from the resulting inequality or the adolescent mental health crisis. I'll argue that these issues, both growing inequality and heightened anxiety over competitive college admissions, set the stage for the *SFFA* lawsuit.

In chapter 2, "*Students for Fair Admissions v. Harvard*: What Exactly Happened?," I will explain how the frenzy of increased competition laid the groundwork for the *SFFA* lawsuits, where Blum and friends alleged that Harvard intentionally discriminated against Asian Americans. I'll unpack the confusion surrounding what is still permissible under law, addressing questions such as: Is there actually a ban on affirmative action and more specifically, race-conscious admissions? Is race-conscious admissions completely dead, or just restricted? Does *SFFA* apply to all of campus life, as claimed by the Trump administration, or just admissions? Should institutions still collect data on race/ethnicity for applicants? Can students talk about race in the application? Did SCOTUS rule that there was intentional discrimination against Asian Americans by Harvard? Do any legal options still exist to defend conventional race-conscious admissions?

Chapters 3 to 6 will discuss policy needs, responses, and initiatives related to the ever-changing admissions landscape. In chapter 3, "Pursuing Diversity in a New Era: Easier Said than Done," I'll discuss existing and evolving approaches to expanding access after the ruling, including considering adversity, life circumstances, and SES in college admissions. Just dropping race-conscious admissions policies is no automatic guarantee that economic diversity, let alone racial diversity, will increase. The situation isn't as simple as "hey, colleges can't consider race directly anymore, so let the floodgates open for low-income students who have been shut out." Greater economic diversity is worth pursuing, but will require much intentionality. We'll look at seeds of hope, such as the UC Davis School of Medicine, and discuss the investments needed to make institutional transformation happen. We'll talk through tools with potential for modest change (e.g., the College Board's Landscape tool, direct admissions), tools that need improvement (percent plans), and tools that probably won't work (lotteries). We'll also discuss research on ways to improve holistic review, such as the use of contextualized measures that compare a metric like GPA to the median score at the high school. Finally, I'll highlight how institutions need to stop practices that undermine diversity.

In chapter 4, "Test-Optional, Test-Required, or Test-Free? The Debate over Standardized Tests," I tackle the hot potato of standardized testing. During the pandemic, an unprecedented number of schools went test-optional, and others like the giant UC system went test-free. In 2024, some elite schools returned to requiring tests. While the SAT was known for being a gatekeeper prior to the pandemic, some elite schools that brought back testing claimed that the SAT/ACT was good for access. Say what? Needless to say, I like to think about the testing debate of the 2020s as existing in two eras: "Before Opportunity Insights" and "After Opportunity Insights." Opportunity Insights is the elite research group headed by Raj Chetty of Harvard University. In this chapter, I'll unpack claims made during both eras, and will argue that the research on testing doesn't point in a singular direction. There's a lot of gray, and people are shaped by their personal perspectives on testing. I'll do my best to walk readers through different angles of the debate, as institutions consider the pros and cons of test-optional, test-required, and test-free admissions. It seems unlikely that required testing will bolster diversity, especially not racial diversity, given decades of research on how race and class aren't interchangeable in admissions.[22]

In chapter 5, "Inequality Beyond Tests: Extracurricular Activities, Letters of Recommendation, and Essays," I will discuss inequality beyond standardized tests affecting college applications. While essays, letters of recommendation, and extracurricular activities have flown under the radar for some time, recent research points to how nonstandardized parts of the application are influenced by inequality.[23] I'll highlight the opportunities and challenges related to these parts of the applications, especially in light of SCOTUS's conclusion that institutions can still consider how race shapes student experiences through the essay. I'll emphasize the importance of admissions systems accounting for context and opportunity when evaluating nonstandardized components.

Chapter 6, "Implications for Campus Life: How Demographic Changes Affect Students' Lives," will address the implications of the ruling for everyday campus life. On the broadest level, the SCOTUS ruling will result in a drop in Black, Latinx, and Indigenous representation at many schools, which is expected to result in greater marginalization, tokenization, and isolation for these students. Projected shifts in both the racial/ethnic and socioeconomic composition of student bodies will affect campus racial dynamics. One key issue is the likely decrease in middle-class Black enrollment at some campuses. Even when admitted, Black students may choose to attend other institutions due to issues in campus racial climate.[24] Middle-class Black students are often a critical "bridge" at historically White institutions, bridging social divides between students from both different economic and racial backgrounds.[25] I will also discuss how programs supporting student body diversity are still fully legal under the ruling, such as residence halls highlighting the experiences of communities of color, racial/ethnic and cultural student organizations, and cultural centers. While the current political landscape is challenging, we must push back against "repressive legalism," where institutions cower to political forces instead of standing up for their missions and values.[26] Finally, I will remind institutions of their crucial responsibility to foster nondiscriminatory environments under Title VI of the Civil Rights Act.

We'll end with a call to reimagine selective college admissions. Admissions is not a culling of the supposed "best and brightest," as some like to think. In reality, it's a process that identifies talented students among those able to pay for attendance, as well as the experiences that got them admitted. Echoing the work of scholars like Lani Guinier and Natasha Warikoo, I'll call for a reenvisioning of "deserving-ness" (as in, who "deserves" to attend a selective institution) driven heavily by societal priorities.[27] We also need greater support for regional comprehensive colleges, minority serving institutions, and community colleges, which do so much of the heavy lifting in postsecondary education. Government and philanthropy must invest aggressively in these sectors, which reach the greatest number of low-income and racially minoritized students. That said, we cannot forget the need for racial diversity within selective institutions as well. Precedent says that when access is restricted in the nonprofit sector, URM students are more likely to end up at for-profit institutions, including those that are known for predatory practices.[28]

Finally, I'll remind students and families that it's not necessarily about where a student attends college, but what they make of the experience that matters the most. Institutions must help enrolled students reap the benefits of higher education. In order to allow students to reach their potential, society has a responsibility to invest in the sectors of higher education that have been traditionally underfunded and under-resourced due to societal inequality and institutionalized racism. At the same time, the selective college sector has a responsibility to move toward disrupting societal inequality, instead of perpetuating it.

Throughout the book, I'll draw on a range of empirical research studies, both quantitative and qualitative, from a variety of authors and sources. As the admissions landscape is rapidly changing, institutions are releasing the results of their own internal analyses on issues like academic performance under test-optional policies, so we'll refer to those where relevant. Nerd alert: We're at an exciting period in admissions research, where tools like natural language processing and machine learning are enabling researchers to study nonstandardized text within massive datasets. These data include hundreds of thousands of applications, allowing us to study components like letters of recommendation at unprecedented scale. Some of the research I'll reference comes from my work at the College Admissions Futures Co-Laborative (CAF Co-Lab), which has been kindly funded by the Bill & Melinda Gates Foundation to conduct research on test-optional admissions and the future of the college application.[29]

A LITTLE BIT ABOUT YOUR TOUR GUIDE

Let me introduce myself as your tour guide through the research. I'm a second-generation Korean American from southwestern Ohio. I grew up within an immigrant community where talking about where "so-and-so" was going to college was a popular topic of conversation. Even at a young age, I could tell that certain places were more valued than others. Still, my high school was pretty laid-back about college admissions, and admit rates were higher in the late 1990s. I don't remember many people being very stressed out about the admissions process—maybe one or two kids, but they were more the exception than the norm. I studied for the SAT with a book and did some practice tests, as did my siblings before me. I was pretty close to going to Ohio State University (no one said "the" back then), the ultimate destination for many at my high school, from the valedictorian to the more lackluster student.[30] Instead, I ended up at Vanderbilt, receiving what used to be a race-conscious scholarship.[31] When I got to college, the University of Michigan admissions cases were making their way through the courts. I became interested in social science research on the educational benefits of diversity related to the cases, which led me to UCLA for my graduate studies.[32]

Once there, I quickly noticed the SAT prep centers that peppered the strip malls of the San Gabriel Valley and other Asian American ethnic enclaves. As someone who grew up thirty minutes away from the region's only (tiny) Korean grocery store, it was fascinating.[33] Living in California made me realize that the Asian American community was incredibly diverse. I met many Asian Americans who had passed through community college, and found out that over 40 percent of Asian American students enroll in community college.[34] My church had a good number of men who had started at UCLA and then left school due to academic challenges. All of these experiences have made me curious as a researcher to understand the different contexts that affect how students approach going to college, especially Asian Americans. My work in the area felt pretty obscure, until SFFA filed suit against Harvard.

In many ways, the book you're reading now is a continuation of my first two books, which both address the intersections between college admissions, racial diversity, and campus life. My first book, *When Diversity Drops: Race, Religion, and Affirmative Action in Higher Education* highlights how major changes in public policy trickle down and affect the everyday lives of students.[35] Beyond the numbers, changes in admissions policy can affect who can be a potential roommate, dialogue partner, lab mate, or life partner. *When Diversity Drops* tells the story of a religious student organization that transformed from a predominantly White group with a largely colorblind outlook to a much more racially diverse group that spoke frankly about race. The group had a hard time sustaining that diversity after the drop in Black enrollment that followed Proposition 209, which ended race-conscious admissions in California.

Students involved in the community I studied went on to found and support multiracial churches and civic organizations scattered around California. One is now a mayor, and many alumni work in jobs where they're trying to enact social change. Many spoke about how critical it was for them to form meaningful interracial friendships during some of their most formative years. After doing talks on the book for a year or two after it came out, I thought the book had lost some of its relevance. It was a cautionary tale of "what could happen." After the Supreme Court affirmed race-conscious admissions in *Fisher I* and *Fisher II*, it seemed like the worst had passed. Unfortunately I was wrong, and so *When Diversity Drops* has popped back into my brain as I think through the repercussions of *SFFA* for campus life.

In my second book, *Race on Campus: Debunking Myths with Data*, I set out to challenge key myths around campus race relations and college admissions.[36] These include the ideas that students of color are to blame for campus racial divides, that Asian Americans are hurt by race-conscious admissions policies, and that universal SAT prep is the answer to inequality. I wrote the book before *SFFA v. Harvard* went to trial in the lower courts, let alone SCOTUS, and also before the widespread adoption of test-optional admissions. Even though many things have changed since the book came out in 2018, it still provides helpful context on issues affecting colleges and universities, so pick up a copy to learn more.

Race, Class, and Affirmative Action: College Admissions in a New Era is sort of a sequel to *Race on Campus*: how to think about the *SFFA* trial and ruling, as well as how to make sense of the research surrounding college admissions. Back when I wrote *Race on Campus*, I had no idea that we would have a worldwide pandemic, leading to the unprecedented adoption of test-optional. I couldn't even imagine test-free admissions. Of course, the landscape around admissions keeps changing, and this book helps document the current moment.

My present day environment also shapes my perspective on admissions. I currently reside in the highly competitive DC/Maryland/Virginia region, a coastal hub for anxious overachievers. The region's largest employer is the federal government (I believe that's still true post-DOGE), so we probably have the highest per capita concentration of high school nerds in the country. Fortunately, much of the country is less intense. Still, more and more people are running on the hamster wheel of competition, status, and upward striving; college admissions is often the culmination of these efforts. Given the affluence that surrounds parts of the DC metropolitan area, it's an interesting place to see how people are playing the admissions "game." What options can money buy? What choices are parents stressing about at earlier and earlier ages? Altogether, it's a prime place to observe some of the brokenness of the system, as well as the need for reform. I'm also the parent of two young children, so I think a lot about topics like extracurricular activities, school context, and the future of testing. Altogether, I'd like to see a saner system for their sake. I also want them to be able to experience the learning and richness that comes from being in a racially and economically diverse community during college. With that, it's time to turn to understanding some of the context influencing how admissions has evolved over time, the backdrop for what would become *SFFA*.

1

Selective College Admissions

A Broken System, Even Before the Supreme Court Ruling

Every summer, high school students around the country work summer jobs, attend sleepaway camp, or circle parking lots for marching band practice. Another lucky group will plunk down $5,000 to $10,000 to develop a research paper, with the goal of boosting their college applications. Beefing up extracurricular achievements is a top priority for students hoping to attend a name-brand institution in the twenty-first century. The high school research industry, detailed in an investigation led by journalist Daniel Golden, is one of the more recent absurdities to hit admissions.[1] Families pay $2,500 to $10,000 to organizations that will match their children with a mentor, often a graduate student or adjunct paid $150 or $200 an hour.[2] The mentor helps them pick a topic and develop a paper, usually over the course of ten to twelve weeks. Collectively, the programs serve an estimated twelve thousand students every year. One admissions officer told Golden: "There are very few actual prodigies. . . . A sophomore in high school is not going to be doing high-level neuroscience. And yet, a very high number of kids are including this." Colleges eat it up. Columbia and Yale specifically encourage students to submit academic research.[3] Organizations like Lumiere Education and Scholar Launch steer students toward a group of "journals" which publish research from high school students, and a number of the journals are run by the organizations themselves.[4] Organizations also support unreviewed preprints, which explains how an article extolling the virtues of Chick-Fil-A landed on the Scholar Launch website before it was removed.

For years, affluent families have used money and connections to try to get ahead in the admissions race. The high school research industry represents a new level of absurdity, a mirror into how some families are willing to do almost anything to help their kids get into an "elite" institution. Despite rising distrust of higher education among sectors of society, many people remain invested in the idea that a college degree, ideally from a reputable, name-brand institution, is a piece of insurance to buffer against the uncertain future. Moving forward, I'm going to use the phrase "name-brand" to encompass both "elite" institutions as well as institutions that are still desirable to students but increasingly competitive, such as state flagship institutions.

Reflecting this dynamic, many families take on considerable debt to make college dreams come true.[5] The Varsity Blues scandal showed how the mega-rich were even willing to break the law to secure spots. Ironically, it's relatively affluent families who are most anxious about admissions and preserving their economic status; *New Yorker* columnist Jay Caspian Kang wryly nicknamed this cohort the "panicking class."[6] In light of the 2008 economic crisis and the general sense that no one really has your back in the individualistic U-S-of-A, a name-brand college education remains desirable. Even if AI is going to take over all of our jobs one day, we still want a nice bumper sticker and sweatshirt to show our friends.[7]

To understand the challenges already facing college admissions before the *SFFA* ruling, we need to take a step back and understand more about how we ended up in the current environment for selective/rejective college admissions. In this era of late-stage capitalism, admit rates are miniscule and rich kids can jump to the front of the line through early decision policies. It's a landscape of strange contradictions, where institutions voiced support for race-conscious admissions and pledge to foot the bill for low-income students, but also defend preferences that mostly benefit White, affluent students. We have taxpayer-supported state institutions spending big bucks to recruit at rich high schools across the country.[8] In a "survival of the fittest" atmosphere, services exist to help students jump through any hoop, from the private college consultant to the high school research industry. Really, it's all a little dystopian.[9]

To better understand this context, we'll cover a few areas. First, we'll review some of the historical "push-out" forces that have kept historically underrepresented populations either explicitly or informally excluded from higher education. Given these dynamics, we'll discuss how conventional race-conscious admissions was a necessary intervention. Next, we'll highlight "pull-in" factors that worked to attract upper-middle-class and rich students, White students, and to some extent, East and South Asian American students. Of course, "push-out" and "pull-in" factors work in tandem, as structures that bring certain students in can lead to others being pushed out.[10] Finally we'll touch on some of the external forces that help explain why college admissions feels so terrible right now, and the implications for society.

HISTORICAL "PUSH OUT" FACTORS: WHERE WE'RE COMING FROM

Both private and public institutions are affected deeply by our country's legacy of racism and segregation.[11] Much of name-brand higher education was literally built by enslaved people, on land seized from Indigenous tribes.[12] Still, it was never meant for them and their descendants. Our country suffers from collective amnesia about how bad our education system has been to people of color over time. It's worth recapping some of the basics: Anti-literary laws made it illegal to teach enslaved individuals to read in most slave states; schools for Black children were systematically underfunded and under-resourced under segregation; and some public school districts closed their doors completely post-*Brown* rather than integrate.[13] Let's not forget landmark lawsuits that challenged segregation affecting Asian American, Latinx, and Native American students. In *Tape v.*

Hurley, which preceded *Brown* by seventy years, the parents of Mamie Tape sued after their daughter and other children of Chinese descent were not allowed to attend Spring Valley Primary School.[14] In *Mendez v. Westminster*, Thurgood Marshall successfully represented Sylvia Mendez, an eight-year old girl who had been turned away from a California "Whites only" public school.[15] We must remember the horrors affecting education for Native American students. These include the forced removal of children from families and the brutal conditions of Native American boarding schools, where children were subject to beatings and sexual abuse.[16]

A pernicious myth persists that Black people and communities do not "value" higher education when in fact they have risked their lives for it. This false but popular belief overlooks how Black individuals attend four-year colleges at higher rates than their precollege economic resources would predict, reflecting how much Black families value education.[17] Over the years, Black communities have persistently supported schools for their youth and fought for the right to learn. Because most postsecondary institutions barred Black students from attending, dedicated educators founded Historically Black Colleges and Universities (HBCUs) to advance the education of Black students. Some predate the Civil War (e.g., Cheney University in 1837, Wilberforce University in 1856, Lincoln University in 1854) and many more followed after the end of the war in 1865. During the nineteenth and even into much of the twentieth century, higher education remained either completely or mostly segregated, with rare exceptions such as Oberlin and Berea College.[18] A very small number of students of color attended historically White institutions outside of the South, but for the most part, these schools remained overwhelmingly White (and White male) for years.

A year before the Emancipation Proclamation and still three years before the end of the Civil War, Congress passed the First Morrill Act of 1862 to fund land grant institutions across the country, with the idea of opening higher education to the (generally, White male) masses and funding institutions that would serve state needs. The federal government gifted funds to the states from the sale of lands taken from Indigenous communities.[19] Black students were shamefully barred from attending many of these institutions well into the twentieth century. Hiram Whittle, the first

Black undergraduate to attend the University of Maryland, College Park (my employer), was not allowed to enroll until 1951, following considerable pressure from the NAACP.[20] With the Second Morrill Act of 1890, funding for land grant institutions was concentrated in Southern states. In a deal struck with Southern Democrats, states were required to either establish a land grant institution devoted to educating Black students (i.e., a HBCU) or show that the state's land grant institution was open to all regardless of race. As compellingly documented by Adam Harris in *The State Must Provide: Why America's Colleges Have Always Been Unequal—and How to Set Them Right*, some states went to astonishing lengths to ignore both of these obligations, opening the door to legal challenges which they fought persistently.[21]

Other efforts to expand access to higher education included the GI Bill (i.e., the Servicemen's Readjustment Act of 1944), whose benefits were often denied to Black veterans; these brave veterans fought for freedom overseas only to have it denied to them at home.[22] Across the country, even when Black students were technically able to attend a school with White students, they were often relegated to second class citizenship. At schools in the Midwest, both public and private, Black students were often not allowed to live on campus, eat in the main dining hall, or use campus facilities.[23] Jim Crow is thought of as a Southern phenomenon, but separation and segregation were still common in other parts of the country. Other students of color also experienced exclusion in campus life. Up until into the 1950s, rules governing historically White sororities and fraternities included "discriminatory clauses against Negroes and Orientals," and more informal segregation continues to persist in Greek life, as it does in other spheres of campus life.[24]

While the historically White sector of higher education dragged its feet to integrate, HBCUs thrived against the odds, punching well above their weight. Over the years, HBCUs played a tremendously outsized role in expanding education to Black students, and they continue to do so today: While they make up only 3 percent of higher education institutions, they educate about 10 percent of all Black undergraduates, almost 20 percent of Black students who graduate, and about 25 percent of all Black STEM degree recipients.[25] In earlier decades, they educated an even greater share of Black students, awarding 35 percent of degrees to Black college graduates in the 1970s.[26] As tremendous as these accomplishments are, HBCUs have been and continue to be under-resourced and underfunded. Separate but equal was a delusion. According to the federal government, sixteen states collectively underfunded (a more polite word for "ripped off") HBCUs by an estimated $12 billion dollars.[27] In Maryland, after years of haggling and litigation, the state settled and agreed to compensate four HBCUs in the state with $577 million.[28] Still, systemic underfunding has left these institutions at a major disadvantage over the years, with endowments being a tiny fraction of endowments at most historically White schools.[29]

RACE-CONSCIOUS ADMISSIONS AS AN IMPERFECT BUT NECESSARY INTERVENTION

The unequal treatment of HBCUs parallels other injustices enacted against communities of color in educational spaces and society. In his famous 1965 commencement speech at Howard University, President Lyndon B. Johnson acknowledged this history when laying the groundwork for affirmative action and, in turn, race-conscious admissions policies. He declared: "Freedom is not enough. You do not take a person who, for years, has been hobbled by chains and liberate him, bring him up to the starting line of a race and then say, 'you are free to compete with all the others,' and still justly believe that you have been completely fair."[30] Universities created programs to expand access, but some initiatives faced legal challenges in the courts, culminating in the 1978 case *Regents of the University of California v. Bakke*. After welcoming an inaugural class made up of all White students, the UC Davis School of Medicine began to reserve a certain number of seats for racially minoritized students. This practice of setting aside seats was struck down in *Bakke*, and the majority of justices rejected the university's argument that the program was needed to remedy historic, societal discrimination. Still, race-conscious admissions survived. Justice Lewis Powell lauded Harvard's holistic, non-quota-based, race-conscious program as an exemplar, and held that universities could still consider race in a nondeterminative fashion based on the educational benefits of engaging in a racially diverse student body.[31]

This rationale, often referred to as the *diversity defense*, was later upheld by SCOTUS majority in the 2003 case *Grutter v. Bollinger*.[32] In some ways, the defense is a roundabout, indirect way to get at the country's legacy of discrimination. In the US, deep educational and residential segregation persists. College is a chance to break the cycle of segregation, and students benefit greatly when engaging across racial/ethnic lines during this critical developmental time period.[33] Well into the twenty-first century, America's schools are still segregated, with one-third of students attending a school where 75 percent or more students were from the same racial/ethnic group, and 14 percent attending one where 90 percent or more were from the same racial/ethnic group.[34] Educational segregation is intertwined with residential segregation, which stems from historic injustices including redlining, the denial of GI Bill housing benefits to Black veterans, and other factors.[35] Part of why engaging across difference is so meaningful and necessary is because of the racial divisions that separate us in the first place.

History and the ramifications of historic racial inequality all speak to the need for race-conscious admissions within higher education, even if the diversity defense only tackles the problem in an indirect way. Conventional race-conscious admissions was (and still is) a necessary intervention given the forces that have pushed racially minoritized students away from selective higher education institutions. Besides the country's history of segregation and exclusion, other push-out forces include the regime of standardized testing that reigned until the pandemic and has since been restored at some schools, unequal access to advanced curriculum, and disparities in college-going support.[36]

Contrary to public perception, conventional race-conscious admissions was never a formula that guaranteed admission for even high-achieving URM students.[37] It allowed admissions professionals to see a student's race/ethnicity and consider it as one of numerous factors shaping a student's experiences, background, and potential to contribute to the university community. Holistic review means evaluating the student as a whole person and not weighing any criteria, trait, or piece of context in a deterministic fashion, including race/ethnicity.

Two things are true. Yes, race-conscious admissions and affirmative action worked. Yes, they couldn't fix everything. In analyzing data on bachelor's degree attainment from the Education Longitudinal Study of 2002, Christina Ciocca Eller and Thomas DiPrete, faculty at Harvard and Columbia, respectively, observe both the achievements and limitations of these policies: "Institutional structures such as affirmative action also play a role in raising black students' BA attainment at the population level. . . . Our own results confirm that higher-quality colleges facilitate higher levels of BA completion among black students, especially among students with higher precollege dropout risk. . . . Additionally, there is persuasive evidence that students who attend selective colleges receive benefits in terms of access to elite jobs and higher wages . . . and that the effects of elite colleges are particularly strong for minority students. . . . Accordingly, affirmative action arguably plays an important role in reducing racial inequality in the long term, despite evidence of persisting discrimination against black elite-college graduates. . . . However, only a relatively small proportion of black students benefit from affirmative action."[38]

As the authors note, race-conscious admissions *has* worked to improve educational and societal outcomes for Black students and other students of color.[39] At the same time, the institutions that use such policies educate a fairly small slice of all Black, Latinx, Indigenous, and Southeast Asian American students, even if those same institutions are highly influential. In order to advance racial equity, we also need to help students of color succeed and graduate from institutions that educate a broader proportion of society, including open-access institutions.

Arguably, many institutions did not maximize the potential of conventional race-conscious policies while they still had them. Affirmative action was pivotal to opening up access to historically White institutions, but not enough was done to strengthen access, even in states with higher support for race-conscious policies. For example, in 1968, the University of Illinois, Urbana-Champaign (UIUC) launched "Project 500" in an effort to diversify. That year, 444 African American students enrolled at

UIUC, experiencing second-class treatment by fellow students and campus administration.[40] You would think that Project 500 was just the beginning, but decades later, the number of Black students enrolled at UIUC hadn't grown much. In 2019, 521 Black students enrolled in the first-year class, 474 in 2018, and as few as 356 in 2014. In 1968, Black students comprised 7.7 percent of the student body, and in 2019, that percentage was even smaller (6.8 percent of the first-year class).[41] The numbers have not changed substantially despite tremendous growth in Black high school graduates in the state.[42] There are a number of reasons that UIUC can cite for low Black enrollment over the years, from bad funding models to a negative campus climate, but it's jarring to note the lack of progress despite the concurrent use of race-conscious admissions and scholarships.

Even before *SFFA*, numerous state institutions were going in the wrong direction with Black enrollment. A report by the late, great Andrew Nichols of Education Trust found that Black enrollment had regressed since the year 2000 at over half of the country's most selective 101 public colleges and universities.[43] Too many schools didn't maximize the potential of race-conscious policies, including race-conscious financial aid, to enroll and support Black students. Things were even worse at schools that couldn't use race-conscious admissions, or chose not to. In Mississippi, in 2021, only 8 percent of undergraduates at the University of Mississippi identified as Black, despite Black students being 48 percent of public high school graduates in the state.[44] In Georgia, 36 percent of public high school graduates were Black, but only 6 percent of undergraduates at the University of Georgia were.[45] Equity gaps also exist in states that used race-conscious admissions before *SFFA*. At UMD, 12.6 to 12.9 percent of undergraduates identified as Black from 2022 to 2024, a number that looks great compared to some other public schools.[46] Still, in the state of Maryland, over 30 percent of individuals identify as Black.[47]

Another reason why race-conscious admissions couldn't live up to its potential is because some schools didn't implement other needed reforms. Sociologists prabhdeep singh kehal, Daniel Hirschman, and Ellen Berrey used fixed effects modeling to analyze enrollment trends for first-year students between 1990 and 2016 at 1,127 selective institutions.[48] They found that at highly selective institutions, using race-conscious admissions was linked with higher Black enrollment. However, at "middle-status" institutions, use of race-conscious policies was linked with lower Black enrollment, especially at the least competitive of selective institutions.[49] In trying to make sense of the finding, the authors suggest that as diversity has become associated with prestige, middle-status institutions adopted race-conscious admissions to emulate their higher-status, more competitive peers. However, some of these institutions may have not implemented race-conscious policies effectively, or at least in a way that supported Black student enrollment. It's also possible that these same institutions didn't change their recruitment, selection, or financial aid policies enough, and just having a race-conscious policy on the books didn't do much on its own. Some institutions may have adopted some form of race-conscious admissions to pay lip service to diversity, while utilizing other policies that undermined equity in admissions.[50]

This "middle-status" group of institutions (competitive but not the most competitive) is the bucket that most state flagship institutions fell into during the 1990–2016 period analyzed.[51] Public middle-status institutions were founded to serve the people and funded by the proceeds of land gifted to them by the federal government, not to mention taxpayer subsidies. Nonetheless, these same institutions engage in plenty of practices that undermine equity and in-state access. Of course, private institutions aren't off the hook at all, and we'll talk about problematic practices used by both types of institutions in the next section.

WHO GETS PULLED IN? HOW RACE AND CLASS AFFECT PRIVILEGE

While race-conscious admissions boosted diversity to some extent, especially at highly competitive institutions, too many schools perpetuated the status quo of "the rich get richer." CAF Co-LAB team member OiYan Poon and colleagues reference Victor Ray's theory of racialized organizations to explain why the status quo persisted, as institutions espoused support for race-conscious policies but advanced policies that undermined equity.[52] As they note, per Ray's theory, organizations claim to be race-neutral, but in reality, "institutions and their mechanisms systemically reproduce racial schemas and unequal distributions and accumulations of public and private resources through mundane organizational routines."[53] The part about inequality being perpetuated through "mundane organizational routines" stands out to me. In other words, racial inequality often persists not because of nasty boogeymen plotting to keep people of color down, but due to everyday policies and practices that perpetuate inequality.

So what are some of these everyday mundane policies and practices that pull in students who tend to have a certain amount of privilege? I'll do a quick, inexhaustive run-through of some of them: legacy admissions, out-of-state recruitment for public institutions, early decision and early action policies, problematic enrollment management practices, and the lack of diversity among admissions professionals. These are all practices that are in theory "race-neutral" but that actually contribute to racial and economic inequality in higher education. Heads up, you'll hear more about other supposedly race-neutral "pull-in" factors like standardized tests and athletic recruitment in chapters 4 and 5, respectively. There's so much to say that they need extra attention.

Legacy Admissions: Even Worse Than It Sounds

We'll start our tour with legacy admissions, which gets a good amount of airtime in the media. Legacy admissions give a student a "bump" if they are the child of an alum; some schools will also include other relations like grandchild or sibling. Yes, it's as ridiculous as it sounds, giving someone a preference due to who is in their lineage. What is this, the Middle Ages? Right now googling "legacy admissions" will spur a flurry of articles about how some colleges are getting rid of these preferences, but we can't forget how bad the problem has been for years. After Maryland, California was the second state to ban legacy admissions in both public and private schools in 2024. Up until very recently, legacy preferences still affected a high number of students at some institutions. For example, the University of Southern California admitted 1,791 legacies for Fall 2023 and Stanford admitted 295.[54] Even if and when legacy policies go away, we still have to deal with the aftermath of their cumulative impact.[55] Economist Sarah Reber and Gabriela Goodman of the Brookings Institution analyzed trends in the 2021–2022 Common Dataset.[56] Of students attending the most selective institutions, 86 percent of students at private institutions, 37 percent of students at publics, and 62 percent of students overall attended schools that still used legacy preferences in 2021. It's jarring how high these numbers are, even in the 2020s. Looking at students from all levels of selectivity, Reber found that 82 percent of students attending private institutions were at schools that used some sort of legacy preference, and 40 percent of all students attended schools that considered legacy status in some way. Let me state the obvious: eighty-two percent of students across the entire private college and university landscape—that's a lot!

In Reber and Goodman's analysis, 30 percent of all public state flagships reported using legacy practices as of 2021–2022. Really, any number over zero is disappointing for public schools. Five dropped the practice prior to the *SFFA* ruling and three dropped it after, leaving six state flagships that still considered legacy status as of March 2024, including, ironically enough, the University of North Carolina, Chapel Hill. Reber and Goodman found that half of state flagships had at least one scholarship for legacy students, including four states that only give funds to out-of-state legacy students (e.g., University of Missouri, up to $21,500), which just struck me as strange. Like "come on, prodigal son, return to the education of your bloodline!" strange.[57] The prevalence of legacy-based scholarships at state flagships is problematic, given what we know about the history of outright segregation and exclusion at our country's land grant institutions. So, if you're wondering why some of these state flagships are so incredibly homogeneous, the persistence of legacy admissions is partly to blame. There has been some momentum following the *SFFA* ruling to get states to ban legacy admissions.[58] Disappointingly, many private schools won't say goodbye to legacy admissions without being forced; it'll take legislation. Getting rid of legacy won't fix everything, but it's philosophically indefensible in this day and age.[59] Ironically, despite the Trump administration's blustering about the need to bring back "merit," so far (as of May 2025), the administration has yet to say anything about legacy admissions.[60] Hmmm.

Nonresident Recruitment: Why State Schools Love Out-of-State Students

Another practice that makes little sense is out-of-state recruitment by public state schools, which spiked in the twenty-first century. For decades, state schools were populated overwhelmingly by in-state students because, well, that's who they were founded to serve. After all, public land grant institutions were charged to educate state residents. Even though too many conveniently forgot in-state residents of color, they generally got the "state" part right. Oh, how times have changed. The percentage of out-of-state students grew notably at forty-eight of fifty state flagship institutions from 2002 to 2015.[61] Who are these students? They're usually White and from affluent backgrounds, which makes sense since (1) public universities go to predominantly White, relatively affluent public and private schools to recruit these students, and (2) the entire point of boosting nonresident enrollment is to collect nonresident tuition, which can be two to three times higher than in-state tuition.[62]

As sticker costs at private schools keep increasing, state flagship tuition for nonresidents seems like a good deal to upper-middle-class families. Sure, it's more expensive than in-state tuition, but it's more affordable than the full cost of private college. I hear this line of thinking a lot from my out-of-state UMD undergraduates, who often hail from wealthy suburbs outside of the Boston and the New York/New Jersey area. Their families make too much to qualify for financial aid, but being full-pay at a private college is still too much. A school like UMD gives them the chance for an out-of-state adventure at a more affordable price, and even better if there's a scholarship involved. Yes, there's money to help families that don't qualify for financial aid! Many states have worked to lure out-of-state students with so-called merit scholarships (a.k.a., enrollment incentives), which can make out-of-state tuition on par with what a student might pay in-state. I'll talk more about "merit" aid in chapter 3, but in a nutshell, it's problematic because it diverts resources from need-based aid.

Places like the University of Alabama are among the worst offenders, allocating more than two-thirds of their total financial aid budget to students who don't actually have demonstrated need. The school went from spending about $12 million on "merit aid" in the early 2000s to over $100 million in such aid in 2014–15.[63] Schools say that throwing "merit" aid at nonresidents will help them in the long run by building up a pipeline of students who will put "The University of X-State" on their list, as students and families swap gossip about who's going where.

So who misses out? In an analysis of data from over one hundred public institutions, growth in nonresident enrollment was linked with lower low-income and URM student representation. Karina Salazar of the University of Arizona, Ozan Jaquette of UCLA, and Crystal Han of UCLA analyzed recruiting data for fifteen public schools, finding that the institutions commonly made more visits to out-of-state high schools than in-state high schools. Further, "out-of-state visits systematically targeted affluent, predominantly white localities."[64] Salazar more closely studied four public schools and found that they engaged in "'recruitment redlining'—the circuitous avoidance of predominantly Black and Latinx communities along recruiting visit paths."[65] All of this activity, both who schools visit and who they don't, affects enrollment. The end product is that nonresidents are 56.6 percent of the student body at University of Alabama, 32 percent at the Ohio State University (OSU), and 45 percent at the University of Arizona, Tucson.[66] These numbers aren't accidental. Schools frequently list specific target goals for nonresident enrollment that are high enough to raise a good chunk of money, but low enough to not raise the ire of the state legislature. In 2023, then-Senator J. D. Vance wrote a letter to the new president of OSU decrying the "rot of 'DEI'" at his alma mater.[67] He closed the letter by saying: "[Ohio State] is one of our country's oldest land grant schools, established to serve the people of the state. I want Ohio State to be successful, but I believe its success depends on serving all citizens of our state, rather than parroting the latest madness to come out of Harvard and Yale." Actually, now–Vice President Vance, the real reason OSU isn't serving "all citizens of our state" isn't because of so-called DEI dogma, but because your alma mater wants to have a third of the student body come from outside of the state.[68]

It's sad to see public universities throw their in-state applicants under the bus because state institutions are best positioned to support state residents. With the lower upfront sticker price, state institutions are a more feasible option for many first-generation, URM, and low-income state residents. Name recognition is especially crucial for first-generation and low-income students. They may have neighbors who attended, or know someone from their high school who went, and these factors can make a college dream feel more possible. Also, state universities are more likely to be within driving distance of home, often a key priority for first-generation, low-income, and URM students.[69] Only time will tell if states will pull back from aggressive out-of-state recruitment, but I doubt it. They've invested too much, and their efforts will continue unless voters decide to do something about it.

Early Deadlines and Associated Perks

Private and public institutions both use early deadlines to lure rich kids, but the process differs depending on the institutional context. At private schools, the role of early decision in perpetuating inequality is pretty blatant. Early decision is binding and generally linked with higher acceptance rates. Even when you control for demographic characteristics, applying early has been linked with a roughly one-hundred-point boost on the SAT.[70] Because students need to commit if admitted, the early decision process privileges students who don't need to compare financial aid packages. Similar to the Disney Genie Pass, if you're willing to pay, you can jump the line.[71] Yes, there are lower-income students who apply and are admitted through the early decision track.[72] Questbridge, an outreach program that matches talented low-income students with colleges, has students apply early.

However, by and large, it's a wealthier crowd that applies early decision. Private institutions are increasingly leaning on the policy. In 2022, half of the classes at Brown and Yale and 66 percent at Tulane were admitted through early decision.[73] College web forums are full of discussions on early decision strategies, since some private institutions have two rounds of early decision, a.k.a. ED I and ED II. It's confusing, which is why people will outsource this stuff to a consultant if they can afford it. Want to be even more confused? There's something called "restrictive early action" (REA) used by Harvard, Stanford, and other schools, where a student can apply through nonbinding, early action to only one school that uses REA. Students can also apply early action to any public school, but they can't apply anywhere early decision. So you could apply to Harvard early, but not Stanford, and you lose your chance to apply anywhere early decision. Phew, that's confusing. Schools see REA as their attempt to level the playing field a bit, but it just reflects how we're really at an absurdly weird moment in the history of college admissions.

Okay, on to early action as used by public schools. At face value, it's less problematic than early decision at private institutions. It's nonbinding and students can compare financial aid packages before making a final choice. These are all good things, but there are still implications for equity. Public universities use early action to lure out-of-state and affluent in-state students. How? By tying early deadlines to prized resources like honors programs, limited enrollment majors (e.g., STEM, business), and "merit" scholarships. Our research team studied two land grant state flagships and found that both institutions rolled out the red carpet for early applicants.[74] Analyzing data on visits to high schools, we noticed that visits to out-of-state wealthy high schools mostly happened during the early fall, allowing the institution to steer students toward the early action deadline with incentives like priority consideration for honors, limited enrollment majors, scholarships, and the like.

Now let's see, who is less likely to apply early? Students who have less socialization and information about the college-going process, including low-income, URM, and first-generation students. Honors colleges and majors/colleges like business and engineering are often some of the more homogeneous spaces at large state universities.[75] Tying such opportunities to early action deadlines is probably part of the problem. Both early decision and early action policies perpetuate racial stratification in a process that is supposedly available to anyone. In reality, both are disproportionately used by groups already privileged in the college admissions process.

Problematic Practices Within Enrollment Management

The field of enrollment management plays a critical, behind-the-scenes role in shaping practices like nonresident enrollment and early decision. Yield and enrollment are difficult to predict, so these units are a mainstay on campus. At the same time, bad things can happen when institutions prioritize status, revenue, and prestige. In best case scenarios, enrollment management leaders can lead their campuses away from problematic practices, and we'll hear about one such leader in the next chapter. At the same time, it's important to highlight practices within enrollment management that can foster inequality, both racial and economic.

Stephen Burd of New America edited the book *Lifting the Veil on Enrollment Management: How a Powerful Industry Is Limiting Social Mobility in American Higher Education*, which documents the evolution of the field.[76] For decades, admissions offices operated fairly independently, making decisions without systematically considering factors like the student's likelihood of accepting an offer or the type of scholarship needed to seal the deal. These practices emerged first at private institutions, but are increasingly popular at public institutions following the 2008 recession.

At their worst, enrollment management practices can bring a for-profit ethos into what is supposed to be a nonprofit environment. Burd explains how when institutions think more like businesses, you have practices like land grant institutions spending money to court wealthy out-of-state schools. The big shift toward early decision? Enrollment management. Greater reliance on massive corporate consultants such as EAB and Ruffalo Noel Levitz? Same, same.

One problematic practice that pulls certain students in while pushing others out is student list buys. Institutions will buy names and contact information from the College Board in order to recruit students. Guess which students they want to recruit the most? Yup, the full pay crowd. Institutions can also target students from historically underrepresented backgrounds, and many do, especially those with high test scores. On the whole though, this practice disproportionately benefits the usual suspects (White, affluent students) and works to maintain the status quo. Since the data is bought from the College Board, institutions generally target students based on test scores, privileging certain populations. Ozan Jaquette, Karina Salazar, Crystal Han, and others are drawing the curtain back on the student list–buy industry and how it perpetuates inequality. Analyzing purchases of student list data from public institutions, they found "student list products systematically exclude students of color . . . discretion in student list purchases can unintentionally exclude students of color at alarming rates."[77]

The Lack of Diversity Among Admissions Professionals

Now for an awkward but necessary topic: how admissions professionals can play a role in reproducing the status quo. People working in admissions are generally wonderful. They're usually passionate about their work. You have to be, to stay in a job where you're so underpaid. That said, because of the low pay, certain people (mostly White) tend to hang around the field longer, while others cycle in and out. The workload of the job is punishing, thanks to heavy travel, high application volume, and low compensation. It doesn't help that admissions professionals get blamed a lot, from the lack of diversity on campus to why Johnny-the-state-legislator's kid didn't get in. Altogether, admissions staff are about 70 to 80 percent White, and least diverse in the upper ranks.[78] In a report from NACAC (the National Association for College Admission Counseling), members stressed the need to diversify leadership ranks, with a special need to retain Black men. Staff of color shared that the burden to support diversity and inclusion training within units and strengthen URM student recruitment is often placed squarely on them.[79]

Unfortunately, the lack of diversity among admissions professionals has likely repercussions for admissions decisions. Professors Nicholas Bowman (a collaborator and friend) of the University of Iowa and Michael Bastedo (who has served on the CAF Co-LAB advisory board) of the University of Michigan conducted a simulation of file review for 311 admissions officers.[80] Participants received three files to review; all three applicants were described as being White men to keep race and gender consistent. The profiles: (1) A traditionally high-achieving, high-SES student; (2) A middle-achieving, high-SES student; (3) A low-SES student with strong grades, who took the most challenging courses offered at his lower-SES high school. Still, the low-SES student's courses were less advanced than those taken by the high-SES student, and his test scores were lower.

In the study, White admissions officers were much more likely to favor admitting the high-achieving, high-SES student versus admissions officers of color.[81] Admissions officers with higher levels of parental education also gave lower ratings to the low-SES student.[82] Interestingly, readers working at their alma mater were less likely to recommend the low-SES student for admission.[83] Commenting on their findings, Bowman and Bastedo note: "These patterns perhaps reflect a comparative lack of interest in equity among these readers and/or a stronger desire to increase academic prestige at their home institution, and thus the perceived value of their own degree. As a whole, such findings may contradict the idealized notion that admissions officers can be trained to provide recommendations that are entirely distinct from their own experiences and identities."[84] Oof, talk about gatekeeping.[85]

At most highly selective institutions, many applications will go through a full-committee read, or at least will be read by more than one person. Still, not all selective institutions have the time and resources for full-committee or multi-reader review. Another concerning trend is the rise of seasonal readers.[86] As the name suggests, seasonal readers are hired on seasonal contracts to support the overworked full-time staff. They are most commonly hired at large state universities, but play a growing role at private institutions. The role of seasonal readers varies. At some institutions they do a first-cull reading of applications, filtering out applications that are unlikely to advance. At others, they have full decision-making power. In 2024 I often saw ads offering about twenty dollars per hour for the gig, sometimes less. At one state flagship, we were told that the seasonal readers were mostly White, retired guidance counselors and other former school personnel.[87] At that institution, there were two Black women and no other people of color in a seasonal reader pool of about 30 people. Considering that the school counselor profession is also known for lacking diversity, concerns related to full-time readers may also apply to the seasonal reader set.

Given the challenges related to the demographic composition of both admissions staff and seasonal readers, some might say that institutions need standardized tests to bring more consistency to the process. However, despite their supposed "standardization," tests can be read and evaluated in a way that overly favors more affluent students, even when test scores are read in context.[88] It's a messy discussion that we'll discuss more in chapter 4.

MORE REASONS WHY TWENTY-FIRST CENTURY ADMISSIONS FEELS OVERWHELMING

Besides the "pull-in" factors I've discussed, other developments have made the name-brand admissions landscape even more complicated. One is simply population growth. The number of public high school graduates is peaking. There were over 870,000 more kids graduating from high school in 2024 than there were when I applied to college in the late 1990s.[89] Higher education has been preparing for an enrollment cliff for some time, and some smaller colleges are closing. However, the demand for name-brand degrees persists, and is not expected to drop even when population growth slows down. Name-brand colleges and universities will do their best to find new markets of applicants. Applications slowing down from China? Well, haven't you heard that India is the next big thing? (I'm not kidding.) Interest in the African international student pipeline has picked up as well, which is long overdue and proof that interest convergence is real.[90] Of course the landscape for international student enrollment is in tremendous flux due to actions taken by the second Trump administration.

The enrollment management industry has contributed to the complexity and lack of predictability in the process, especially with the use of analytics attempting to predict who's going to attend and what type of enrollment incentive students need to commit. There's a bewildering chicken-egg phenomenon, where students feel like they have to apply to more schools to have a better chance of having more options, but then application numbers are inflated and institutions have a harder time predicting yield, which makes everything seem more arbitrary. Then the next round of students applies to even more schools because they want some insurance in an increasingly unpredictable landscape. The role of enrollment management grows in order to try to bring some order to the chaos for institutions, but the process still feels complicated and stressful for families.

I'm fond of Common App, which has been a great research collaborator. At the same time, the ability to use one application to apply to numerous institutions has added to the complexity of admissions. More state institutions have joined Common App in recent years. They were slower to join at first, a relic of the years when more people held on to the logical and sane notion that public state flagships were for the people of the state. Some public institutions joined the Coalition, a consortium of institutions that wanted an application process prioritizing equity.[91] Then someone realized that institutions were getting more applicants through the Common App (900+ institutional members versus 170-ish for the Coalition), so more state flagships joined Common App, making it easier for out-of-state students to apply. Application numbers have gone up, admit rates have gone down, nonresident enrollment has increased, and enrollment management teams are pleased. In-state students and families are mostly frustrated, as schools that used to be a more reliable admit for traditionally high-achieving students feel more out of reach.[92]

THE RAT RACE: THE FALLOUT FOR MENTAL HEALTH AND SOCIETY AT LARGE

The admissions world was already complicated pre-2020. Still, the pandemic and teenage mental health crisis made things even harder. Scholars and pundits alike debate the cause of the ongoing mental health crisis. Is it (a) smart phones; (b) climate change; (c) structural racism; (d) school shootings; or (e) all of the above?[93] Some like *Atlantic* writer Derek Thompson have named the high pressure environment of competitive college admissions as a contributor, at least for young people in more affluent regions.[94] Over twenty-five years ago, William Fitzsimmons, Dean of Admissions at Harvard College, commented: "Many of us are concerned that the pressures on today's students seem far more intense than those placed on previous generations."[95] Gen Z and Gen Alpha will wonder what the Gen Xers and elder millennials were so stressed about back then. In the late 1990s and early 2000s, admit rates at many "elite" institutions were still fairly generous—over 30 percent of applicants got into Cornell and almost 50 percent into the University of Chicago.[96] Vanderbilt admitted about 50 to 60 percent of students in the late 1990s.[97] In 2023, they admitted 5.6 percent of applicants.[98] How things have changed.

Back when I started writing this book in 2023, I thought a lot about Naomi, a family friend who was working on her college applications at the time. Despite an almost perfect academic record and impressive accomplishments, she expressed feeling "hopeless" about the future. Over text, she lamented: "It seems that nowadays even if I do all I can, it might still not be enough in the end to get into one of my dream colleges." Naomi is not alone in her worries, and many teenagers are anxious about their college prospects, even though well-meaning adults will try to remind them of the ethos behind Frank Bruni's bestseller, *Where You Go Is Not Who You'll Be: An Antidote to College Admissions Mania*.[99] The current system produces stressed out kids at a time when bathing the brain in stress-related hormones is one of the worst possible things for adolescent development.[100] The mental health crisis reflects how young people are reacting to the punishing process of feeling crushed, poked, and prodded into a system where they're constantly having to prove their worth. There's a sense that the process is endless, but necessary to gain economic security in a society that promises nothing.

When I ask my undergraduates to describe their experiences applying to college, I hear a lot of sighing: "Stressful." "Exhausting." "Terrible." "I still feel burnt out." More and more, these young people look world-weary when reflecting on their experiences. Naomi also spoke to the toll of a heavy activity and academic load on mental health, saying "sadly enough, the stress of comparing grades and extracurriculars with my friends has made me lose a lot of confidence in my own abilities." Fortunately, she got into her top pick. While I'm thrilled for her, I wish the process could have been gentler. We should want students coming to college with energy to burn, not already feeling burnt out. The current system isn't serving anyone well, from either an equity or mental health perspective. Sure, our little knowledge-worker bees from privileged backgrounds will take calculus a year or two earlier than previous generations. Still, what good is it if young people are burnt out?

The strange irony is that amidst the rat race, there actually are plenty of options for young people to receive an excellent postsecondary education. Back in 2021, only about 222 of the over 4,000 postsecondary institutions nationwide accepted fewer than 50 percent of students.[101] There are still plenty of schools that accept the majority of applicants. It's easy to get tunnel vision and focus more on schools with the most name recognition. People have heard of these schools, so more people apply, and they become even more competitive. This dynamic speaks to why name-brand schools have an even greater obligation to recruit and enroll students from historically excluded backgrounds. Someone coming from a lower-SES background is going to have to rely more on name recognition when figuring out where to apply to college, versus someone whose college consultant can identify schools that are lesser known, but still excellent.

WRAPPING IT UP

When schools become more competitive, they become even more desirable and prestigious. Frustrated students aren't thinking about population trends and targets for revenue generation when they're wondering why college admissions feels so disheartening these days. Unfortunately, this lack of awareness, while understandable, has made some students and families wonder if they were rejected because of race. No one blames athletic or legacy preferences; instead, race is the easy target. It doesn't help that there are well-organized forces encouraging the idea that students are rejected because of race. Feeding into this confusion, when organizing the *SFFA* case, Ed Blum put up recruitment websites asking: "Were you rejected from Harvard? It might be because you're the wrong race."

From day one, there was much misunderstanding and confusion about what was at stake in *SFFA v. Harvard*, and that confusion persists after the ruling. Now that we've highlighted the inequality and anxiety within admissions, we can turn to the case that represents the convergence of these two issues. What happens when a bunch of stressed-out and confused students meet an old-ish White guy who tells them that they didn't get into Harvard because of race? What happens when the White guy says that together, they can combat (supposed) discrimination against Asian Americans, when the bigger agenda is to destroy the ability of colleges and universities to consider race/ethnicity in admissions altogether? You probably already know the unhappy ending, but keep reading to find out more.

2

Students for Fair Admissions v. Harvard

What Exactly Happened?

Like many in the higher education community, I spent way too much time in June 2023 clicking "refresh" on *SCOTUSblog.com*, eager to find out the ruling. Finally on June 29, 2023, the bombshell dropped. The majority opinion issued by Chief Justice John Roberts deemed that the programs at Harvard and UNC were unconstitutional and violated the equal protection clause of the Fourteenth Amendment.[1] It was a heavy day for the higher education community.

Reading the opinion, I realized that things had been doomed from the start. The majority opinion referred to "race-based admissions" instead of "race-conscious admissions." In the words of Eric Hoover of the *Chronicle of Higher Education*: "'Race-based admissions' is a made-up nonsense term."[2] That one-word modification reflects a world of difference between how the SCOTUS majority viewed the admissions programs at Harvard and UNC, and the reality of how conventional race-conscious admissions actually worked. "Race-based admissions" suggests that race is a determinative factor in admissions decisions; that checking a certain box for one's race/ethnicity all-but-guarantees whether someone gets in or not. In contrast, the process is much more nuanced in conventional race-conscious admissions, with race being one of numerous factors considered in understanding who an applicant is and their potential contributions to the student body.

Unfortunately, it didn't take long for people to misread the opinion. Immediately, the state attorney general of Missouri announced that the ruling applied not just to admissions, but scholarships and even employment, despite the ruling's silence on both.[3] Of course, SFFA founder Ed Blum contributed to the mess by sending cease and desist letters to 150 institutions around the country, demanding that schools take away "any definition or guidance regarding 'underrepresented' racial groups," another issue not discussed at all in the SCOTUS ruling.[4] The headlines themselves didn't help: "The Death of Affirmative Action" (NPR),[5] "The Supreme Court Has Killed Affirmative Action" (*The Nation*);[6] you get the idea.[7] Things reached a new level of chaos in 2025 when the Trump administration began referencing *SFFA* in an attempt to wipe out programs related to diversity, equity, and inclusion.[8]

Needless to say, confusion persists after the ruling. In this chapter, I'll address key points of the ruling and questions like: Is there actually a ban on affirmative action, and more specifically, race-conscious admissions? Does the ruling in *SFFA* apply to all of campus life? Can students talk about race in their essays or extracurricular activities? Can institutions still collect applicant data on race/ethnicity? Did SCOTUS rule that there was intentional discrimination against Asian Americans by Harvard? What legal options remain for institutions that want to advance racial diversity?

IS RACE-CONSCIOUS ADMISSIONS DEAD?

Here, the devil is in the details. Yes, the SCOTUS majority ruled that the programs used at Harvard and UNC-Chapel Hill were unconstitutional. However, campuses may still consider how students discuss race as relevant to their experiences or identity in the application. Big takeaway: Race-conscious admissions isn't dead; it's restricted. Let's rewind a little. In

Regents of the University of California v. Bakke (1978), SCOTUS disallowed the practice of allocating seats for racial/ethnic groups. Yes, quotas have been illegal for decades. Still, SCOTUS affirmed programs like Harvard's, which evaluated students holistically by considering race as one of numerous parts of a student's background. Measures like giving an applicant extra points for being of a particular race/ethnicity have been illegal since *Gratz v. Bollinger* in 2003, when SCOTUS rejected the undergraduate admissions program at the University of Michigan.[9] In the companion case *Grutter v. Bollinger*, SCOTUS upheld the law school's practice of using race-conscious holistic review, where race was considered in understanding an applicant's context, but not tied to points. This type of holistic review has been the norm for conventional race-conscious admissions at a wide array of institutions for decades.

In *Grutter*, SCOTUS affirmed that race/ethnicity could still be considered during the admissions process based on the educational benefits linked with engaging with racial/ethnic diversity. Critically, this rationale was not explicitly struck down in *SFFA*. Some legal scholars argue that *Grutter* was effectively gutted by the majority opinion, but others contend that the ruling does not depart radically from *Grutter*.[10] In their article about the ruling, Benjamin Eidelson and Deborah Hellman (of Harvard Law School and the University of Virginia School of Law, respectively) comment, "In particular, we have tried and failed to identify a principle, implicit in *SFFA*, that would vindicate the perception of the opinion as a fundamental departure from the Court's precedents in this area."[11] Altogether, the ruling in *SFFA* presents a somewhat contradictory situation, where the SCOTUS majority referred to *Grutter* as the precedent, but voiced doubt that any institution could meet the standard of strict scrutiny issued in *Grutter*. The majority opinion contended that goals like training future leaders were laudable, but argued that they "cannot be subjected to meaningful judicial review" through metrics or other means.[12] Others contend that critical mass and dynamic diversity are documentable and measurable, but the SCOTUS majority disagreed.[13] Justice Roberts commented on how universities can still define their missions, and didn't challenge the ability of institutions to pursue goals related to diversity, equity, and social mobility.

The majority opinion explained what is and isn't permissible on the route to advancing institutional goals. Out: consideration of race/ethnicity as related to an applicant's demographic data as one of many factors. In: institutions can still consider individual discussion of how race has affected applicants' lives in other parts of the application like the essay. Justice Roberts famously wrote: "At the same time, nothing prohibits universities from considering an applicant's discussion of how race affected the applicant's life, so long as that discussion is concretely tied to a quality of character or unique ability that the particular applicant can contribute to the university."[14] Later in the opinion, he repeated the sentiment, writing clearly that "nothing in this opinion should be construed as prohibiting universities from considering an applicant's discussion of how race affected his or her life, be it through discrimination, inspiration, or otherwise."[15]

In reading the majority opinion, it's easy to imagine that Justice Roberts and friends had a certain image of policies being determinatively race-based at Harvard, UNC, and others. In this flawed understanding, people think that race-conscious admissions is a set of formulas or near-automatic admissions decisions where students were being treated more as members of categories than individuals. The SCOTUS majority told institutions that they can only consider discussion of race when it illuminates something about the applicant, which admissions committees were already doing for the most part.[16] The term *mansplaining* (SCOTUS-splaining?) comes to mind: "You guys need to start thinking how race affects people's lives! Treat people as individuals and not categories!" Admissions offices: "We already do this!" Under conventional race-conscious admission policies, readers generally weren't making race-based decisions (e.g., simply admitting an applicant because of their race, or admitting certain students over others based just on race). Instead, a reader might have been impressed by a student's compelling narrative about how being Black, Asian American, or whatever race/ethnicity shaped their resilience, commitments, or insights. At the same time, admissions committees could have rejected another student of the same race/ethnicity—even one who also discussed racial/ethnic identity—based on any number of additional considerations.

Justice Roberts emphasized how experiences related to race are supposed to reflect individual character traits valued by institutions: "A benefit to a student who overcame racial discrimination, for example, must be tied to that student's courage and determination. . . . In other words, the student must be treated based on his or her experiences as an individual—not on the basis of race."[17] SCOTUS's mandate represents a strange parsing of traits, an attempt to separate one's race from a student's "experiences as an individual." It's a sort of backwards attempt at colorblindness, where experiences and discussion tied to race can be considered, but only when framed as being what one "experiences as an individual." The "individual" characteristic (e.g., courage, determination) is presented as something that exists in a supposedly race-neutral, detached space.[18] In reality, the lines are much blurrier. Individual traits do not necessarily exist in a space that is somehow magically detached from race. Try as they might, even the SCOTUS majority (sort of) recognized this complex reality, as noted by Eidelson and Hellman: "*SFFA* revealed that the Court's conservative majority could not live with its own abstract commitment to colorblindness."[19]

Following the ruling, media headlines blared variations of "affirmative action is dead," but Justice Roberts said that universities can still consider student discussion of race. Understandably, people are confused. Parsing Roberts's words, the greenlight phrase that sticks out to me is "discussion of race," versus consideration of race through demographic information in tandem with any discussion of race by the applicant. Following the ruling, race-conscious admissions is greatly restricted because understandably, not every person of color wants to discuss race in their application. At the same time, affirmative action and race-conscious admissions aren't dead following the SCOTUS ruling, although they're certainly weakened and restricted.[20] Eidelson and Hellman comment on how *SFFA* is not a particularly colorblind ruling: "Roberts made it clear that *SFFA* has not purged all traces of race consciousness from the college admissions process—and he expressly contemplated that some manner of dialogue with regulated universities over the pivotal lines would therefore continue. . . . Despite its sometimes strident rhetoric, there were certain forms of race consciousness that even [the SCOTUS] majority did not want to condemn."[21] Their article is a fascinating read that unpacks the race consciousness that still exists in admissions even after the verdict.

Regardless of what any political administration says, the ruling in *SFFA* clearly states that institutions can still consider student discussion on race and racial identity in admissions. Consideration of *discussion* of race is the thread on which race-conscious admissions hangs following *SFFA*. Do we need a new name, like "race-discussion-aware admissions"? I personally like "race-sensitive admissions," which Eidelson and Hellman reference in their article.[22] Another thing to consider is that other legal options exist to defend a more conventional version of race-conscious admissions, where admissions reviewers could consider applicant data around race/ethnicity as relevant context. We'll discuss that option toward the end of the chapter.

DOES THE *SFFA* RULING APPLY TO ALL OF CAMPUS LIFE?

On January 21, 2025, President Trump ordered the federal government to wipe out illegal efforts to advance diversity, equity, and inclusion.[23] The key word here is *illegal*. Despite the scary wording, there are many ways to advance diversity, equity, and inclusion that remain perfectly legal. Wedged into the order is a mandate for the attorney general and the secretary of education to issue guidance on how states and higher education institutions receiving federal funds (basically, everyone) should act "regarding the measures and practices required to comply" with the ruling in *SFFA*.[24] A few weeks later, Craig Trainor, Acting Assistant Secretary for Civil Rights within the US Department of Education, released the infamous "Dear Colleague" letter claiming that *SFFA* somehow applied much more broadly to "all other aspects of student, academic, and campus life," from campus housing to graduation ceremonies.[25] Say what?

Lawyer Art Coleman of EducationCounsel blasted the "Dear Colleague" letter, calling its interpretation of *SFFA* "skewed and incomplete."[26]

Professor Liliana Garces also noted that the "content of the current letter widely expands, without any legal authority, the parameters of the court's decision in *Students for Fair Admissions v. Harvard*."[27] Altogether, the executive order and letter show how the far right is attempting to exploit the ruling in *SFFA* to advance its agenda. As written in a memo by a group of law faculty on the continued legality of diversity, equity, and inclusion-related initiatives, "Contrary to the Trump administration's suggestion, [*SFFA*] does not render [diversity, equity, and inclusion] initiatives legally suspect."[28] As noted by the authors, the ability of institutions to define their own missions and goals remains protected by the First Amendment.

Ironically, even Ed Blum doesn't think that the ruling in *SFFA* applies much beyond admissions, although he's eager to continue his destructive work.[29] Coleman commented: "By its terms, *SFFA* concerned the higher education admissions context—not, as the Acting Assistant Secretary appears to claim, a ruling that swept all issues of hiring, training and programming within its ambit."[30] The Trump administration's Department of Education later applied *SFFA* to deem consideration of race in various admissions-adjacent contexts (e.g., scholarships and outreach programs) illegal, although the courts have yet to rule on the issue. In *Inside Higher Ed*, I wrote about how these particular programs are vulnerable, but not illegal.[31] Regardless, to say that the ruling somehow creates the legal basis for barring a slew of programs is going way too far.

CAN STUDENTS (AND COUNSELORS, AND TEACHERS) STILL TALK ABOUT RACE IN THE APPLICATION?

Okay, back to college admissions. To make it crystal clear, the response to the question "can students, counselors, and teachers still talk about race/ethnicity in the application" is an unequivocal yes. SCOTUS did not prohibit students and supporting adults from talking about anything on the application. The essay is still a prime place to discuss anything related to a student's background and context. Some institutions have given encouragement in this area, from direct questions about racial/ethnic identity to broader questions on overcoming challenges. Students usually can select from among different questions, so they can choose to veer as close to or far away from talking about race as they want to.

Unsurprisingly, there are mixed feelings floating around about the heightened prominence of the essay. Even before the ruling, many didn't like the idea of students feeling pressured to "sell" their trauma or highlight hardship. Also, race might be highly relevant to a student's life, but maybe they want to write their essays on something random like knitting. Yes, that was me.[32] I thought constantly about race from a young age, and started a diversity-awareness club at my high school—a cutting-edge extracurricular for late 1990s Ohio! At the same time, I didn't feel compelled to write about race in my main essay, and thought I could write a pretty good essay about knitting. Would I have felt differently if I was going through the process today? Quite possibly.[33]

Overall, the SCOTUS majority ruling reduces some of students' freedom to write about whatever they want, which is concerning. That's what we're left with for now, which means that institutions have a responsibility to pay attention to how students talk about race, "be it through discrimination, inspiration, or otherwise," in the application, and also to make sure that "discussion is concretely tied to a quality of character or unique ability that the particular applicant can contribute to the university," as stated in the ruling.[34] Once again, the latter phrasing doesn't differ substantively from what many admissions staff were already doing prior to the ruling—considering how race shapes student lives in nonformulaic ways.[35]

So what should educators and mentors tell students about these new murky waters? Students should feel comfortable talking about whatever they want in their essays, to tell the stories that explain who they are and that help an admissions committee get to know them beyond their resumes. If a student feels comfortable, they should not shy away from talking about the influence of race on their life, their context for opportunity, and what they might contribute to the campus community. Bottom line: Students should feel free to talk about race in any way that seems relevant; rest assured, they have the freedom to say whatever they want.

Of course, artificial intelligence is currently disrupting how we think about pretty much everything. How long the essay will stick around in a post-AI era is anyone's guess, but given the specific attention to essays in the SCOTUS majority opinion, it seems important to protect the space. Whether institutions will rely more on supplemental questions versus the main essay due to concerns about AI in the essay is anyone's guess. In 2024, Duke University announced that they would no longer give the essay a numerical score given concerns about AI and ghostwriting from college concierges.[36] However, they'll still read the essay for insights into the applicants, which sounds like they're trying to keep the door open for the type of discussion highlighted by Justice Roberts.

Now for the rest of the application. Extracurricular activities weren't mentioned at all in the majority opinion, but similar dynamics apply. Students should feel comfortable listing anything, and should not hesitate to highlight activities related to race/ethnicity, racial justice, culture, heritage, and the like. In general, additional description is helpful for people reading applications. For example, many readers know that Jack and Jill is a civic organization supporting leadership development for African American youth, but not everyone does. Ditto goes for a student's Lion Dance troop, MEChA chapter, and the like.[37] It's also important to list activities that are not viewed as traditional "extracurricular" activities, but that contribute somehow to one's household or community. These include translating for grandparents, taking care of siblings, and being in charge of household chores.

Recommendation letter writers should not hesitate to talk about culture, background, identity, race/ethnicity, socioeconomic status, and any other relevant student experiences. A concern before the *SFFA* trial was whether the ruling would bar a teacher from writing about race as relevant to student experiences, such as an Asian American student starting a club to combat anti-Asian violence. Letter writers should just proceed as they normally would, providing all relevant information. Admissions committees can once again apply the same consideration of how experiences and background context related to race/ethnicity are tied to traits valued by institutions, such as overcoming adversity, demonstrating leadership, and contributing to society. We'll discuss extracurricular activities and letters more in chapter 5.

SHOULD INSTITUTIONS STILL COLLECT DATA ON RACE/ETHNICITY?

Yes, yes, yes! I wish that we didn't even have to address this question. MIT had a sharp drop in racial diversity the first admissions cycle post–SCOTUS ruling. In a Q&A following the announcement, they acknowledged: "[MIT] did not solicit race or ethnicity information from applicants this year, so we don't have data on the applicant pool."[38] My jaw dropped when I read the statement. MIT of all places should know how critical data is when engineering (sorry for the pun) any sort of solution to a problem. Missing race/ethnicity data on applicants is hugely problematic because the institution doesn't even have an idea of who's applying in the first place. I'm sure that Ed Blum is thrilled, since he didn't even address the collection of applicant data in the threatening letter that he sent to 150 institutions shortly after the ruling. Instead, he just urged institutions to separate "checkbox" data from actual file review, which institutions were already planning to do.[39] MIT unnecessarily went the extra mile. MIT uses its own application and not the Common App, unlike most selective schools. Thus, we can only hope that most schools still collected race/ethnicity data for applicants, which is easy to separate from file review. (You'd think that MIT of all places could figure this out.)

Do schools in states that already had bans on race-conscious admissions still collect and analyze data on race/ethnicity? Absolutely. California is constantly pumping out reports and policy memos to understand the demographic composition of the pool.[40] Data like the number of applications submitted by different racial/ethnic groups is critical to guide policy and practice. So yes, keeping a close eye on race/ethnicity in the applicant, admitted, and yield pools is essential for institutions, and institutions should not shy away from having frank conversations about how things are playing out in admissions cycles following the SCOTUS ruling.

In his letter to 150 institutions, Blum demanded that institutions "prohibit your admissions office from preparing or reviewing any aggregated data (i.e., data involving two or more applicants) regarding race or ethnicity." In his point-by-point response to Blum's letter, David Hinojosa of the Lawyers' Committee for Civil Rights responded: "Universities can use their discretion in including aggregated data regarding the race or ethnicity of applicants as part of a lawful race-conscious admission program. For other admissions programs, nothing in the opinion forbids universities from monitoring admissions demographics. They simply should not make admissions decisions based on an applicant's race."[41]

The question of whether institutions can still collect data on the race/ethnicity of students, both applicants and enrollees, is crystal clear. The SCOTUS majority opinion says nothing about data collection, period. Regarding enrollment data, institutions receiving federal aid are required under various laws and statutory requirements to report demographic data to the Integrated Postsecondary Education Data System, so they have to collect it.[42] Of course, data collection and reporting is being upended by the Trump administration, but the federal mandate remains. The ruling in *SFFA v. Harvard* had nothing to do with this type of data collection, and institutions should continue business as usual in data collection and reporting obligations.

A CARVE OUT FOR MILITARY ACADEMIES

An interlude to address one of the more baffling aspects of the majority opinion: the exemption for military academies. In *SFFA*, the SCOTUS majority commented: "No military academy is a party to these cases, however, and none of the courts below addressed the propriety of race-based admissions systems in that context. This opinion also does not address the issue, in light of the potentially distinct interests that military academies may present."[43] Technically, conventional race-conscious policies *could* exist at our nation's military academies, because the SCOTUS majority viewed entities like West Point, the US Naval Academy, and others as having unique interests. Secretary of Defense Pete Hegseth decided to ax race-conscious admissions at the academies, which he conveniently didn't mention during his confirmation hearing.[44]

While the SCOTUS majority recognized the needs of the military, Ed Blum was less sympathetic. The paint had barely dried on the SCOTUS ruling before he and SFFA decided to file suit against the US Naval Academy, the US Air Force Academy, and West Point. SCOTUS declined to take up the West Point case and in December 2024, a federal district court upheld the Naval Academy's use of race-conscious admissions.[45] Thus, a future secretary of defense could decide to bring conventional race-conscious admissions back in the military academies.

Under the Biden administration, the US government filed a brief in *SFFA* arguing that race-conscious admissions supported compelling interests within the country's military academies.[46] The military has a complex history related to race. During the Vietnam War, major tension brewed due to the lack of diversity among military leadership, as noted in the amicus brief filed in *SFFA* by thirty-five retired top military leaders in support of race-conscious admissions.[47] For all of its issues, the military has worked hard to recruit, retain, and promote a racially diverse leadership over the years, knowing that the stakes are too high to ignore.

Race-conscious admissions has made a difference for the military, and not just because it supported diversity within the military academies. Writing in the *Hechinger Report*, reporter Olivia Sanchez explained how race-conscious policies at civilian institutions played an important role in diversifying military leadership.[48] Graduates of US military academies make up less than 20 percent of all military officers. The remaining portion, over 80 percent of military officers, receive their required bachelor's degree at civilian institutions through the Reserve Officer Training Corp (ROTC) or postgraduation officer training programs. For a stronger and more diverse military, you want to maximize the pool of highly educated URM individuals graduating from well-resourced civilian institutions. Thus, restricting race-conscious policies at civilian institutions has ramifications for the military's talent pool. Places like

Harvard and UNC, with their active ROTC programs, matter for the future of the military and national security. Besides the military, the Department of Homeland Security, FBI (Federal Bureau of Investigation), CIA (Central Intelligence Agency), and others rely heavily on civilian higher education to graduate students from a wide range of backgrounds, both racial/ethnic and economic. They need students who have experience grappling with difference, working in diverse teams, and thinking critically—outcomes linked to engaging with a racially diverse student body during college.[49] As Justice Sotomayor pointed out in her dissent in *SFFA*: "To the extent the Court suggests national security interests are 'distinct,' those interests cannot explain the Court's narrow exemption, as national security interests are also implicated at civilian universities."[50]

The ruling in *SFFA* allows military academies to pursue diversity more directly because people's lives are at stake in the military. Still, it limits options for when people's lives are at stake outside of the military. Do a quick online search for "diversity saves lives" and you'll find numerous articles documenting how racial/ethnic diversity literally saves lives in the medical field. Doctors of color, including those from Black, Latinx, and Indigenous backgrounds, are pivotal to the health and literal survival of racially minoritized communities. Writing in *Stat News*, Usha Lee McFarling noted that a study published in *JAMA Network Open* was "the first to link a higher prevalence of Black doctors to longer life expectancy and lower mortality in Black populations."[51] Disturbingly, the authors of the article found that half of the nation's counties don't have a single Black primary care doctor.[52] Relatedly, an analysis of births in Florida from 1992 to 2015 suggests that when "Black newborns are cared for by Black physicians, the mortality penalty they suffer, as compared with White infants, is halved."[53] Troublingly, "Black newborns die at three times the rate of White newborns," a travesty in a country as affluent and well-resourced as ours.[54] Yes, diversity saves lives, and the phenomenon goes beyond the military. It affects education, public health, the criminal justice system, and more.

HOW DID SCOTUS RULE ON THE ASIAN AMERICAN DISCRIMINATION QUESTION?

Harvard lost, and its admissions program was struck down. Does that mean that the SCOTUS majority agreed with SFFA that Harvard intentionally discriminated against Asian Americans? Not necessarily, although it's easy to assume so. Charges of intentional discrimination against Asian Americans ate up the headlines when Blum and friends filed *SFFA v. Harvard* in 2014. Asian Americans were critical to the branding and image of the case from day one. Blum recruited SFFA members through a website featuring young Asian Americans looking studious, with the words NOT FAIR written on top. Williams College graduate Michael Wang became a key spokesperson for the case. He had filed earlier complaints of discrimination with the US Department of Education after getting rejected from several competitive institutions before *SFFA v. Harvard* was filed. Wang couldn't join *SFFA v. Harvard* as a plaintiff, but he basically became the face of the case since none of the real SFFA plaintiffs wanted to go public.[55] Ironically, Wang later expressed mixed emotions about his role in the case as he came to recognize the continued need for some version of race-conscious admissions.[56]

In the end, Justice Roberts side-stepped the Asian American question. The decision to strike down Harvard's admissions process doesn't mean that the SCOTUS majority fully endorsed SFFA's claim of intentional discrimination. To explain why, let's rewind a bit. *SFFA v. Harvard* distinguished itself as the most high-profile effort to bring Asian Americans into the debate on race-conscious admissions. While previous litigation (*Grutter, Gratz, Fisher v. University of Texas I* and *II*) relied on White women with somewhat unexceptional resumes, Blum finally realized that Asian Americans with 1500+ SAT scores were more sympathetic plaintiffs. At the heart of the case was the question of whether Harvard intentionally discriminated against Asian Americans, which is different from issues of implicit or indirect bias affecting the admissions process, even though the phenomena are sometimes conflated.

SFFA's lawyers argued that Harvard violated the Equal Protection Clause of the Fourteenth Amendment and Title VI of the Civil Rights Act of 1964, which forbids institutions that receive federal funds from engaging in discrimination. In the original complaint filed in the US District Court (District of Massachusetts), SFFA argued that Harvard was using race as more than a "plus" factor: "Each applicant for admission is not evaluated as an individual. Instead, race or ethnicity is the defining feature of the application. That is especially true for Asian-American applicants. Only using race or ethnicity as a dominant factor in admissions decisions could account for the remarkably low admission rate for high-achieving Asian-American applicants."[57] SFFA's claims gloss over the fact that Harvard has a remarkably low admission rate in general, and the admit rate for White applicants who were not athletes, legacies, or children of donors/faculty was on par with the admit rate for Asian Americans.[58]

Overall, the burden of proof was on SFFA to show that Harvard had a game plan to keep the Asian American student population down. In the District Court hearing, SFFA highlighted how Harvard sent mailers encouraging students in "sparse country" (i.e., areas of the country with fewer Harvard applicants) to apply, and used different score thresholds to determine who got a mailer.[59] Evidently, White students who scored a 1310 or higher got a mailer, as did Black, Latinx, and Indigenous students if they scored at least an 1100. Asian Americans needed a 1380 to get a letter. (Cue dramatic music: Dun dun dun!) Harvard countered that the test score minimums for outreach mailers were context dependent. White kids based in urban areas needed higher test scores than Asian Americans to get a mailer.[60] Hey, postage is expensive. Let's not forget that getting an outreach mailer encouraging someone to apply is totally different from being admitted to an institution. Still, SFFA still made a big deal about the issue. Another big controversy was the issue of the *personal rating*, which took up so much space in the media that I'm going to give it its own section below.

When the case went to the Supreme Court, the Asian American discrimination question became less prominent, and the team behind *SFFA* doubled down on trying to wipe out the precedent in *Grutter* that affirmed diversity as a compelling interest that could justify consideration of race. In the original filing, SFFA listed its request that the court overturn cases affirming conventional race-conscious admissions as the sixth grievance on a laundry list of issues; they didn't even specifically mention *Grutter*.[61] Blink twice, and it's easy to miss. In contrast, when they asked the Supreme Court to take up the case, they got right to the point. Right after the title page under "Questions Presented" is: "Should this Court overrule *Grutter v. Bollinger*, 539 US 306 (2003), and hold that institutions of higher education cannot use race as a factor in admissions?"[62]

In breaking down reactions to the ruling, I'm going to rely on the helpful reporting of *Harvard Crimson* writers Cam E. Kettles and Claire Yuan, who spoke to legal experts Jonathan Feingold (Boston University School of Law), Vinay Harpalani (University of New Mexico School of Law), and Kimberly West-Faulcon (Loyola Law School).[63] Kettles and Yuan observed that overall, the SCOTUS ruling "did not disturb a lower court decision that Harvard had *not* [emphasis added] illegally discriminated against Asian American applicants." Feingold stated: "The Supreme Court—the majority, at least, in Justice Roberts' opinion—ignored or avoided . . . the legal claim that Harvard was intentionally discriminating against Asian Americans." In a similar vein, Harpalani commented: "They didn't really disturb the finding that there was no intentional discrimination against Asian Americans."[64] The *Crimson* reporters observed how SCOTUS spoke positively about the process at Harvard, despite striking it down: "Instead, the Court's majority opinion called Harvard's admissions practices 'well intentioned and implemented in good faith,' praising the 'commendable goals' behind the process."[65]

So what did the ruling in *SFFA* actually say about Asian Americans? Not that much, considering that the entire lawsuit was supposed to be about Asian Americans. Yes, we're so invisible that we got mostly ignored in a Supreme Court ruling that's supposed to be all about us. Two justices issued concurring opinions that danced around the Asian American question. Justice Clarence Thomas, notoriously against affirmative action, didn't even mention Asian Americans until page 43 of his opinion, when he argued that Asian Americans should not bear any shared responsibility for discrimination against Black people.[66] He seemed to forget that (1) no one had really made that point; and (2) in the Harvard case, no one defended race-conscious admissions based on societal discrimination. Justice Gorsuch talked about how unfair it was that an industry of consultants has sprung up to help Asian American applicants "downplay their heritage to maximize their odds of admission."[67] Such trends only speak to how applicants are reacting to the cutthroat world of competitive college admissions, versus what admissions offices are actually doing.

Now let's see how the majority opinion, issued by Justice Roberts, discussed the Asian American issue: "First, our cases have stressed that an individual's race may never be used against him in the admissions process. Here, however, the First Circuit found that Harvard's consideration of race has led to an 11.1 percent decrease in the number of Asian-Americans admitted to Harvard. . . . And the District Court observed that Harvard's 'policy of considering applicants' race . . . overall results in fewer Asian American and white students being admitted.'"[68]

Does that quote mean that the First Circuit concluded that race was being used against Asian Americans in admissions? No. Let's go back to the First Circuit opinion. When the First Circuit referenced "11.1 percent," it was basically to roll their eyes at SFFA. SFFA made a big deal about how Asian American representation at Harvard might increase from about 24 percent to an estimated 27 percent (11.1 percent difference) without race-conscious admissions.[69] The First Circuit noted that the effect was similar to the one attributed to race-conscious admissions in *Grutter.*[70] In turn, they noted that the "11.1 percent" statistic was being used "to make the impact of Harvard's use of race appear more significant than it is."[71] Yes, an institution might have somewhat lower percentages of non-URM groups under race-conscious admissions, a dynamic recognized in *Grutter.* In 2023, the SCOTUS majority conflated that slight statistical effect with the phenomenon of someone's race being "used against him in the admissions process."[72] Similarly, in the next part of the opinion, the SCOTUS majority deemed Harvard's race-conscious admissions as being responsible for a somewhat lower number of White and Asian Americans being admitted—and saw that pattern as being analogous to someone's race being used against them.

Under the precedent set in *Grutter* and upheld in *Fisher I* and *Fisher II*, an institution of higher education has the ability to consider race/ethnicity in a favorable light as long as the institution meets the criteria related to strict scrutiny and narrow tailoring.[73] That approach extends to Asian Americans, some of whom testified at trial about how they benefited from Harvard's admissions process. Sally Chen, a 2019 Harvard graduate, noted that "she believes she benefited from Harvard's race-conscious admissions policies because she was admitted despite her less-than-perfect SAT scores and GPA. In her view, [Harvard] College evaluated many factors, including the 'role of her race in her life experiences and achievements' and looked at her as a 'whole person.'"[74] Being able to see someone's race/ethnicity as part of someone's life experiences isn't the same thing as using someone else's race/ethnicity against them, despite the claims of the SCOTUS majority.

How numbers ebb and flow in any given year is not an automatic signal of discrimination or of someone's race being used against them. Similarly, the lower courts noted how numbers might shift in the absence of race-conscious admission, but did not pin the phenomenon to the issue of intentional discrimination. Both the US District Court and the First Circuit Court rejected the charge of intentional discrimination after diving deeper into the claims made by SFFA. In the end, the SCOTUS majority relied on the simplistic explanation that any recognition of race had to be a negative for some applicants if it had the potential to work as a positive for others.

Overall, "SFFA's goal, West-Faulcon said, was to have the Supreme Court conflate 'race used for the purpose of inclusion and race used to exclude.'"[75] West-Faulcon and Harpalani agreed that SFFA used the attention-grabbing claim of illegal discrimination to mobilize support for the case, especially among Asian Americans. However, once they made it to the Supreme Court, there was a bait-and-switch, as noted by West-Faulcon: "At the Supreme Court level, *SFFA* shifted from any focus on white advantage compared to Asian American penalty, and shifted to 'Please overrule *Bakke* and

Grutter. Please make it so Harvard and UNC have no capacity to be race-conscious for purposes of inclusion.' . . . The question of whether Asian Americans were the victims of intentional race discrimination was never really the point for SFFA."[76] Ultimately, the strategy worked—and the question of whether Asian Americans were intentionally discriminated against fell by the wayside, having served its purpose of getting the case to the highest court in the land.

ASIAN AMERICANS AND THE PERSONAL RATING

Even though *SFFA v. Harvard* became more about trying to overturn *Grutter* than the Asian American question over time, many still wanted to know what SCOTUS thought about the question. By framing admissions as a "zero sum game," SCOTUS chose to view consideration of race as analogous to discrimination. However, many Asian Americans reject that viewpoint, recognizing the continuing significance of race. Historical and contemporary discrimination motivates many Asian Americans to work for a society that reflects the true diversity of the country, where everyone has the chance to thrive and use their gifts to contribute.[77] Concurrently, many believe that this vision will not be achieved through solely colorblind means.

In *Race on Campus*, I challenged the claims made by SFFA in their initial filing to the US District Court, but the expert reports in the case came out right as the book went to press. Thus, I wasn't able to address the big question of why Asian American applicants received a slightly lower personal rating than White applicants, and whether the discrepancy was evidence of intentional discrimination by Harvard. Unfortunately, misinformation and confusion on the issue persist. You may remember the headlines that popped up, like CNN's "Lawsuit: Harvard Ranks Asian American Students Lower on Personality Traits."[78] SFFA attorney Cameron Norris highlighted the issue in oral arguments before SCOTUS: "Asians should be getting into Harvard more than whites, but they don't because Harvard gives them significantly lower personal ratings."[79] Damning words, but are they true?

Let's recap what these ratings actually are. Harvard assigned several ratings to applicants: an academic rating, an extracurricular rating, an athletic rating, a personal rating, and an overall rating. The lower the number for the rating, the better. Ratings were not used in a determinative fashion, and getting all 1s and 2s didn't guarantee admission. Still, having low ratings (e.g., more 1s) was correlated with a higher probability of admission. Think of the ratings as a shorthand that helped admissions staff guide discussion as they sifted through hundreds of applicant files. Some commentators referred to the personal rating as the "personality rating" or "personality score."[80] Without more context, it's easy to assume that Harvard thought that Asian Americans had "substantially worse personalities than those of any other racial group."[81] SFFA rode the momentum of the confusion, with SFFA attorney Norris proclaiming in oral argument: "Harvard ranks Asians less likable, confident, and kind."[82]

As often is the case, the truth is more complicated. First, the personal rating was a lot more than a so-called personality score. As explained by Harvard, the personal rating was "based on all parts of the application, including essays, letters of recommendation, and interview reports."[83] The rating considered potential contributions to the community at Harvard, as well as "to society as a whole after graduation."[84] In retrospect, the personal rating should have been called "the other stuff rating" or something similar, because it's supposed to reflect features that aren't captured as much in the other ratings. The personal rating included a scale related to certain traits such as integrity, helpfulness, reaction to setbacks, and concern for others. *However, the scale was not the entire personal rating*; it was just one of the many pieces of information that could inform the personal rating. Further, Harvard never released data for how students ranked on the personal traits subscale—there would have been even bigger headlines if they had. Thus, the (slightly) lower personal ratings for Asian Americans could exist for reasons besides the personal trait subscale. Unlike what Norris claimed, we don't actually know if Harvard ranked Asian Americans as "less likable, confident, and kind." I haven't been able to dig up any evidence supporting that specific assertion after combing through both expert reports.

Unlike the personal traits subscale, we *do* have data on scores assigned to letters of recommendation, which are part of the personal rating. Asian Americans received slightly lower ratings on letters from counselors and teachers than White applicants.[85] This pattern was true both overall and for students with the same level of academic performance. Why would Asian Americans get lower ratings on letters of recommendation, when they received the strongest extracurricular and academic ratings from admissions staff? There's an explanation: Asian Americans are much more likely to attend public schools, where counselors are overloaded and have much less time to write highly individualized letters of recommendation. With my collaborator Sooji Kim, I found that almost 75 percent of Asian Americans whose top college pick was Harvard or a similarly elite, highly selective institution attended public school.[86] However, among White students whose first choice was a place like Harvard, only 56 percent attended public school.

Differences between public and private school likely affect the letters that applicants receive. You'll hear more about this in chapter 5: Private schools often have numerous advantages when it comes to letters of recommendation, including smaller student-to-counselor ratios and relationships with admissions counselors at elite institutions.[87] In contrast, in one study, researchers found that counselors from large, public high schools were notably more likely to reuse text from letters for their students, likely due to their heavy caseloads.[88] The essay also probably affected the personal rating. We don't have data from Harvard on any scores assigned to the essay, if any were assigned. Quite possibly, White applicants were more likely to have private college consultants who would help guide (or near ghostwrite) essays.

So yes, there are multiple unfair conditions that help explain why Whites had slightly stronger scores on the personal rating than Asian Americans. Still, that doesn't mean that Harvard was intentionally discriminating against Asian Americans by slamming their personalities.[89] Similarly, Judge Burroughs concluded: "To begin at the end, the Court sees no evidence of discrimination in the personal ratings save for the slight numerical disparity itself. The statistical disparity is relatively minor and can be at least partially explained by a variety of factors including race-correlated inputs to the rating such as teacher and guidance counselor recommendations. Just as the Court cannot explain the variations in the academic and extracurricular ratings, it cannot definitively explain the difference in the personal ratings, but it finds that the disparity is small and reflects neither intentional discrimination against Asian American applicants nor a process that was insufficiently tailored to avoid the potential for unintended discrimination."[90]

Judge Burroughs tackled the question of intentional discrimination much more carefully than the SCOTUS majority, getting into the weeds of the expert reports and considering alternative explanations for hypotheses. She refuted stereotypes about Asian Americans, writing: "The Court firmly believes that Asian Americans are not inherently less personable than any other demographic group, just as it believes that Asian Americans are not more intelligent or more gifted in extracurricular pursuits than any other group."[91] In pushing back against pseudoscience and entrenched stereotypes, she made a powerful statement about how talent and achievement aren't exclusive to any single community.

Overall, SFFA's claim that Asian Americans were less likely to get into Harvard because Harvard thought they were "less likable, confident, and kind" is arguably based more on speculation than on data and evidence. As Judge Burroughs noted in her opinion: "SFFA did not present a single admissions file that reflected any discriminatory animus, or even an application of an Asian American who it contended should have or would have been admitted absent an unfairly deflated personal rating. . . . This would strongly suggest that Asian American applicants were not discriminated against relative to white applicants and were therefore not unduly burdened by Harvard's admissions program."[92]

When you hear about someone with outstanding grades, test scores, and accomplishments, it's easy to forget that there are thousands of students around the country who have similarly high-caliber accomplishments. A 1600 and lots of special extracurricular activities are great, but still no guarantee of admission. Despite the competition, many Asian Americans *are* admitted to Harvard, and many incredibly strong students of all races/ethnicities are rejected. Asian Americans who joined SFFA may have felt that the deck was stacked against them, but as I discussed in the last chapter, the admissions scene is incredibly challenging for everyone. As I write this in 2024, over 870,000 more students are graduating from high school now than in the late 1990s.[93] Not everyone is aiming for Harvard, but many will try. At the end of the day, Asian Americans will find that the intense competition in admissions is here to stay, even after the SCOTUS ruling. Perfect test scores and strong accomplishments will never guarantee admission. In the end, SFFA took advantage of confusion about the personal rating to rally support for their case. Still, not much is going to change for Asian Americans and competitive college admissions.

ARE ANY LEGAL OPTIONS LEFT? I'M GLAD YOU ASKED

Do any legal options exist for bringing back conventional race-conscious admissions? At some institutions, there is no substitute for being able to directly consider a student's race/ethnicity during the admissions process. Once again, "direct" does not mean "determinative." "Direct" refers to being able to see a student's race/ethnicity and consider how it may have shaped their context for opportunity, as well as potential contributions to campus and society. The SCOTUS ruling leaves us with more indirect options to consider students' experiences with race through the essay and other parts of the application.

Still, other options exist to defend even a more conventional, direct (not determinative) version of race-conscious admissions—basically, what we had prior to the *SFFA* ruling. A report issued by the Congressional Research Service (CRS), the nonpartisan research service that supports Congress, acknowledged that an institution could draw up such policies to remedy past racial discrimination *exhibited by the institutions themselves.* Report author April Andersen, an attorney for CRS, wrote: "Additionally, other Supreme Court precedent recognizes that remedying educational institutions' past discrimination is a compelling government interest distinct from the interest in fostering student-body diversity that the Court appeared to reject in *Students for Fair Admissions.* Accordingly, an institution could still take action (including, perhaps, race-conscious action) to remedy its own past racial discrimination. Remedying general, societal discrimination, however, is not an adequate compelling government interest. In the *Students for Fair Admissions* case, the schools did not claim to be remedying past discrimination. . . . Accordingly, it is unclear whether institutions could succeed on a remedial theory."[94]

As Andersen notes, remedying the historical discrimination of a specific institution could be a viable compelling interest to justify race-conscious admissions. There is no shortage of US higher education institutions still affected by legacies of exclusion and discrimination. It would be an impressive show of leadership to see an institution adapt race-conscious policies to address and remedy those injustices. Yes, it's unlikely to happen in the current political environment of the mid-2020s, but we never know what could happen in the future.

One type of remedial defense didn't work in *Bakke* (addressing societal but not institution-specific discrimination), but others exist. In her article "Affirmative Action after *SFFA v. Harvard*: Other Defenses," legal scholar Kimberly West-Faulcon outlined no shortage of possibilities for how institutions could defend conventional race-conscious admissions based on the need to address and remedy institution-specific discrimination.[95] She discussed how such arguments could be supported by previous cases: "[*City of Richmond v. J. A.*] *Croson* is the Supreme Court decision that colleges and universities should look to for the evidentiary standard for demonstrating a compelling interest in remedying institution-specific race discrimination or an institution's 'passive participation' in race discrimination by another entity that impacts its selection and inclusion of non-Whites. The *Croson* remedial defense has long been available for a university that seeks to rectify systemic exclusion of historically disproportionately excluded racial groups that stems from that university's own past or ongoing institution-specific forms of race discrimination. But, it has gone unused in the higher education context."[96]

In *City of Richmond v. J. A. Croson*, the SCOTUS majority deemed that a minority-owned business contracting initiative run by the city of Richmond violated the Equal Protection Clause.[97] (You can read more about the specifics of the case in the endnotes.) Richmond had justified the program based on societal discrimination writ large. While SCOTUS rejected the city's rationale, it offered guidance on how the city could've properly justified a remedially based, race-conscious hiring initiative. West-Faulcon notes a detail that should pique the interest of universities: "So, additionally, the *Croson* decision identifies a remedial defense that does not require colleges and universities to prove themselves to have been guilty of race discrimination. . . . Colleges and universities can show that they have 'essentially' become 'passive participants' in a system of racial exclusion by an outside industry, such as the standardized testing industry."[98] The concept of passive participation is throwing a huge bone to institutions. They don't have to show that they acted maliciously, just that they were victims of the times. Of course, if they're willing to step up to own their own responsibility as institutions, even better, but schools may be less eager to do that.

Intriguingly, Justice Kavanaugh quoted directly from *Croson* when commenting on the continuing effects of racial discrimination. In his concurring opinion filed in *SFFA*, he commented: "To be clear, although progress has been made since *Bakke* and *Grutter*, racial discrimination still occurs and the effects of past racial discrimination still persist. Federal and state civil rights laws serve to deter and provide remedies for current acts of racial discrimination. And governments and universities still 'can, of course, act to undo the effects of past discrimination in many permissible ways that do not involve classification by race.'"[99] The quotation in the last part of Justice Kavanaugh's comments is from Justice Scalia's concurring opinion in *Croson*. In *Croson*, Justice Scalia and the SCOTUS majority affirmed the use of race-neutral options to pursue accessibility, and it looks like Justice Kavanaugh was trying to do the same here in *SFFA*: recognize the enduring effects of racial discrimination but signal his preference for race-neutral routes to diversity.

Naturally, the question of the legality of race-neutral methods to advance diversity remains, and I'll talk about that issue more in the next chapter. If you can believe it, in his concurring opinion in *SFFA*, Justice Thomas referenced *Croson* to say that nothing is stopping institutions from giving admissions preferences to identified victims of discrimination if they so desire—a technically race-neutral practice.[100] Seriously! Keep reading to find out more. Still, besides justifying race-neutral methods, *Croson* provides valuable insights into how a campus can defend a race-conscious admissions program based on the need to address institution-specific discrimination.

Other defenses for race-conscious admissions exist. West-Faulcon dubs one "the preservation of federal funding" or "the Title VI compliance" defense. Basically, under Title VI, institutions that accept federal funding (pretty much everyone) cannot exclude anyone, or deny them the associated benefits of participation, due to race, color, or national origin.[101] She argues that the dwindling Black student population at many state flagship institutions "imposes potential Title VI statutory legal liability on flagship 'public ivy' campuses that are in the midst of returning to the days of excluding Blacks altogether."[102] According to West-Faulcon, specific institutions, including those in states that banned race-conscious admissions prior to *SFFA*, could justify race-conscious admissions programs as part of their obligations under Title VI.[103] These obligations include both preventing exclusion and promoting inclusion.

The CRS report notes how Title VI addresses the issue of disparate impacts. Anderson writes: "Some agency interpretations of Title VI could require that schools consider whether their policies disadvantage minority applicants, even inadvertently. . . . A Title VI federal funding recipient's actions might violate Title VI regulations if they have a disproportionate racial effect."[104] It's common sense that institutions should steer clear of policies that put racially minoritized applicants at a disadvantage. Still, legacy admissions, preferences for athletes, and out-of-state recruitment are still going strong as I'm writing this in the mid-2020s. It'd be ideal for institutions to move away from these policies on their own, but the CRS report highlights how Title VI could be used to hold institutions accountable if they continue using policies that disproportionately disadvantage URM students.

WRAPPING IT UP

Overall, the SCOTUS majority did not explicitly overturn *Grutter*, and some scholars highlight how the ruling in *SFFA* is more sensitive to race than commonly thought. In striking down the programs at Harvard and UNC, the SCOTUS majority highlighted issues like the lack of an expiration date for programs and the perceived fuzziness of metrics for evaluation. That said, the end result is *restriction* of race-conscious admissions, versus total destruction. In the end, the SCOTUS majority side-stepped the question of whether Harvard was intentionally discriminating against Asian Americans. Still, SFFA got some of what it wanted. SFFA successfully co-opted Asian American concerns about discrimination to garner media attention and public support, while dealing a significant blow to institutional efforts to advance diversity. Consideration of race-related experiences and identity still continues through the essay and other parts of the application.

Importantly, other legal options remain to defend conventional race-conscious admissions. They include justifying such policies due to institution-specific discrimination, as well as institutions' obligations to prevent exclusion under Title VI. If institutions want to support diverse and inclusive learning environments, they have a serious responsibility to consider these options. Unfortunately, some institutions are bending over backwards to appease Ed Blum. We need courageous action and leadership. Institutions still have legal options to consider race/ethnicity as one of numerous factors in admissions, although the current political climate is admittedly challenging. For the time being, the means to support diversity in higher education have changed, but not the ability of institutions to define and live out their missions related to access and opportunity. In the next chapter, we will discuss the tools that higher education institutions have available to them as they attempt to recruit and enroll diverse student bodies.

3

Pursuing Diversity in a New Era

Easier Said than Done

Shortly after the ruling in *SFFA v. Harvard/UNC* came out, President Joe Biden called on institutions to not "abandon their commitment to ensure student bodies of diverse backgrounds and experience that reflect all of America."[1] Continuing, he declared: "What I propose for consideration is a new standard, where colleges take into account the adversity a student has overcome when selecting among qualified applicants . . . adversity should be considered . . . because we know too few students of low-income families, whether in big cities or rural communities, are getting an opportunity to go to college." Biden's words were a helpful pep talk. Still, taking adversity and socioeconomic status into account isn't a "new standard" in selective college admissions. Prior to the *SFFA* ruling, institutions didn't just consider race *or* class, they always had leeway to consider *both* in understanding a student's context. The two categories are inextricably intertwined, and low-income students of all racial/ethnic backgrounds received considerable preferences in admissions even before *SFFA*.[2]

Still, boosting any type of diversity in higher education is easier said than done. For years, Richard Kahlenberg, a decades-long advocate for solely class-based affirmative action, has made it sound easy: Drop race, and not only will you get more economic diversity, but you'll get just as much racial diversity.[3] The logic was that if you made it harder for some students of color to get in, you could just swap them out with low-income students, and institutions will still have plenty of racial diversity. Plenty of poor kids of color to go around! I'm being sarcastic here, but that's basically the argument of Kahlenberg's 1996 book on the subject, *The Remedy: Class, Race, and Affirmative Action*.[4] His proposed "remedy" made it sound like there were massive numbers of low-income students just waiting in the wings eager to enroll once conventional race-conscious admissions got the boot. Of course, things are a lot more complicated. As noted in the *New York Times*, "income is a relatively weak proxy for race in admissions."[5] The absolute number of low-income White and Asian American students notably exceeds the absolute number of low-income URM students, even if higher proportions of Black, Latinx, and Indigenous students come from low-income backgrounds. Drops in campus diversity in states like California and Michigan, as well as at schools like MIT, Johns Hopkins University, Boston University, Carnegie Mellon University, and others show how there is no simple substitute for being able to consider race in the admissions process.

You can't just wave a magic wand and hope that low-income students are going to come flocking. Yes, there are many low-income talented students "undermatched" in admissions, meaning that they end up at a less selective school but could attend a more selective (i.e., richer) one.[6] However, getting more low-income students to enroll in name-brand institutions is not a quick or easy fix.[7] Increasing economic diversity within higher education is still a worthy goal, and efforts to boost economic diversity will sometimes overlap with efforts to recover racial/ethnic diversity. In this chapter we'll talk about some of the challenges and possibilities related to policies that seek to boost diversity. We will walk through what the research says in terms of what different initiatives do (or don't do) for both economic diversity and racial/ethnic diversity, highlighting the difficulties of advancing either, let alone both.

BOOSTING ECONOMIC AND RACIAL DIVERSITY: CHALLENGES AND POSSIBILITIES

Before I dive into different approaches to boost diversity, I need to address a key question: Can we still pursue diversity through "race-neutral" approaches? The question feels strange because for decades, conservatives supported race-neutral approaches like percent plans and class-based affirmative action. However, we are not living in normal times, and even race-neutral approaches to pursuing diversity are under attack. To date, the most prominent attacks have been on the admissions program at Thomas Jefferson High School for Science and Technology in Fairfax County, Virginia (a.k.a. TJ). TJ is not a college or university, but the case has potential repercussions for higher education. The admissions system at TJ is basically a percent plan where up to 1.5 percent of each middle school in the county can attend TJ; the county also eliminated the $100 application fee. The percent plan boosted both racial and economic diversity. Under the percent plan, the number of low-income Asian Americans admitted to TJ increased considerably, from one student in 2020 to fifty-one students.[8] However, some Asian Americans were unhappy because the percent plan resulted in fewer seats for kids from feeder middle schools in the county, so they sued. For more details on TJ, check the endnotes.[9] The District Court ruled against Fairfax County, but the Fourth Circuit Court of Appeals ruled in favor of the TJ policy. The Supreme Court declined to take the case, which means that the Fourth Circuit ruling still stands.

In May 2025, the Trump administration launched a Title VI investigation into TJ, and there's some big talk saying that even race-neutral approaches to diversity are forbidden under our current regime.[10] However, scary as the bluster is, we have to remember reality. SCOTUS declined to hear the TJ case and let the lower court ruling stand, basically affirming the use of race-neutral methods to pursue diversity. As pointed out by Kahlenberg in an op-ed, Justices Alito and Thomas weren't fans of the TJ admissions system, but none of the other conservative justices joined their dissent.[11] In his concurring opinion in *SFFA*, Justice Kavanaugh quoted directly from Justice Scalia's comments in *Croson* affirming the use of race-neutral methods to pursue diversity. Believe it or not, even Scalia affirmed such approaches. So yes, connecting the dots, SCOTUS is fine with using race-neutral policies to pursue diversity, even with the current conservative majority.

Okay, now let's address the challenges of increasing diversity in a system that has privileged White and wealthy students for so long. Given the entrenched nature of inequality, economic diversity is not an automatic by-product of dropping or severely restricting race-conscious admissions. Increases in low-income student enrollment don't happen without a lot of intentional work and investment. At the University of Michigan, it took over a decade following Prop 2, the state's ban on race-conscious admissions, to see much growth in low-income student enrollment.[12] Low-income students made up only 16 percent of the student body in 2017 (Prop 2 passed in 2006), and inched up to 19 percent in 2022, thanks to initiatives like the Go Blue Guarantee (free tuition for families with incomes of $75,000 or less, inaugurated in 2018) and the HAIL (High Achieving Involved Leader) scholarship.[13] Some schools boasted of increases in Pell-eligible students after the first admissions cycle post-*SFFA*, but those upticks were mainly due to how the formula for eligibility changed versus institutional efforts.[14]

The example of the American Talent Initiative (ATI) reflects how challenging it can be to achieve economic diversity. Funded by billionaire Mike Bloomberg, ATI rolled out to much fanfare in 2015, with the goal of increasing economic diversity in selective institutions. The organization pledged to enroll fifty thousand more low-income students at the 355 institutions (including non-ATI members) that graduate more than 70 percent of students by 2025. Colleges excitedly signed on, happy to be in the company of elite peers like Yale and Princeton. From the 2015–2016 to 2021–2022 academic years, ATI member institutions collectively enrolled about 7,713 low-income students, falling short of goals. Progress has been nonlinear and was disrupted by the pandemic. In their 2022 annual report, ATI noted how members actually enrolled 507 fewer low-income students in the prior year, showing how progress can sometimes be one step forward, two steps back.[15]

ATI noted the challenges to progress: "Despite the initiative's early success, ATI members collectively lost ground toward the 50,000-by-2025 goal from 2019–2020, nearly returning the initiative's Pell enrollment levels to 2015–16 totals."[16] Things have been even worse at non-ATI institutions. From 2015 to 2021, the enrollment of Pell-eligible students at non-ATI schools declined by 12,225 students.[17] Things got somewhat better in 2023, but as of midyear 2025, ATI had yet to post the 2024 report.[18] Hopefully it's updated by the time you're reading this. Altogether, since 2016, ATI schools have enrolled an additional 18,100 low-income students.[19]

For ATI schools, the most growth in absolute numbers occurred at large state universities. The University of Illinois, Champaign-Urbana (UIUC) enrolled 1,688 Pell Grant recipients from 2015 to 2022, and the University of Michigan enrolled 1,386 Pell Grant recipients during the same period.[20] The increase at Michigan is tied to the HAIL scholarship effort that I'll discuss later; UIUC started the Illinois Commitment in 2018, which provides four years of tuition for students with household incomes of $67,100 or lower and $50,000 or less of household assets.[21] Of note, UIUC has had the Illinois Promise program since 2005; the program covers tuition, food/housing, books, supplies, and fees for students with $0 expected family contribution, as well as a fifth year of support if needed.[22] Growth has occurred at smaller institutions as well, like Washington University and Claremont McKenna.[23]

To its credit, ATI isn't trying to hide the news that progress has been nonlinear. Changes in economic diversity are not going to happen overnight; barriers to expanding opportunity are stubborn, complex, and entrenched. It's still worth the effort, even when institutions have lost the tool of conventional race-conscious admissions. Yes, restricting race-conscious admissions is bad for economic diversity, and not just racial diversity. To recap from *Race on Campus*, Sean Reardon of Stanford University and colleagues found that campuses would have the most racial *and* economic diversity if they gave strong consideration to both race and class in admissions.[24] Counterintuitively, they'd have more economic diversity when considering both race and class, versus only weighing economic background strongly.[25] Sometimes you need to consider race to identify economic disadvantage. After all, we don't just have a wealth gap in the US, but a racial wealth gap.

The *New York Times* asked Reardon to run simulations of how elite colleges could attract diverse classes following the decision in *SFFA*.[26] Scenarios that only gave preference for income, as well as income plus poverty, yielded the least diversity.[27] In another scenario, Reardon considered what would happen if campuses favored students who outperformed peers of similar backgrounds: "This strategy identifies, for example, a student who has an 1100 SAT score—but whose score is 250 points above the typical student who also goes to a high-poverty high school and who has low-income parents who didn't attend college. This strategy also discounts some of the wealthiest students whose 1400 scores look less impressive when compared with their equally well-off peers."[28] In this scenario, 17 percent of admitted students would be from low-income backgrounds. Black and Latinx students would be an estimated 25 percent of admitted students. He also looked at the potential effects of expanding the applicant pool through significantly ramping up recruitment at high schools that are predominantly Black and Brown.[29] If somehow we could wave a magic wand to get these students to apply, and also examine their accomplishments in the context of opportunity like in the latter scenario, then 23 percent of admitted students would be from low-income backgrounds, and 32 percent of admits would be Black or Latinx.

These simulations are admittedly simplistic. Right now high school recruitment often favors predominantly White, affluent high schools, which is basically the opposite of the final scenario described by Reardon. Getting all of these students to actually apply would require a tremendous effort. Also, these are simulations of admitted students, versus projections of enrollment or actual enrollment patterns. Just because students are admitted doesn't mean that they'll attend. Even with a good financial aid package, there are plenty of reasons why some students don't want to go to a college that feels like a country club. Consider scenes from the Yale holiday dinner, captured on TikTok. Students uploaded clips showing elaborate ice sculptures, opulent spreads of lobster and sushi, Vegas-style acrobats walking around on stilts, and gingerbread houses as tall as a grown adult.

The captions say a lot: "Yale holiday dinner is basically the capitol party from the hunger games"[30] and "yale [*sic*] holiday dinner accidentally radicalized me #yale #marxism #socialism #ivyleague."[31] It's not hard to imagine a prospective student watching the clips and feeling that they wouldn't fit in at Yale.[32]

Reardon's simulations show how institutions need to do more than give additional favor to low-income students based on income and high school context. The additional step of considering a student's accomplishments relative to their peers is a powerful lever, as is getting more students to apply.[33] It's also important to recognize that meaningful change is not going to happen from a single measure; it's going to take the combination of many changes and reforms. While there is no "magic wand" that will fix admissions, the hope is that many incremental changes will add up. In the next sections, I will highlight policies that may affect economic and/or racial diversity. First we'll look at an exciting example of institutional change, the University of California, Davis (UC Davis) School of Medicine. After that, we'll review policies that are more incrementally successful (e.g., Landscape), policies that need improvement (e.g., percent plans), and policies that are ineffective or downright counterproductive.

CHANGE IS POSSIBLE: THE UC DAVIS SCHOOL OF MEDICINE STORY

Change is possible, but institutional change will require top to bottom investment, from funding to student support and climate. One promising exemplar of what's possible is the UC Davis School of Medicine (UCDSOM). Transformation at UC Davis didn't happen overnight. Prop 209 (California Proposition 209) passed in 1996, banning race-conscious admissions in the state. Racial diversity plummeted at UCDSOM after Prop 209. The ballot initiative didn't boost economic diversity either: There wasn't suddenly an influx of low-income students enrolling now that UCDSOM couldn't consider race/ethnicity. The percentage of URM students was a dismal 8 percent in 2000; it continued to bounce between under 10 percent to under 20 percent from 2001 to 2009.[34] Around 22 percent is the national average.

Mark Henderson, who helped coordinate much of the change, became associate dean of admissions and outreach in 2007. Around 2010, the numbers began to climb, to 26 percent in 2010, 36 percent in 2014, back down to 30 percent in 2018, and an impressive 52 percent in 2020.[35] The numbers shift a bit from year to year, but UCDSOM has clearly pulled away from the pack in terms of institutional change. For the class of 2026, 14 percent of students identified as Black, 30 percent as Hispanic/Latinx, 42 percent as first-generation college students, and 84 percent from economically disadvantaged backgrounds.[36] This change is even more poignant when you consider that UCDSOM was the site for the historic *Regents of the University of California v. Bakke* case in 1978.

Change didn't happen through just one big thing: It required a multifaceted approach. Step one was diversifying the admissions committee and staff. Yes, the people who read and evaluate applications matter, as research from the undergraduate sector shows.[37] UCDSOM poured money into scholarships, about $12 million. They deemphasized MCAT scores, and started relying heavily on a measure of socioeconomic disadvantage that incorporates eight measures: whether a student received a fee waiver for the medical school application, if they spent their childhood in an underserved region, if they ever received family assistance, income, contributions to family earnings, need-based aid received during college, the family's contribution to funding college, and parental education.[38]

This measure is more complex and multifaceted than leaning just on income, or even some combination of income, parental education, and neighborhood. That said, UCDSOM doesn't just look for students who scored high on the measure. The institution realized that if it wanted to attract highly talented students from economically and racially diverse backgrounds, it needed to become the type of school that these students would want to attend. It set up specialized pathways to train students to serve underserved communities, from an accelerated three-year primary care program to working with Native/Indigenous communities to supporting migrant workers in California's Central Valley. All are incredibly critical needs. UCDSOM worked to improve their institutional climate, diversify the faculty, and support students.

Some of the changes at UCDSOM are specific to medical schools, but most of the general ideas are broadly applicable. Walking the talk on institutional transformation is hard. Seeing as how too many schools are taking their sweet time to drop practices like legacy admissions, I'm not optimistic that many institutions are willing to make the investments needed for significant change. Undergraduate institutions have a choice in who they want to educate, and the way they structure admissions and recruit students says a lot about their value systems. Of course, minority-serving institutions have been walking the talk for over a century. As UCDSOM shows, change is possible within the historically White sector of selective higher education if the leadership and investment are there. I'm not sure it is, but I'd love to be proven wrong.

INCREMENTAL CHANGE: LANDSCAPE AND OPPORTUNITY ATLAS

Now that we've looked at one example of transformational change, we can look at other initiatives that can support incremental change. You can think of them as the à la carte menu of options. A growing number of selective institutions were using the College Board's Landscape tool, which is linked with modest gains in economic diversity but not racial diversity. Sadly, the College Board decided to kill Landscape in September 2025, right as this book went to press. I've decided to keep the section for posterity's sake; it's a very disappointing move. Funded and supported by the College Board, Landscape provides information related to the high school and the student's neighborhood.[39] You may remember the initial branding of the tool as an "Adversity Score" before it was renamed in 2019. While Landscape existed before the SCOTUS decision, it gained attention postruling as one of the few tools with a decent amount of research behind it. Policymakers love to point to something and say that it's "evidence-based." Use of Landscape has been linked with about a 3 to 5 percentage point increase in the probability of admission for low-income students, but not increased racial diversity.[40] These studies predate the SCOTUS ruling, but it's unlikely that much will change when campuses can't consider race in the way they did in earlier years.[41]

One study led by Zachary Mabel of the Georgetown Center for Education and the Workforce analyzed data from forty-three schools that used Landscape.[42] Use of Landscape was not linked with an increase in low-income student *enrollment* (versus admission) for most of the schools in the sample. However, nine of the forty-three institutions had increased low-income student enrollment, and most of those nine schools indicated that they used Landscape to help allocate scholarship funds. According to Mabel and team, just adding Landscape as a "mechanical function" did little for enrollment outcomes. Still, "the evidence suggests that some colleges were better positioned to yield students on the margin of enrolling (potentially due to their underlying attractiveness unrelated to Landscape), more successful at identifying and accepting marginal students likely to matriculate, used Landscape in particular ways to incentivize matriculation, or combined Landscape with other institutional policies to do the same."[43] In other words, just using Landscape and calling it a day won't do much to boost low-income student enrollment. Colleges need to be serious about boosting need-based financial aid and outreach to help Landscape live up to its potential.

Ideally, Landscape can facilitate a more consistent review of applicants by providing a consistent set of measures reflecting socioeconomic challenge or privilege. The makeup of who actually reads applications varies widely from campus to campus, from a smaller group of full-time admissions professionals to a large pool of seasonal readers. Hopefully, training will sink in well, but people may digest the information and apply it differently. Reader background can also shape evaluation, as we discussed in chapter 1. Making tools like Landscape a regular feature of the application review can prime admissions readers to be thinking about a student's environment as a standard part of the review process, versus leaving it to chance. Plus it's free, so there's no excuse not to use it.

Much of the research on Landscape has been led by Professor Michael Bastedo, director of the Michigan Admissions Collaboratory, whom we met in chapter 1. In one study that set the stage for Landscape, Bastedo and Nick Bowman (a friend/collaborator) conducted a randomized controlled trial to see whether providing more information to evaluators was linked with admissions outcomes.[44] In the "limited-information" condition, admissions officers received some information about high schools, such as graduation rates. However, in the "detailed-information" condition, readers received more information about the high school to help put an applicant's accomplishments in context: the median SAT/ACT score of the high school and the applicant's GPA percentile within the high school.[45] Altogether, those who participated "in the detailed-information condition were 13 to 14 percentage points (i.e., 26%–28%) more likely to recommend admitting a low-SES applicant from an underserved high school than those in the limited-information condition, although the limited-information condition provided significant details about family SES and high school context."[46]

If the items in the detailed-information condition sound familiar, well, you're looking at the foundation for what would later become Landscape. Bastedo is characteristically modest about the tool, noting: "We don't expect to be able to move the needle in a huge way, but we hope it continues to go in the right direction."[47] I appreciate that Mike is of the "a lot of little things can add up and make a difference, but there's no magic wand" camp. While Landscape is no magic wand, it's probably a step in the right direction, especially when paired with serious investments in financial aid and efforts to broaden the applicant pool. I'm curious to see whether adding measures like the racial/ethnic breakdown of the school, neighborhood, and zip code or Census tract, as well as other measures related to race, could be useful to admissions readers as additional context.

Another tool worth looking at is the Opportunity Atlas, which is accessible for free at https://www.opportunityatlas.org/. The Atlas is a collaboration between the team at Opportunity Insights and the US Census Bureau. Viewers can see data on outcomes related to social mobility at the neighborhood and county levels, as well as parse out trends related to mobility for specific subpopulations. Yale used the Opportunity Atlas as a supplement to Landscape and managed to avoid a major regression in URM student enrollment in the first year after the SCOTUS ruling, so it may be worth looking at.[48] In particular, data on outcomes related to specific racial/ethnic groups is helpful contextual information.

DON'T FORGET TO DO THIS: ADVANCING DIVERSITY THROUGH OUTREACH AND YIELD

Institutions should also pay attention to outreach and yield. Regarding yield, it's one thing to admit students; it's another thing to get them to come. One promising effort is partnering with cultural centers and student organizations to encourage admitted students to enroll. These efforts are nothing new. I still remember making the T-shirt for the official "Asian Student Recruitment Weekend" (a.k.a. ASRW) at Vanderbilt, my alma mater, before it morphed into "Mosaic Multicultural Student Weekend." Back then, the institution would send invitations to admitted students of color encouraging them to attend the weekend. In the current political climate, this type of direct approach is vulnerable to scrutiny, although the ruling in *SFFA* doesn't mention outreach efforts. However, institutions can still host yield events in partnership with ethnic student organizations and/or cultural centers. They need to allow any interested student to attend, or apply if the program warrants a selection process. Programs can be advertised through websites, mailers, or emails highlighting different ways that students can get to know the institution after being admitted.

Institutions can learn from outreach events hosted by institutions following the SCOTUS ruling. Not too long after the ruling was announced, Yale hosted a program, "Yale in MOHtion," which flew in interested high school seniors to attend Yale's Multicultural Open House (MOH).[49] MOH features programming from Yale's Afro-American, Asian American, La Casa, and Native American Cultural Centers. Importantly, MOH is open to anyone who wants to attend. Students apply to the fly-in part of the program, and priority is given to those who would not be able to afford to attend MOH if not for the fly-in program, which covers expenses. There you have it, folks: a program that's open to everyone that showcases parts of campus that are of interest to many students—yes, it can be done.

INCREMENTAL CHANGE, BUT STILL IMPORTANT: IMPROVING HOLISTIC REVIEW BY CONSIDERING CONTEXTUALIZED GPA

Other work by Bastedo and colleagues highlights the potential of using contextualized GPA in admissions. The issue is important given debates about whether test scores or GPA are a better predictor of college outcomes. Contextualized GPA is a metric that reflects a student's GPA in relation to other GPAs at the high school, versus raw GPA, the traditional score that goes up to 4.0 (unweighted) or 5.0 (weighted). Bastedo's team analyzed a database of 2.3 million students from a Midwestern state, which included data from all public high schools and the state's fifteen public colleges and universities.[50] The dataset also included ACT scores for all students; the state requires that all students take the ACT as juniors. The dataset included both raw and contextualized GPA; contextualized GPA represented the student's GPA in relationship to the median GPA of the high school.[51]

Contextualized GPA and raw GPA were the strongest predictors of student success outcomes (first-year college GPA, first-year retention, four-year graduation), followed by ACT scores and curriculum rigor. Of note, contextualized ACT was a stronger predictor of student success outcomes than raw ACT score, but contextualized GPA outperformed both. In the study, "contextualized GPA had a stronger, more consistent relationship with college success than did contextualized standardized test scores; this trend was found across all fifteen institutions in our study sample."[52] Importantly, findings on contextualized GPA were consistent across the state's fifteen institutions, including one with an admit rate of under 20 percent.

Intriguingly, curriculum rigor was not a standout predictor of college success outcomes. Along with ACT-related measures, "the effect sizes associated with these variables of interest are much lower in comparison to those associated with high school GPA-related variables."[53] Admissions readers consider whether students are taking the most rigorous courses possible, but maxing out on AP courses may matter less for collegiate outcomes than people might think. Taking some advanced coursework is valuable, but given the "survival of the fittest" atmosphere of some high schools, students might benefit from a little breathing room instead of just taking the highest-level courses for the sake of having them.

Bastedo's team also looked at trends for low-income and URM students in another study, finding that both raw and contextualized GPA outperformed the ACT, both raw and contextualized, as a predictor of student success outcomes.[54] Curriculum rigor variables were not a significant predictor of GPA in half of the fifteen institutions for URM students, and "ACT scores, both raw and contextualized, do not show a consistent, significant association with college graduation and retention across institutions in our sample [for URM students], and the effect sizes of estimates are small."[55] Given that both raw and contextualized GPA consistently predict success outcomes across populations and institutions, Bastedo and team suggest that providing both data points to admissions readers is helpful. Providing contextualized GPA would also be helpful in light of critiques that GPAs are difficult to compare due to grade inflation.

INCREMENTAL CHANGE: TEST-OPTIONAL AND TEST-FREE ADMISSIONS

I'll touch more on testing policy in the next chapter, but I want to include a quick discussion here to highlight the potential of test-optional and test-free policies for broadening access. Our CAF Co-LAB research team found that such policies were associated with an increase in Black student enrollment at mid-selective institutions during the pandemic.[56] In some but not all models, test-optional was associated with greater enrollment of low-income students at highly selective institutions. Some institutions argue that requiring test scores will help them identify high-scoring, low-income students with the potential to succeed. The concern is that under test-optional, these students didn't submit test scores that were on the lower end of the testing percentile range for the institution. I'll unpack this reasoning more in chapter 4, but two quick points. First, some institutions seem to assume that the same type of students will still apply under test-required policies, which may or may not happen. In our work, test-optional was linked with a clear increase in applications. Second, if test-required admissions is better for access, why was low-income student enrollment so low under test-required policies pre-pandemic?[57] Test-optional and test-free policies aren't the best at predicting who will get hired by McKinsey or attend an Ivy for graduate school, which has been noted in pro-testing arguments.[58] Still, if a goal is broadening access, test-optional and test-free policies may be a helpful tool.

INCREMENTAL CHANGE: DIRECT ADMISSIONS

Direct admissions is a newish kid on the block. Traditionally, students can only be admitted to the institutions that they apply to, but figuring out where to apply can be daunting. Looking back, creating my college list was a somewhat haphazard process. The list consisted of schools where I knew people at, some I heard of thanks to my siblings, our state flagship, one where I had done a summer camp, and a few known for giving scholarships. Down the road as I met people who had gone to other schools, I thought to myself "hm, maybe I should have applied there," but the school wasn't on my radar. Random as my list was, I benefited from knowing a lot of people who had gone to college, seeing two siblings apply, and attending a high school visited by elite institutions.[59]

Now imagine a student at a high school that doesn't get a lot of college visits and who doesn't know many people who went to college. How will they build their list? Here's where the College Board would plug the SAT because of the marketing and outreach materials that some students receive due to their scores. Yes, colleges do buy lists, but as the research of Ozan Jaquette, Karina Salazar, and Crystal Han shows, it's usually affluent students who benefit: Schools want applicants who can pay the bills.[60] Even if marketing materials sometimes reach low-income students, moving from marketing to an actual application is another uphill climb. Numerous factors discourage too many students from applying, from sticker shock to fear of not getting in.

In direct admissions, students are offered admission up front, or are told they'll be admitted if they apply. Instead of hoping that students will apply to your institution, you tell them up front: Congratulations, you've been admitted! The programs are a good fit for institutions that want to expand access or boost enrollment. Direct admissions has been adapted in states like Georgia, Idaho, Virginia, Hawaii, New York, and Minnesota. Some programs are run directly through the institution or state system; others are facilitated through vendors like Common App or Niche. Taylor Odle of the University of Wisconsin, Madison and Jennifer Delaney of the University of California, Berkeley have been tracking the impact of programs. In one study of six colleges that made offers through Common App, getting a proactive offer of admission was linked with being 12 percent more likely to apply to the institution.[61] Students were told that they were accepted but still had to submit a simplified version of an application. They were proactively given a fee waiver and the impact was stronger for racially minoritized, low-income, and first-generation students. However, students were not more likely to enroll than their control group peers, likely because of financial barriers. In Idaho, a direct admissions initiative was linked with a 4 to 8 percent increase in first-time, undergraduate enrollment, but had no effect on low-income student enrollment. Growth was highest in the two-year, open access sector.

Direct admissions has some promise, but affordability is still a key barrier. Increasing low-income student enrollment is not an easy fix, even when you directly go to students and admit them proactively. Beyond the financial cost of college, low-income students have to weigh the cost of lost wages from not working full-time. Direct admissions holds a valuable lesson for more selective schools: Just admitting students is not enough—there are so many challenges that impede actual enrollment, let alone retention.

INCREMENTAL CHANGE, WITH INTRIGUING POTENTIAL: DIRECT/PUSH-OUT FINANCIAL AID

Another "direct" practice with potential is direct financial aid, or *push-out* financial aid packages. These packages offer students scholarships, or even just an estimated cost of attendance, before they formally apply. Like direct admissions, the emphasis is on reducing friction in the process, telling students up front *before* they apply what they can expect to pay.[62] A key example is the HAIL scholarship piloted at the University of Michigan. Michigan told targeted students up front that if they applied to Michigan and were accepted, they would receive a full-tuition scholarship.[63] There was no requirement to prove eligibility through receiving a Pell Grant, even though most of the students ended up receiving one. In other words, the possibility of the scholarship offer was *pushed out* to students, making them feel one step closer to being able to attend Michigan.

In a study run by researchers at Michigan, low-income enrollment increased only when students were told they'd get the scholarship if accepted. No significant increase occurred when students were told that they needed to be accepted *and* have eligibility confirmed through FAFSA (Free Application for Federal Student Aid) to get a full-tuition scholarship.[64] The difference between the two formats seems negligible, but having to prove eligibility is another hoop for students to jump through. The success of HAIL, with no proof-of-eligibility, shows that reducing friction in the admissions process is vital for expanding access. Notably, push-out financial aid can make a difference even without students being guaranteed admission.

Selective colleges have not experimented much with push-out financial aid offers, but this area is ripe for innovation and research. While some public institutions offer free tuition for students with certain household incomes or who are Pell-eligible, most require proof of eligibility. Students must apply first, then confirm that they're Pell-eligible if admitted, versus telling students up front that they'll receive the scholarship if admitted. The latter scenario is ideal for reducing friction. I would like to see more experimentation with push-out offers from private institutions, given the intimidatingly high sticker prices. Institutions, both public and private, should consider more targeted outreach to low-income students, proactively telling them the expected cost of attendance. Using metrics like attendance in high schools with a high percentage of free and reduced lunch, institutions could send mailers or electronic communication to push out estimated or actual aid offers to students. Later in the chapter, we'll discuss a study where researchers tested the effectiveness of direct financial aid packages combined with guaranteed admission, joining two approaches to reduce friction and increase certainty in admissions.

As I type this, the financial aid landscape is still a bit of a mess with the botched FAFSA rollout of 2024, which unfortunately made an already confusing process even more complicated.[65] Right now the onus is still on the student and their family to wrangle with a school's net price calculator, which may not provide accurate, easily digestible information. In theory, net price calculators sound great: Families type in information about their finances and receive an estimated cost of attendance. However, a team led by Laura Perna of the University of Pennsylvania found multiple problems with net price calculators, from the calculators simply not working to "incomplete and misleading presentations of information."[66] Net price calculators are often difficult to use, especially for low-income families. Phillip Levine, an economist at Wellesley College, noted: "[Net price calculators] often use tax jargon and require inputs from tax forms. The fear and confusion that those tax forms generate is often enough to scare away potential users."[67] Further, going to each institution's website and entering in the information one at a time is a cumbersome process. Ideally we would have a streamlined and centralized system where a student, parent, or guardian could enter the information once and receive the results for a larger list of institutions. If we can have dating websites that can do this, surely we can do better with financial aid. Levine started the tool MyinTuition to help simplify the process, but there's still room for improvement.

NECESSARY, BUT NEED IMPROVEMENT: FREE TUITION AND LOAN REDUCTION PROGRAMS

As noted, more public institutions have rolled out "free tuition" programs to low-income students. To the upper middle-class or rich person, free tuition sounds like an incredible bargain. However, to many low- or moderate-income families, college costs are still daunting even without tuition. At some state institutions, estimated room and board costs exceed tuition. For example, in my home state of Ohio, room and board at the Ohio State University (OSU) in 2023–2024 was $14,382 while in-state tuition was $12,859. Even with scholarships or additional grant aid, the average net price for a family making $30,000 or less was an estimated $7,759 per year, which is a huge share of a low-income family's finances.[68] Some students take out loans to cover costs, but others will decide that a four-year institution isn't worth it. So yes, "free tuition" can be a good first step to attract students, but it doesn't guarantee that students will enroll.

In general, loan reduction programs like free tuition programs have been linked with increases in low-income student enrollment, but not increased URM student enrollment.[69] Once again, measures to boost economic diversity don't automatically translate into greater racial/ethnic diversity. Another issue is that most programs cover only four years, but time-to-degree is shaped by both race and class. Many students from affluent high schools come in with AP credit that speeds up time-to-degree.[70] Due to disparities in academic preparation, Black, Brown, and low-income students are less likely to come in with AP credit. Oftentimes they have less socialization around choosing a major and career path, which can result in switching majors more and prolonging time-to-degree. Finally, they're more likely to experience challenges that make college graduation take longer, like having to leave school during a family crisis or working during college to help support relatives. To go back to OSU as an example, the four-year graduation rate for Black students who started in Fall 2019 was 54.9 percent, versus 74.1 percent for White students.[71] However, most free tuition programs are not responsive to that reality, meaning that participating students can still end up with substantial unmet need.

To be more effective, free tuition programs should include options for a fifth or sixth year if a student is making consistent progress toward graduation. Ideally, financial aid programs would meet all demonstrated need, although few public institutions do. The less friction in the program, the better. One institution that we studied showed us what *not* to do: They announced their free tuition with glowing press releases, but we had a hard time finding any information on the program on the institution's website. You really had to dig, and that was even with us intentionally looking for information on the program. Execution matters. Previous iterations of the Excelsior Scholarship in New York provide another cautionary tale. The program had a limited impact both in the two and four-year sector due to having too many hurdles, restrictions, and requirements for participation.[72]

Culturally and linguistically responsive outreach for programs is also needed. Just like direct admissions, an institution can't assume that an accepted student will actually come even if tuition is covered. In fact, they shouldn't even assume that eligible students will even apply. Of course it never hurts to have a billionaire provide additional funding to support student needs beyond tuition, such as in the Dell Scholars Program at the University of Texas at Austin (UT Austin). Still, institutions need to go out in the community and help students from high-need areas know about programs. It's a tall order, but one worth pursuing to widen opportunity for talented in-state students.

While we're talking about money, what about race-conscious scholarships? The *SFFA* ruling said a lot about university admissions, but was silent on financial aid and scholarships. That didn't stop state officials in Missouri and Kentucky from immediately rescinding race-conscious financial aid and scholarship programs. Technically, such programs remain legal, being unaddressed by the ruling in *SFFA*. After the ruling, Western Illinois University revoked a race-conscious scholarship, saying that they were required to do so by the ruling. After outcry, someone realized that the ruling didn't actually say anything about scholarships, and the scholarship was restored.[73] Ed Blum himself has said that he does not think the ruling in SFFA applies to scholarships, although he doesn't think race-conscious financial aid would survive in court.[74] In this litigious day and age, race-conscious scholarships are often seen as a vulnerability for campuses, even though these scholarships have been so incredibly vital over the years. Many programs already proactively shifted from "minority scholarships" to scholarships for students committed to supporting and advocating for diversity. Likely, in the years to come, institutions that have already not made the switch will do so.

WHY NOT? REPARATIONS AND RECOGNIZING VICTIMS OF DISCRIMINATION

I've sat in a lot of conversations about "what do we do post-*SFFA*?" over the last few years. Let me tell you, there's no way to make a higher education policy conversation more awkward than to bring up reparations.[75] Fortunately for you, I'm not afraid to dive into an awkward conversation, so I'll address it—why not special consideration, in both admissions and scholarship funds, for those who are descendants of enslaved peoples?[76] Much of higher education was built and sustained by enslaved peoples and their descendants. Justice Brett Kavanaugh concluded that such policies would not be based on race.[77] Ironically, too many institutions have defended legacy preferences for years based on family ties and connections, while generally ignoring the other generational ties that have sustained their institutions.[78] Depending on the design of such programs, reparation-oriented programs might affect only a limited number of students (e.g., Georgetown's scholarship program, which has supported about twenty individuals over the years), but broader programs are possible.[79] Once again, when there's a will, there's a way.

The door is also open for policies that don't involve so-called racial classification but consider how students are affected by discrimination. In his concurring opinion in *SFFA*, Justice Thomas commented: "Even today, nothing prevents the States from according an admissions preference to identified victims of discrimination. See *Croson*, 488 U. S., at 526 (opinion of Scalia, J.) ("While most of the beneficiaries might be black, neither the beneficiaries nor those disadvantaged by the preference would be identified *on the basis of their race*" (emphasis in original))."[80] The ins and outs of how being a victim of discrimination would be determined are complicated, but still, options remain. I guarantee that bringing up the idea with your legal counsel would make them squirm, but hey, the idea is right there in *SFFA*.

NEEDS IMPROVEMENT: PERCENT PLANS

One popular policy idea circulating after the SCOTUS decision is the idea of percent plans. Percent plans have been around for some time. The best-known one was enacted in Texas following the state's ban on race-conscious admissions in 1997. What was initially the "Ten Percent Plan" has evolved into the "Top 6 Percent Plan" as seats have become scarcer at UT Austin. California and Florida also instated versions of percent plans following state bans on race-conscious admissions. Percent plans are attractive because they're easy to understand at the surface level: Students who fall into the top *X* percent of their graduating high school class qualify to attend.[81] However, key differences exist between the plans used in Texas, California, and Florida, so it's worth reading the fine print. In Texas, the student can choose any Texas public institution. In California, landing in the top 9 percent and completing the University of California (UC) A–G curriculum requirements gets you a spot in a UC institution, but not necessarily your top pick. In Florida, being in the top 20 percent of your high school class and completing required coursework will get a student into one of the state's twelve institutions, but once again, not necessarily their top choice.

Historically, conservatives liked percent plans because they are technically race-neutral.[82] Prior to the SCOTUS ruling, many saw percent plans as inferior to race-conscious admissions in terms of diversity outcomes. Just being admitted to UT Austin wasn't enough to make everyone go, due to cost, concerns about campus culture, or other factors.[83] In California and Florida, being a top-ranked student gets someone admittance to a state institution but not necessarily one's top choice, so the impact on the states' most selective campuses was limited.[84] Institutions in these states generally saw steep drops in Black and Latinx enrollment following enactment, with some recovery over the years. However, many institutions were unable to recoup the racial/ethnic diversity they had prior to the adoption of the percent plan.[85] Even when institutions did recover some of the numbers, any growth was outpaced by the parallel growth in youth populations of the state, especially for Latinx students. Finally, percent plans didn't help graduate and professional education (e.g., law, medicine, business), which suffered from drops in diversity.

On their own, without any other structural changes like massive investments in financial aid, percent plans don't appear to do much for economic diversity. Analyzing implementation in California, Zachary Bleemer, an economist at Princeton University, concluded that "the combination of these results suggests that, at least as implemented by the

University of California system, top percent policies and [race-neutral] holistic review have minimal impact on the enrollment of lower-income students at selective universities."[86] At UT Austin as well, there wasn't much growth in economic diversity for years following the instatement of the Ten Percent Plan.[87] While the plan was lauded for bringing in some students from high schools that rarely sent students to UT Austin, key barriers to enrollment still remained for many students eligible to attend. In short, admission was not enough.[88]

Prior to the *SFFA* ruling, conventional race-conscious admissions was still legal in most states, so we had the luxury of comparing race-conscious policies to percent plans and concluding that percent plans were an inferior option. Now according to Stella Flores, professor at Boston College and an expert on percent plans, "the counterfactual has changed." Conventional race-conscious admissions is no longer an option, which necessitates giving percent plans a closer look. While less than ideal, percent plans may be better than the option of "doing nothing" following the ruling. Also, already-existing plans in Texas and other states aren't going away, so it's worth thinking about how such plans could be improved.

Flores points out that one issue in Texas is that "the university assumes that with percent plans that the students will come to them." It's easy to assume that if a student is admitted, they will come (rephrasing *Field of Dreams* here) because, hey, who wouldn't want to attend the state flagship? However, that isn't always the case for students, especially low-income students. How can universities encourage more enrollment from low-income students admitted through percent plans? Matt Giani of UT Austin led a team (including Flores) that investigated a "direct-to-student intervention that proactively guaranteed low-income students free tuition, on-campus housing, and a housing scholarship at the University of Texas at Austin. The intervention increased application rates for the full sample, but only increased enrollment at the university among students eligible for automatic admission, for whom the intervention nearly doubled enrollment (43% vs. 24%)."[89] The treatment effect on enrollment for low-income students admitted through a percent plan is really notable, showing how guaranteed admissions is not enough for low-income students: They need more support up front to come. Giani and colleagues comment: "Our results suggest caution in the use of financial certainty for students unlikely to be admitted to universities. However, they underscore the promise of these interventions for low-income students, even those who are guaranteed admission."[90] Their work reflects the potential of direct, push-out financial aid packages discussed earlier in the chapter. The context differs somewhat from the HAIL scholarship intervention we discussed, and we need additional research on various approaches to reducing friction in admissions and financial aid to inform policy.

Flores also suggests improving percent plans by pairing them with more proactive measures such as culturally and linguistically responsive outreach. It's an uphill task that will require major coordination with school districts and community-based organizations, but certainly one worth pursuing to reach students who are hesitant to attend UT Austin and other institutions, even if guaranteed admission.

PROBABLY NOT GOING TO WORK: LOTTERIES

One of the more popular ideas I've heard for college admissions reform is to use lotteries. A quick Google search turns up articles on the idea in *Vox*, *Forbes*, *The Hill*, and others.[91] A headline in *The Atlantic* proclaimed "Lotteries May Be the Fairest Way to Fix College Admissions."[92] Lotteries are fairly easy for people to wrap their minds around, and the (surface level) simplicity is appealing. Given that admissions feels like a crapshoot anyway, why not make the process officially random by entering interested and eligible students who meet a certain GPA or test score threshold into a lottery, and then sample by the desired makeup of the class? Some think that lotteries would lighten some of the mental load of applying to college by making the process feel less personal.[93] Lotteries are also appealing in light of incidents like the Varsity Blues scandal, where wealthy parents paid mastermind Rick Singer to bribe officials and fake accomplishments to get their children into prestigious colleges. Aunt Becky, how could you.

Lotteries seem like a nice, simple solution in the abstract, but how would they affect the selective college landscape? Earlier work concluded that lotteries would not do much for racial/ethnic diversity, although one scenario resulted in an increase of low-income students.[94] That study used a minimum SAT threshold of 900, which seems low for selective colleges. Similarly, in another study, researcher Rebecca Zwick used a minimum GPA of 2.8 and a SAT of 1000 as minimum criteria.[95] In Zwick's study, URM student enrollment went up by a modest 2 percentage points when only GPA was used as a criterion for eligibility. In both studies, graduation rates would likely drop due to the low eligibility thresholds used.

More recently, Dominique Baker at the University of Delaware, and our friend Mike Bastedo of the University of Michigan, explored the question by using robust simulation models, samples of relatively recent college applicants, multiple eligibility criteria, consideration of institutional selectivity, and stratified sampling by gender and income.[96] Dominique is a collaborator, friend, and codirector at CAF Co-LAB who served as an assistant dean of admissions at her alma mater, the University of Virginia. Baker and Bastedo tested a bunch of different scenarios, looking at what would happen if eligibility for the lottery were based on GPA, the SAT, or some combination of the two. They conclude: "Our results show reductions in the proportion of students of color and low-income students across most lotteries . . . with no other changes to the admissions process, it does not appear that the lottery-eligible pools of students would automatically create more racially or economically diverse classes at selective institutions."[97] Additionally, they noted that "year-to-year simulations of an admission lottery suggest that, in some years, lotteries would create severe reductions in the racial and economic diversity of an incoming class . . . if increasing the number of low-income students attending selective institutions is a goal, including a college entrance exam as part of lottery eligibility makes attaining this goal exceptionally difficult."[98] The duo looked at whether stratifying the lottery by income or gender would make a difference.[99] Stratifying by income could result in more economic diversity, but not any increase in Black and Latinx enrollment.[100]

Baker and Bastedo's simulations are helpful in understanding the ramifications of different eligibility criteria for diversity if lotteries were to be used. The authors used SAT and GPA thresholds (in the 25th and

50th percentile for both) that are generally lower than the typical test scores and GPAs at selective institutions, especially highly selective institutions. Even when using lower thresholds for eligibility, lotteries don't come out looking so great on diversity outcomes. They may be less appealing to selective and highly selective institutions who want students who have higher GPAs or test scores *and* who add to the diversity of the student body, which lotteries seem to have trouble replicating. Overall, it doesn't seem that lotteries are the magic wand solution that so many are hoping for to create radical change in admissions.

STOP DOING THIS STUFF: RACE-CONSCIOUS SCHOLARSHIPS FOR MOSTLY WHITE KIDS (A.K.A. "MERIT" AID)

Now for stuff that institutions need to *stop* doing. Post-*SFFA*, most institutions have yet to move away from funds informally earmarked for White, as well as upper-middle-class and flat-out rich students. These funds, which go by the loftier label of "merit" aid, are basically subsidies that disproportionately go to more affluent and White students, and in some cases, Asian Americans.[101] Instead of helping needy students, they tend to reward the dividends of privilege. Of course campuses don't want to outright label them as scholarships for mostly White kids, but that's essentially what they are. You can also think of them as enrollment incentives, as they attempt to lure students away from the competition. In this day and age, even people who are legitimately rich often don't feel rich, and everyone loves a scholarship. Say an institution has $80,000 they can allocate toward aid. They could give it all to one low-income student, allowing them to attend without cost. Or they can give out a $20,000 "merit" award to four wealthier students, who will each pay $60,000 to attend. Guess which option is more attractive? No wonder many institutions allocate more of their dollars toward "merit" versus need-based aid. This type of practice used to be more common at private institutions, but unfortunately it has spread to public schools as well.

Stephen Burd of New America, a DC-based think tank, has been one of the most prolific writers on the subject, documenting the negative consequences of "merit" aid for both racial and economic equity. Examining 134 public research and land-grant institutions in 2014–2015, he found that 28 percent spent at least half of their aid budget on non-needy students; only 13 percent reported allocating under 10 percent of aid to non-needy students.[102] Many schools spent huge sums on "merit" aid, including the University of Alabama ($101 million), Ohio State University ($62 million), Indiana University ($56 million), the University of Michigan ($50 million), and others. Imagine what could happen if most of that money went toward students with demonstrated financial need?

In the world of enrollment management, many argue that "merit" aid is essential to bring in richer students whose tuition payment can help subsidize low-income students. However, it *is* possible to walk away from so-called "merit" aid while expanding economic diversity. Under the leadership of now retired Vice President of Enrollment Management Monica Inzer, Hamilton College decided to stop awarding merit aid in 2007, and shifted funds to need-based aid.[103] In an interview with the *Chronicle of Higher Education*, Inzer commented: "The faculty said, 'Merit scholarships are how we get the smartest kids in our class, right?' And I said, 'Actually, we're not admitting the smartest kids because we don't have enough money.' It was a real challenge to try and convince this community that merit aid, in fact, wasn't what was getting us the smartest students, and that having more need-based financial aid would help us do that."[104] Alumni have responded enthusiastically; it turns out actually committing to a set of values can make people open their pocketbooks more.[105]

STOP DOING THIS STUFF: LOPPING LOW-INCOME STUDENTS

Next on our list is the deeply uncomfortable truth of how students can be denied due to their inability to pay under "need-aware" policies. "Need-blind" schools admit students without consideration of whether they can pay or not.[106] Being branded as a need-blind institution can help attract low-income applicants, but doesn't guarantee economic diversity. A school could be "need-blind," but not offer enough financial aid to students. "Need-aware" institutions may reject some students due to their inability to pay, while giving some special consideration to full-pay students, a.k.a. "perks for rich kids." Need-aware institutions may justify their actions by providing adequate funding for the lower-income students they do admit, even if they turn some away due to finances.[107]

Debate continues over which type of policy better serves students and institutions. The ideal situation is need-blind admissions where institutions meet full financial need. In her interview with the *Chronicle*, Inzer pointed out that even though Hamilton went need-blind in 2010, the goal was access, and not being need-blind for the sake of being need-blind.[108] Inzer described how cutting students worked at Hamilton before it went need-blind: "Hamilton met full need, but when it ran out of money, it ran out of spots for students who needed money, because the college was need-sensitive. At the same time, the college was trying to entice students who didn't need money. So I was like, wait a minute, the difference between the kid we're not admitting because he needs financial aid, and the student we're giving merit aid to because they don't need financial aid, is razor-thin."[109]

In 2017, a reporter for the Lafayette College student paper (jazzily called *The Lafayette*) noted: "Just under 200 applications were turned down because the student could not pay tuition."[110] That number is a sobering reminder of how money can directly shape opportunity. Lafayette allowed Jeffrey Selingo to observe them rejecting students based on inability to pay, which he documented in his book *Who Gets In and Why: A Year Inside College Admissions*.[111] Kudos to Lafayette for drawing back the curtain on a troubling practice. Lafayette is an ATI member and is trying to boost low-income student enrollment. Their current president Nicole Hurd founded the College Advising Corp and is passionate about college access. They sit in a paradoxical spot of being committed to meeting 100 percent of demonstrated need, but still making some decisions based on the ability to pay.

THE START/STOP COMBO: WHAT INSTITUTIONS NEED TO CONSIDER

Campuses can't just adopt tools like Landscape, visit a few more urban high schools, and call it a day. Instead, they need to figure out what their "start/stop" combo should be. The start/stop concept is simple. Every institution needs to *start* doing certain things while also *stopping* other things. Most of the "start" initiatives that I discussed in this chapter are linked with incremental change. Still, if you combine a number of them, the cumulative impact will support progress.

The "stop" list includes but is not limited to recruitment redlining, demonstrated interest, early deadlines (both early decision and early action preferences for limited enrollment majors like business or engineering, honors colleges, etc.), legacy admissions (really low-hanging fruit but still entrenched), "merit" aid, and athletic preferences. As noted by the Georgetown Center for Education and the Workforce, "unless selective colleges eliminate admissions preferences for legacy applicants, student athletes, and other privileged groups, they will be unlikely to achieve the levels of racial/ethnic and class diversity that our models suggest are possible."[112]

Each "stop" measure is linked to incremental change, and once again, the cumulative impact of ending all of these practices would be notable, although other inequities would persist. For example, Amherst College ended legacy preferences in 2022. Without a bump for legacies, the percentage of legacies in the first-year class dropped from an average of 11 percent in previous years to 6 percent.[113] Are all of the spots not filled with legacies now filled with students from historically excluded backgrounds? Not automatically, but now there's a little more wiggle room and flexibility in the class to attract different types of students. Equally important, Amherst and other institutions that have dropped legacy don't have to defend a practice that's incredibly hypocritical for any institution that claims to care about equity and diversity. The team at Opportunity Insights estimates that 24 percent of the admissions advantage accrued to students from the top 1 percent of household incomes is related to these students being more likely to be recruited athletes, and 40 percent is related to legacy status.[114] Given that there are so many forces that make the playing field unequal, doesn't it just make sense for institutions to ditch the ones that they have control over?

WRAPPING IT UP

All right, we have covered a lot, from the inspiring example of institutional transformation at UC Davis School of Medicine to options that can advance more incremental change. Restricting race-conscious admissions won't automatically result in economically or racially diverse campuses. Institutions must invest heavily in expanding opportunity for low- and moderate-income students of all racial/ethnic backgrounds. Leaders should know that some solutions that sound promising at the surface level (e.g., lotteries) may not facilitate diversity. Other initiatives like free tuition programs for low-income students need additional tailoring to better serve populations. Efforts to reduce friction in the process, such as telling students that they'll receive a scholarship if admitted (versus requiring proof of eligibility), are promising. Institutions also need to try combining approaches, such as guaranteed admissions and guaranteed financial aid, as there is no single initiative that will fix all of our problems.

On the legal front, institutions need to remember that pursuing diversity through race-neutral means has the green light from the Supreme Court, despite heated rhetoric from certain camps. There's also a case to be made for connecting reparations to admissions, as well as favoring victims of discrimination. Both ideas have been recognized by conservative Supreme Court justices (Justices Kavanaugh and Thomas, respectively) as defensible ways to advance diversity that don't need to involve racial categorization, so the methods could quite possibly withstand legal challenges. Yes, it's out-of-the-box thinking, but it is worth considering as institutions explore options.

Beyond things schools can start doing, there are also numerous things that schools need to stop doing. Practices like legacy admissions and athletic preferences are counterproductive to equal opportunity, and institutions need to scrutinize practices that privilege certain groups over others. For years, standardized tests were criticized as a practice that perpetuated inequality in admissions, but the test-optional movement turned everything upside down. We'll explore this issue more in the next chapter.

4

Test-Optional, Test-Required, or Test-Free? The Debate over Standardized Tests

Once upon a time, the idea that standardized tests could be optional in college admissions seemed impossible. For so long, test scores were an entrenched, taken-for-granted part of applying to college. Your SAT or ACT score could open or close doors for you. Growing up, I remember a friend determined to attend an elite school. Over the months he grew increasingly stressed when he couldn't break past a certain score. In the end, he attended a perfectly good state school, and later, Harvard Business School. (He had better luck with the GMAT.) On the alternate side, I had unremarkable scores on practice tests, but ended up scoring much higher on the actual test.[1] Suddenly I felt more competitive at certain schools, and the score helped me land a generous scholarship. If we had been born a few decades later, our experiences applying to college may have looked different.

When test-optional admissions came on the scene, it felt like a fringe movement isolated to a few liberal arts colleges. Eventually, hundreds of schools went test-optional, but tests still dominated.[2] Some name-brand schools like the University of Chicago went test-optional before the pandemic, but it seemed impossible that the Ivies would follow. Then again, there are a lot of things we never could've imagined before COVID. With the virus running rampant, it seemed unwise to stuff students into a room for hours. The list of test-optional schools faithfully maintained by Fairtest.org exploded that year, from large state schools to the entire Ivy League. After vaccines came out in 2021, only a small number of schools, like state schools in Georgia and Florida (politics), Georgetown University (does everything old school), and the Massachusetts Institute of Technology (well, MIT), went back to requiring test scores. In 2024, Dartmouth, Brown, Harvard, and Stanford joined them. Some state schools decided to require testing again, like the University of Texas at Austin, which admits mainly on class rank anyway. Others formally adopted test-optional, like the University of Michigan. About eighty institutions went test-free, meaning they didn't want to see your test scores at all. By fall 2024, over two thousand institutions still didn't require the SAT or ACT.[3]

As part of the College Admissions Futures Co-Laborative (CAF Co-LAB) team, I've been studying the impact of test-optional policies over the last few years thanks to the support of the Bill and Melinda Gates Foundation. This work has involved combing the research and observing institutional responses as the debate over testing continues to evolve. The answer to whether institutions should require the SAT/ACT is fuzzier than some might think. In this chapter, I aim to show the gray behind the research on testing, arguing that existing research doesn't point schools in a single clear-cut direction. Researchers, faculty, and policy makers can look at the same research but come to different conclusions about what we should do. People's worldviews and experiences influence whether they see testing as helpful or less relevant.[4] Some hope that testing will facilitate equity, while others see it as a gatekeeper.[5]

Let me help walk you, dear reader, through the different conversations around testing. We'll start by noting the pros and cons of test-optional policies. Next, we'll discuss different arguments advanced by the test-required camp after over 2,000 institutions adopted test-optional during the pandemic, examining two eras that I like to think of as "BOI" (Before Opportunity Insights) and "AOI" (After Opportunity Insights). Finally we'll discuss the test-free movement, a new frontier in the testing debate.

Regardless of an institution's specific testing policy, it's critical that institutions actively work to recruit and enroll low-income and URM students through increased investments in financial aid, proactive outreach, and the like. That said—spoiler alert—I'm going to argue that greater flexibility around testing is helpful to support access, especially following the SCOTUS ruling. Requiring standardized tests but not being able to consider race is very different from requiring tests but having conventional race-conscious admissions. After all, inequities affecting standardized tests are a key reason why race-conscious admissions policies needed to exist in the first place.

TEST-OPTIONAL: PROS AND CONS

The most comprehensive study of pre-pandemic test-optional adoption was conducted by Christopher Bennett, a researcher at RTI International.[6] Bennett analyzed data from one hundred private institutions, and found a suggested uptick in URM student enrollment after schools went test-optional, from 10.3 percent to 11.9 percent.[7] The increase from 10.3 percent to 11.9 percent sounds small, which may be why Jill Barshay of the *Hechinger Report* wrote that Bennett's work showed that "test-optional didn't do much to diversify college student populations."[8] Still, that 1.6 percentage point gain in URM student enrollment is roughly equivalent to an increase of 10 to 15 percent.[9] Over email, Zachary Bleemer, an economist at Princeton, described Bennett's study as finding "large increases in URM enrollment when schools go test-optional, mostly driven by middle-selectivity schools. . . . Those estimates are considerably larger than both top percent policies and holistic review."[10] In his work, Bleemer found that race-conscious admissions in the UC (University of California) system increased URM enrollment by 20 percent; percentage plans increased it by 4 percent, and holistic review by 7 percent.[11] When you compare test-optional to other initiatives attempting to boost diversity, it looks more impressive.

Earlier work on test-optional (circa 2015) did not find gains in enrollment for URM or low-income students among early adopters of test-optional, which were generally small liberal arts colleges.[12] The finding disappointed some advocates, but reflected how test-optional policies have limited effectiveness without broader changes in need-based financial aid and campus climate. Our CAF Co-LAB team analyzed data from the widespread adoption of test-optional at selective and highly selective institutions during the pandemic.[13] Associate Professors Kelly Rosinger of Pennsylvania State University and Dominique Baker of the University of Delaware led the work. Both are well-positioned to tackle the topic, having previously worked in admissions. Kelly was a coauthor on the 2015 paper that found no effect linked with test-optional at liberal arts colleges, a nuanced finding that frustrated some advocates.[14] Her willingness to publish the findings despite the mixed reactions speaks to her integrity as a researcher. Both are meticulous and careful not to overstate results.[15] Because the duo has been studying and mulling over test-optional for years, they insisted on including finely grained variables like whether an institution was test-optional for scholarships, which required a lot of work to verify.[16]

Analyzing data on application and enrollment outcomes from IPEDS (the Integrated Postsecondary Education Data System), we found a significant increase in Black student enrollment at institutions with mid-level selectivity. In some but not all models, adopting test-optional was linked with increases in low-income student enrollment at highly selective institutions. We also found wide variation in how test-optional was implemented. Some schools were test-optional only for students who met certain criteria, such as test-optional for a GPA of 3.0 or above. Gains in Black student enrollment were most pronounced at schools that extended test-optional to scholarships and didn't restrict who could apply test-optional, suggesting that *how* test-optional was implemented at institutions made a difference.

Why would test-optional make a particular difference for Black student enrollment at institutions with mid-level selectivity? Likely, being test-optional makes more of a difference at schools that previously weighed test scores more or used them as a weed-out factor, even if the institutions concurrently used holistic admissions. Schools that are selective but not highly selective fall more into this category.[17] You can imagine that public state universities might be prone to using test scores as a weed-out factor more given their high application volume.

To note, our work is based on admissions predating the SCOTUS ruling, so most of the institutions in our sample used race-conscious admissions. However, we can observe shifts in testing policy in states that already banned race-conscious admissions before the pandemic. In the UC system, people are pretty happy with test-free admissions, which I'll address at the end of the chapter. The University of Michigan has seen some small upticks in Black enrollment since going test-optional.[18] Whether gains can be credited to test-optional is hard to say, but Michigan is satisfied enough to stay test-optional. We also surveyed admissions professionals on their experiences adopting test-optional or test-free admissions during the pandemic. Most reacted positively, saying that it gave them more flexibility to admit students from historically underrepresented backgrounds.[19]

Of course, test-optional has some limitations. Without broader changes in financial aid policy and campus climate, effectiveness can be limited. Another complication is confusion over whether to submit test scores or not. Low-income, first-generation, and URM students are less likely to have college coaching to help decipher the pros and cons of score submission. In contrast, some affluent parents talk about looking up the percentage of students submitting test scores at schools in the Common Data Set (CDS) to help them decide whether their child should submit or not.[20] While the CDS is publicly available, who has the know-how or the time to look up this type of information?

Relatedly, some elite schools expressed concern that hundreds of low-income students did not submit scores that could have made them competitive applicants, perhaps because the scores were on the lower end of the listed percentile range (i.e., the 25th to 75th percentile of scores for enrolled students). It's a compelling concern, but does it justify requiring test scores? In this next section, we will unpack that concern, and further explore defenses of required testing.

THE CASE FOR REQUIRED TESTING: THE BEFORE OPPORTUNITY INSIGHTS (BOI) ERA

As mentioned before, I like to think of the testing debate in two eras: BOI (Before Opportunity Insights) and AOI (After Opportunity Insights). Opportunity Insights is a highly regarded research group directed by Raj Chetty of Harvard University. BOI refers to the period when almost all selective schools went test-optional during the pandemic, from 2020 to late 2023, before Opportunity Insights entered the debate. During this time, most elite institutions seemed fairly content with test-optional. BOI, test-optional made sense given the pandemic, and seemed like an important option to keep given the uncertainty of *SFFA v. Harvard*. Let's not forget the national reckoning around race following the murder of George Floyd in 2020. Institutions scrambled to announce racial equity taskforces, and our country's wretched history with race was front and center. Loosening the grip of standardized testing, a historical barrier, was in sync with the mood of the country.[21] Unfortunately, we all know what followed: the backlash that swung back hard against efforts to advance diversity, equity, and inclusion.

BOI, pro-testing arguments focused on the idea that testing could help identify talented lower-income students. For example, MIT's Dean of Admissions Stuart Schmill stated that "most students can study for these exams using free tools at Khan Academy, but they (usually) can't force their high school to offer advanced calculus courses, for example."[22] While Schmill's statement is technically true, gains associated with Khan Academy's free SAT prep program have been largely overstated, as documented by journalist Paul Tough.[23] Basically, the program led to a "rich get richer" effect where students who already had more access to resources were the ones who benefited the most from the Khan Academy program. Inequality affects not just who takes test prep but who benefits from it, as I discuss in *Race on Campus*.[24] In one study, East Asian Americans were the only group with statistically significant gains from taking test prep.[25]

Besides test prep, there are other inequities affecting tests. Affluent students are more likely to take the test multiple times to improve their scores.

Rich (oftentimes White) families go the extra mile to secure accommodations that give their children extra time to take the test.[26] Justifying required testing due to the availability of Khan Academy is like saying that the playing field is equal because we have YouTube.[27] In a study examining the effectiveness of an online ACT prep program, researchers commented: "Results indicate that simply granting a population of students access to a self-directed test preparation product such as [ACT Online Program] would not be sufficient for improving the college readiness of this population, as many of these students would not make adequate use of the product."[28]

Another issue raised BOI was the idea that test-optional undermined the "SAT/ACT for all" movement, which some view as helpful for identifying talented low-income students. Taking the SAT or ACT is required in twenty-five states as a graduation requirement.[29] Some lower-income students take the SAT/ACT due to graduation requirements and score well, which puts them on the radar of colleges. Commonly cited is Joshua Hyman's study on how requiring the ACT boosted the identification of college-ready students in Michigan.[30] In the study, for every ten low-income students who scored "college-ready" on the ACT (an ACT score of 20 or higher, or the equivalent of a 1060 on the SAT), another five scored at or above the same threshold once Michigan required that students take the ACT during school hours.[31] Hyman's study got some good press thanks to his adviser Sue Dynarski, who wrote about the study in the *New York Times* and other outlets.[32]

Hyman's study shows the potential of low-income students to attend college. At the same time, is it clear-cut evidence that universities should require the SAT/ACT when students apply to college? Not really. Having students take a standardized test is one way to identify students with the potential to succeed in college. However, that test doesn't have to be the SAT or ACT. States already require students to take plenty of tests during high school, and if needed, those tests can be used to identify students and encourage them in the college-going process.[33] Of course there are advocates who argue against mandatory standardized testing in schools, and their arguments have merit. High schools should encourage students to plan for a postsecondary pathway regardless of test scores. Still, if high school assessments are going to remain, they can help guide state policy without four-year institutions requiring scores.

During the BOI era (early 2020s), professors like Jonathan Wai of the University of Arkansas and Kathryn Paige Harden of the University of Texas at Austin amplified the idea that SAT/ACT requirements are helpful for talent identification, but they didn't get much traction. Wai studies gifted education, and there's lots of controversial history there regarding testing.[34] Harden is a psychologist who uses genetics to examine inequality; her work has been critiqued for overemphasizing the role of genetics in educational attainment.[35] The College Board went on a PR blitz, worried that the SAT had lost its death grip on the nation's teens. In 2022, Priscilla Rodriguez, senior vice president at the College Board, gushed that "students want to take the SAT to show what they've learned and to connect with scholarships and colleges."[36] Who knew that the SAT was a bucket list item for America's teenagers? I suspect that the College Board was concerned about California's swing to test-free admissions. The organization commissioned a survey, and trumpeted the results on its website: "70% of students and 57% of parents prefer SAT/ACT to be optional for admissions."[37] It's hard to believe, but BOI, the College Board seemed more afraid of states considering test-free admissions, versus test-optional. All I can say is that it was a very different time.[38]

THE AOI ERA: OPPORTUNITY INSIGHTS ENTERS THE CONVERSATION

Okay, so that was the landscape of the BOI era. Things started to shift in fall 2023, when Dartmouth adopted a "test-preferred" stance. There were whispers that Dartmouth felt that academic performance from students admitted via test-optional was subpar, and was thinking about bringing back required testing. Forget other reasons for academic challenges, such as the pandemic or issues with the campus climate.[39] There are graduation rates to worry about, gotta screen out the riff raff! Indeed, *U.S. News & World Report*'s shift to consider the graduation rates of Pell Grant recipients made some institutions scramble. (What, we have to graduate students and not just admit them?) Some find it easier to take chances on low-income students with better test scores, versus those whose accomplishments are demonstrated in other areas. Using test scores to weed out students is easier than having to transform an institution to better support students.

A few things happened in January 2024 that kicked off the era I dub AOI (After Opportunity Insights). As the name suggests, the unifying factor was some connection with Opportunity Insights. In the words of reporter Liam Knox of *Inside Higher Ed*, "Opportunity Insights research . . . blew up what seemed to be a solidifying test-optional status quo."[40] Most academic research gets swallowed up by a black hole or at best, just read by other academics. When Chetty and friends do a study, the *New York Times* creates an interactive feature for readers to explore the findings.[41] In January 2024, Opportunity Insights released a policy brief arguing in favor of standardized tests, coauthored by John Friedman of Brown (codirector at Opportunity Insights) and two faculty from Dartmouth, economist Bruce Sacerdote and sociologist Michele Tine.[42] That same month, a group of Dartmouth faculty, including Sacerdote and Tine, released a report on test-optional at Dartmouth.[43] Around the same time, David Leonhardt wrote an article, "The Misguided War on the SAT," in the *New York Times* that referenced the Opportunity Insights brief on testing, as well as other studies written by Opportunity Insights.[44] Leonhardt used to serve on the advisory board of Opportunity Insights.[45] Anyone see a pattern here?

Now don't get me wrong, Opportunity Insights does important work. But there are statistics, and then there's the interpretation of statistics, which informs what people should do with the data. Numbers rarely speak for themselves, but people can speak for numbers. Sometimes the policy conclusions are clear cut; other times they're hazier. Someone who believes strongly in the value of testing might see the numbers and conclude that bringing back tests is a slam dunk. Another person more skeptical about testing may see room for disagreement. Similarly, people have different ideas around how people should be selected for rare and prestigious opportunities like attending an elite college, or I don't know, working for Opportunity Insights!

Quick but relevant tangent before we turn to the Dartmouth report, Opportunity Insights policy brief, and *New York Times* article: Nell Gluckman and Francie Diep published a piece on Opportunity Insights in the *Chronicle of Higher Education* entitled "Does Raj Chetty Practice What He Preaches?"[46] They discussed the selection criteria that Opportunity Insights used prior to 2021 to hire staff (at least prior to 2021), which raises questions about the worldview that the team brings to their work on standardized tests. Gluckman and Diep documented how Opportunity Insights used a nine-point rubric to screen applicants for their predoctoral fellowship, a competitive and prestigious position. Up to two of the nine points came from the applicant's alma mater. Graduating from a school with an average math SAT score of 790 or higher could result in the applicant receiving two points. If one's school's average score was 750–789, the applicant got 1.5 points. Applicants received just one point if their school was in the 700–749 range. To clarify, it's not two points for the applicant having an SAT math score of 790 or higher, it's for graduating from a school where the average SAT math score is 790 or higher. Originally, just thirty-five institutions fell into the "two point" category. The vast majority of colleges and universities fell into the zero-point range. Guess what else could get someone two points? Having perfect grades. (Your own grades, not your peers' grades.)

The rubric offers a peek into the value that Opportunity Insights ascribes to testing, as well as their perspective on what metrics should drive evaluation. Opportunity Insights has since expanded their list of schools linked to two points to about seventy institutions, and says they're committed to advancing applicants from different backgrounds regardless of how they score on the rubric. Still, there weren't any Black predoctoral fellows at Opportunity Insights until 2021. Chetty defended the team's approach: "'If you're trying to do the best research,' he said, 'the reality is, I think it is valuable to hire students from top colleges.'"[47] I admire Chetty's work, but we have different perspectives about how to assess talent.[48] If you want to read more about my own perspective on testing, see the endnotes.[49] Without further delay, let's dive into some of this work released by Dartmouth,

Opportunity Insights, and Leonhardt. A lot of it overlaps, so I'll try to bundle the issues covered.

GPA for Score Submitters Versus Non-Submitters: Can They Do the Work?

A key part of the AOI-era debate revolves around college GPA—specifically, the difference between students who didn't submit scores ("non-submitters") and those who did. Opportunity Insights/Dartmouth kicked off their brief with the issue: "Finding #1: Students with higher SAT/ACT scores are more likely to have higher college GPAs than their peers with lower scores."[50] So did non-submitters drag the Ivies down the drain? Not really. In the Dartmouth report, first-year GPA for non-submitters was something like a 3.45, which doesn't sound that terrible.[51] Maybe there's some grade inflation, but then score submitters' grades would be inflated too. Analyzing data from Ivy Plus students (the Ivies plus Stanford, Duke, University of Chicago, and MIT), the Opportunity Insights/Dartmouth team predicted that someone with a 1600 SAT score would have a GPA .43 points higher than someone with a SAT score of around 1200. Similarly, the Dartmouth-specific analysis predicted that non-submitters would have a GPA of 3.4–3.5, and someone with a perfect SAT score would probably land in the 3.8–3.9 range. Leonhardt also featured the GPA issue in his article, with a graph showing that non-submitters would end up with (on average) a 3.25 GPA and 1600 scorers would land a 3.75.[52] To Leonhardt, this finding is a compelling pro for keeping tests.[53]

If you think about it, the differences in GPA aren't that drastic considering that these analyses compare two pretty different groups: students who felt like their scores weren't strong enough to submit, and those who literally got perfect SAT scores. The GPA gap is unsurprising, and it's not huge. The gap slims down in the Dartmouth report when comparing non-submitters with students who got a 1500: about 3.45 for non-submitters, a 3.60 for the latter group.[54] A difference, but not that big. As noted by Yale's Dean of Admission Jeremiah Quinlan, "students who have been admitted to Yale without test scores have done relatively well in their Yale courses."[55]

Sure, the collegiate GPAs for submitters versus non-submitters differ somewhat, but is it that terrible to have some students carry a B or B+ average in college? The issue feels like a relative nothingburger in the grand scheme of things. I still remember how it wasn't that hard to end up with a lot of Bs in college. If I hadn't studied abroad, I would have ended up with a lower GPA despite my decent SAT score.[56] Yes, differences exist in collegiate GPAs. Still, students who choose not to submit test scores aren't flunking out for the most part, and they also make key contributions to the campus community.

So there's an unsurprising difference between the GPAs of non–score submitters versus someone coming in with a 1600. Is that reason to go back to requiring test scores? Places like Dartmouth and people like Leonhardt say yes: If test scores tell us something about how students will do in college, then in their view, everyone should submit them. Others disagree: Non-submitting students aren't tanking, and most are doing "relatively well," to quote Dean Quinlan. Perhaps it's not a big deal for an institution to have more B/B+ students, especially if the policy opens the door for a more diverse applicant pool.[57] Overall, there's room for disagreement. To note, Dartmouth didn't think that test-optional diversified their applicant pool, but that was only as related to SES; the institution didn't comment on racial/ethnic diversity.[58]

It's also worth shifting the conversation from what a non-submitter won't bring (a 1600) to remembering what talents and traits they could bring to an institution. Half of Black and Latinx students applying via Common App are choosing not to submit scores, as well as plenty of White and Asian American students.[59] Likely, there's still a lot of talent within that pool of students. Some institutions want "all of the data" available, but others are comfortable with measures like contextualized GPA, a stronger predictor of academic success outcomes than test scores in some studies.[60] They may also be concerned that test score inclusion, even when contextualized, may advantage more affluent students, as research suggests.[61] Is more information always better? Maybe it depends on the type of information and how it affects the reader.

Leonhardt quoted Brown's president Christina Paxson as saying: "Careful statistical work by one of Brown's faculty members shows that students with higher SAT or ACT scores are less likely to encounter academic difficulty at Brown."[62] That's no surprise given the strong correlation between wealth and the SAT, as well as how race and class are linked to K–12 education. Newsflash: If you're financially comfortable enough to not have to work twenty hours a week during college . . . you'll probably have more time to study.[63] It would also probably be accurate to say: "Careful statistical work shows that students at Brown who attended private high schools that cost $30,000–$60,000 a year are less likely to encounter academic difficulty at Brown." That's great, but does that mean that you want a university full of those students? Does that mean that students that face academic challenges have no place being at Brown?

Generally absent from debates on GPA for submitters versus non-submitters is any discussion of the institution's responsibility to support students who demonstrate high potential but experience challenges adjusting to college. I once heard Ruth López Turley, Professor of Sociology at Rice University, speak about what it was like to attend Stanford as a first-generation college student from a low-income background. Her first year was full of less than ideal grades. As time went on, she learned the ropes of the institution and adjusted to the workload. She went on to earn a PhD at Harvard, and has done incredible work through Rice's Kinder Institute for Urban Research. Not every student is Ruth López Turley, but her story speaks to the importance of investing in students from different levels of academic preparation.

The Usefulness of High School GPA: Do We Need Tests to Make Admissions Decisions or Not?

Next up in the AOI-era debate is the usefulness of high school GPA as a predictor of college outcomes. The Opportunity Insights/Dartmouth team didn't mince words on this one: "Finding #2: High school GPA does a poor job of predicting academic success in college."[64] Their brief features two figures. One has a neat and tidy diagonal line showing the positive correlation between SAT score and first-year college GPA within a sample of Ivy Plus institutions, controlling for race and income. The higher the SAT score, the higher the first-year GPA. The second figure shows a flatter (though still trending slightly upward) line displaying the correlation between high school GPA and first-year GPA. It indicates that on average, once you control for demographics, a high school GPA of 3.1–3.4 predicts a college GPA of a little under 3.5. Coming in with a 3.9 or higher from high school predicts a college GPA of a little over 3.5. The authors conclude that test scores provide a better sense of what a student's GPA will be during college than high school GPA.

Arguably, the headline claiming that GPA does a "poor job" of predicting success is alarmist. Another take is that the second figure shows that students across the board tend to do pretty well in college. Challenging a pro-testing piece written by Opportunity Insights member Professor David Deming of Harvard, Professor Jake Vigdor of the University of Washington highlighted how retention was basically identical between test-optional and test-required cohorts at Dartmouth, Brown, and Yale. He tweeted: "Here's another sentence you won't read in @ProfDavidDeming's article: 'In their quest to keep low-income enrollment numbers up, without the benefit of test scores, colleges took unreasonable chances on unqualified students.' Because, again, there's no evidence this is true. . . . It's a fairly open secret: getting into Ivy League schools is hard. Staying in them is pretty easy."[65]

Economist Jesse Rothstein, the Carmel P. Friesen Chair in Public Policy at UC Berkeley, slammed Leonhardt's take on the Opportunity Insights/Dartmouth analysis in an unpublished letter to the editor: "[Leonhardt] shows only that at a few 'Ivy Plus' colleges, SAT scores predict college grades better than do high school GPAs. This is unsurprising—Harvard could fill its class with 4.0 GPAs, leaving little room for GPAs to predict variation in college success. There is no basis to think this generalizes beyond a tiny slice of higher education."[66]

Other researchers have come to different conclusions from Opportunity Insights about the value of high school GPA. Saul Geiser was the director of admissions-related research for the UC system for years. In analyzing UC data, he consistently concluded that high school grades in college prep courses were a stronger predictor of student outcomes in the UC system than test scores, with SAT scores explaining slightly under 2 percent of the variance in first-year grades.[67] As discussed in chapter 3, contextualized GPA was a stronger predictor of college success outcomes than ACT scores (raw or contextualized) for fifteen institutions in a Midwestern state.[68] Both the Midwestern and UC datasets differ from the Ivy Plus data, although both contain selective institutions, including UC Berkeley and UCLA in the UC system. Both systems are more representative of the broad swath of higher education weighing the future of testing policy, versus the Ivies. The UC's approach of focusing on high school GPA in college prep courses may yield insights that differ from those of studies that just look at the entire high school GPA.

So yes, this is another area where implications for policy are unclear based on the data. Some schools will decide that they want test scores to inform their review; others will decide that GPA or contextualized GPA in combination with other factors provides enough information—with or without tests. There's no one-size-fits-all solution. Caltech (the California Institute of Technology) is an interesting case of a school that experimented with test-free admissions for a few years but decided to bring back required testing. When using test-free admissions, Caltech stated that their "rigorous internal analysis . . . indicates that standardized test scores have little to no power in predicting students' performance in the first-term mathematics and physics classes that first-year students must take as part of Caltech's core curriculum. Further, the predictive power of standardized test scores appears to dissipate as students progress through the first-year core curriculum."[69] Interestingly, when Caltech announced the move back to test-required admissions, they didn't refute any of their earlier analysis.[70] Instead they talked about how the faculty advisory committee thought that tests would provide useful information during holistic review, and they wanted all of the information possible to make decisions. It's an understandable decision, but one that also likely reflects values ascribed to testing (e.g., that it's "objective") held by the faculty on the committee. Others might be concerned that requiring the SAT/ACT can lead to decisions that overreward higher scores.[71]

What Type of Low-Income Student Do Institutions Want?

Another talking point advanced in the AOI era is the idea that test-optional is somehow bad for low-income students. In their report, Dartmouth faculty estimated that hundreds of students with SAT scores of 1400 or above from less advantaged high schools didn't submit scores, thinking the scores weren't competitive.[72] However, Vigdor showed on Twitter that low-income student enrollment was actually up at schools like Dartmouth and Brown for test-optional cohorts.[73] While the absolute number of low-income students was slightly down at Yale, the share of the cohort receiving need-based financial aid increased slightly at all three schools.[74] Still, based on all of the hype on test-optional supposedly hurting low-income students, you'd think that they disappeared when schools went test-optional. They didn't. They were still there at institutions despite the devastation of the pandemic, and sometimes even in greater numbers.

Yes, it's concerning that some low-income students were overlooked because they didn't submit scores. Still, the argument that test-optional is bad for low-income students is puzzling, considering that low-income student enrollment was pretty much the same or even better under test-optional at elite institutions. Reading between the lines, the subtext seems to be: "We admitted some minority/low-income kids without test scores. Their accomplishments were pretty amazing because duh, we admitted them, but whoops, they're the type that might end up with B+ GPAs in college. There were others who had 1400s but didn't submit scores. Moving forward, we'd like more of them!" Sure, institutions can want more students from historically underrepresented backgrounds with higher test scores, why not. However, given that non–score submitters can do the work, why can't institutions try to admit more of *both* types of underrepresented students if they're so hungry for diversity?

Dartmouth may have missed some lower-income students with higher test scores. However, by going back to tests, they might miss out on another type of lower-income student—one with strong talents and achievements, but lower test scores. The Dartmouth team commented on this particular group in a January 2025 working paper: "The beneficiaries of this failure to submit scores by [lower-income] high achieving students appear to be lower scoring disadvantaged students who are admitted at higher rates when they do not submit their scores."[75] For more on the paper, check the endnotes. I'm guessing that these "lower scoring disadvantaged students" were pretty impressive if Dartmouth admitted them. Given the constraints on institutions following *SFFA*, institutions can't afford to lose out on either type of outstanding student, lower or higher scoring—why can't they admit both?

Even if going back to required score submission helps enroll some low-income students (I'm not sure it will, but let's hope for the best), policies that boost economic diversity don't necessarily do the same for racial/ethnic diversity.[76] Race and class aren't interchangeable in admissions.[77] Requiring standardized tests without the tool of race-conscious admissions is a very different situation than pre-pandemic, when institutions required tests but could consider race more directly. MIT is adamant that the two scenarios are not meaningfully different, but the stark drop in their URM student enrollment in the first admissions cycle after the ruling suggests otherwise.[78] Inequities affecting SAT/ACT scores are a key reason why race-conscious admissions was necessary to begin with. Of course some test-optional schools also experienced sharp drops in Black enrollment following the ruling, but it's possible that declines would have been even worse without test-optional.

Institutions shouldn't assume that even if "hundreds" of lower-income students with higher SAT scores are admitted, the students will actually enroll.[79] Numerous barriers to access remain. Dartmouth has ramped up some of its financial aid initiatives, which is a good thing. To attract and enroll the broadest range of students, institutions could remain test-optional but provide language on admissions websites encouraging students to submit scores above 1400 or so if they come from a lower-income background. They can conduct more outreach to lower-SES high schools to help students understand that test scores are read in context. They could even set up AI chatbots that advise students on whether they should submit scores or not. There are numerous ways that schools could tackle this issue without going back to required testing. Elite schools that have gone back to required testing make the SAT sound like a magical elixir that's going to radically change higher education. However, we had required testing for decades before the pandemic, and we know what it does.[80]

Another consideration: While providing more context about a low-income student's SAT score boosts their likelihood of admission, the same goes for affluent students. In a study by Bastedo and colleagues that simulated the admissions process, both low-income *and* affluent students were more likely to be admitted when additional context was provided about their SAT scores.[81] Affluent students were more likely to be admitted even when the score was high (e.g., 1500s), but not exceptionally higher than their peers. The extra boost given to low-income students from reading the score in context was basically canceled out by the more affluent students also getting a boost. As observed by the authors, "Because these effects were similar in magnitude across applicants, applicants from low socioeconomic backgrounds did not differentially benefit from providing more robust contextual information about test scores in this experiment."[82] Low-income students benefit from having scores read in context, but they do not benefit "differentially" because rich kids also benefit.[83]

Bastedo and colleagues comment that "providing additional context about students' SAT scores leads to more positive evaluations, regardless of socioeconomic background, suggesting that such information may not serve to 'level the playing field' between higher- and lower-SES students in the admissions process. . . . Given unequal educational opportunities and the fact that SAT scores are highly correlated with a student's SES, this type of selection behavior overwhelmingly benefits economically advantaged students who attend highly resourced high schools where average SAT scores tend to be higher, thus contributing to a concentration of wealthy students at selective colleges and universities."[84] Overall, rich kids are more likely to benefit from having higher test scores because there are many more of them (both rich kids and rich kids with high test scores) in the applicant pool.

What Are Tests Good For?

Let's unpack Leonhardt's discussion of Opportunity Insights' research in his *New York Times* article "The Misguided War on the SAT." The piece doesn't do much to bolster the case for required testing. In bold text, Leonhardt proclaimed: "Test scores are strong predictors of student outcomes after college." So what outcomes? Attendance at an elite graduate school and working at a prestigious firm.[85] Really? That's why we should bring back required testing? Opportunity Insights' findings are no surprise. Attending an elite graduate school is closely related to scoring well on the GRE, LSAT, MCAT, or whatever test, which is highly correlated with scoring well on tests in general. Working at a prestigious firm is strongly linked with attending an elite graduate program, which once again is related to scoring well on tests. To top it all off, all three—high test scores, elite graduate school attendance, and working at a prestigious firm—are correlated with wealth.[86]

So yes, test scores predict certain outcomes, but why should those outcomes drive testing policy for an entire applicant pool? Test scores are great for seeing who will join the army of consultants that often makes pretty bad decisions with disturbingly large repercussions.[87] They're less suited for predicting who wants to pursue teaching, combat homelessness, or fight for an underserved community. High test scores and commitments to public service aren't incompatible. Still, to defend required testing because scores predict who's likely to work for McKinsey seems weird at best and misguided at worst. In a letter to the editor responding to Leonhardt's piece, Rebecca Steinitz of Arlington, Massachusetts, wrote: "But in 2023, is our definition of success still limited to elite graduate schools and prestigious firms? Might an M.I.T. graduate become an incredible high school physics teacher or a creative coder? Might people who get B's at Harvard or U.C.L.A. be capable of having fulfilling, productive, dare I say successful lives?"[88] Well said, Rebecca.[89]

Testing Policy, Sector, and Selectivity: What Matters?

One last note before we move to test-free admissions: considerations related to test-optional at highly selective (a.k.a. rejective) institutions versus schools with mid-level selectivity, as well as thoughts on public versus private institutions. On occasion, Opportunity Insights and friends note that their findings are most relevant to elite, highly selective institutions, although mentions are easy to miss.[90] At times, caveats related to sector and selectivity are downplayed, making it sound like everyone should go back to required testing. In our "TL;DR" world, it's easy to overlook the nuances of the debate. As a result, trustees at XYZ state institution, which admits the majority of applicants, will demand that XYZ go back to requiring tests because, dang it, if Harvard has done it, it's good enough for us.

If you haven't been able to tell, I think there's a perfectly fine case for keeping test-optional admissions even at hyperrejective private schools. At the end of the day, test scores seem to be more of a "want" versus a "need" in admissions review. Would having test scores for everyone make the process more efficient? Probably, but not necessarily in a good way. Does it make it easier to prescreen people for McKinsey? Sure. So part of the hyperrejective sector of higher education has decided to go back to required testing—so be it. For everyone else, from other highly selective institutions to schools categorized as "mid-selective," test-optional or even test-free admissions is a more than viable option. While the gains related to diversity aren't revolutionary, they're notable, and we need all of the help we can get post-*SFFA*.

A funny story about institutional priorities and how they drive the ship: I once interviewed a senior admissions leader who supported test-optional admissions, but whose school had gone back to required testing. They said that the only way their school would go back to test-optional is if the football coach demanded it. At first I thought it was a joke, but they were serious. Coaches want every recruitment advantage they can get, and some players might not want to sit down for the test (who does?) given the plethora of places that don't require one. So yes, Harvard and friends are back to testing now, but we know how they love their athletic teams. You never know what might happen as institutional priorities evolve.

TEST-FREE ADMISSIONS: A NEW FRONTIER

With some schools going back to required testing, others are moving in the opposite direction: conducting admissions and scholarship decisions without test scores, a.k.a. test-free admissions. The idea seems daunting, but the UC system, which is the country's largest selective public system of higher education, has used test-free admissions since Fall 2021. Overall, they seem satisfied with the move. As of Fall 2023, eighty-six institutions around the country used test-free admissions, from UC Berkeley to small private institutions like Reed College.

First, some background on the UC system's move to test-free admissions. The 2019 lawsuit *Smith vs. Regents of the University of California* set the stage for a radical rethinking of testing policy. *Smith* argued that the use of standardized tests in college admissions violated students' rights, given the role of testing in perpetuating racial inequality.[91] Around the same time, UC President Janet Napolitano and the UC Academic Senate's Academic Council commissioned a faculty committee, jazzily named the "Standardized Testing Task Force," or STTF, to write a report on the use of tests in UC admissions.[92]

The STTF recommended that the UC keep standardized tests for the time being. They contended that test scores facilitated access to the UC for some students who would not otherwise qualify. (Preview: They technically did, but only for a pretty small group of students who attended UC Merced.) Here's the surface-level version of the process: STTF highlighted that 22,613 students qualified for UC admission due to a statewide index that included standardized test scores, versus Eligibility-in-Local-Context ("ELC"), where students qualify by being in the top 4 to 9 percent of the high school class.[93] Thousands of the 22,613 were from historically underrepresented backgrounds.[94] In both paths, students get an offer to at least one UC, but it's not necessarily their top choice. The UC still does holistic review of applicants, which influences *where* students receive an offer.

Whoa, wait, are you telling me that standardized tests were helping URM students gain access to the UC? Not really. On the surface, that tidbit seems like a compelling reason to keep tests. Commentator Caitlin Flanagan latched on to the point when blasting the UC for moving to test-free in a piece subtly titled "The University of California is Lying to Us."[95] However, economist Sarah Reber, formerly at UCLA and now at the Brookings Institution, found that out of the 22,613 UC-eligible students, only 168 actually ended up at a UC, which was UC Merced for all of them.[96] The STTF made it sound like SAT scores were a huge pathway to access the UC, but ultimately, the number of students accessing the UC through test scores versus ELC was much smaller. Reber blasted the STTF report's enthusiastic spin on the statewide index: "The report's conclusion that 'the SAT allows many disadvantaged students to gain guarantees of admission to UC' . . . is misleading; facilitating the admission of a few dozen students to a single campus does not point to a compelling need for the SAT."[97]

Others argued that the STTF report exaggerated the predictive power of the SAT. The report's authors bolded the following: "Admissions tests add substantially to UC's ability to predict student success beyond the predictive information in high school grades alone."[98] Saul Geiser, former director of admissions research for the UC, challenged the STTF's conclusion: "One of the major claims of the report . . . is that SAT and ACT scores are superior to high-school grades in predicting how students will perform at UC. . . . When student demographics are included in the model, the findings are reversed: High-school grades in college preparatory courses are actually the stronger predictor of UC student outcomes. . . . The advent of holistic review in UC admissions has added substantially to the amount and quality of applicant data available to admissions officers. In real-world admissions, the question is not what SAT/ACT scores add to high school grades alone, but what they add to the large body of other academic and socioeconomic information already available from the UC application."[99] Geiser further observed that SAT scores explain a little under 2 percent of variance in first-year grades in analyses of UC data. His point on "real world admissions" is compelling, as policy makers consider how much is really added by tests in the application.

When the pandemic hit, the UC system considered going test-optional, but a California court ruled that doing so during the pandemic would discriminate against students with disabilities. In the end, the pandemic combined with litigation drove UC's move to test-free admissions. They seem pretty happy so far, and the UC system has admitted some of the most diverse classes ever, with high retention rates.[100] It's challenging to isolate the effect of test-free admissions, given all of the concurrent change in students' lives during the pandemic, as well as other promising developments in the UC system. For example, at UC Berkeley, Director Femi Ogundele has been lauded for instating a number of changes related to recruitment, outreach, and evaluation.[101] In some but not all of the models that our team ran, test-free admissions, relative to test-required admissions, was linked with higher enrollment of Black, Latinx, and low-income students.[102] Ripple effects of being test-free may show up in future years, as institutions cultivate and expand relationships with different high schools. Students and families may be drawn to UC schools because of the message sent by test-admissions.

In 2021, Gary Clark, Director of Undergraduate Admissions at the University of California, Los Angeles (UCLA), described his observations of going test-free: "At UCLA, the move to test-free certainly had an impact on both our application volume and the makeup of our applicant pool. Some of our largest increases came from underrepresented and high-performing students, as measured by both unweighted and weighted GPA. . . . The increases in apps from these communities and from top performing students tells us that there were strong students each year who may have been scared off by the middle 50 percent of our test scores."[103] In 2023, the UC Board of Admissions and Relations with Schools (BOARS), which oversees admissions for the system-wide UC Academic Senate, noted: "Though not initially endorsed by BOARS, elimination of standardized tests have demonstrated a way in which UC can lead in advancing access and opportunity for the state's students."[104]

Our CAF Co-LAB team studied a group of admissions professionals working at test-free schools. The vast majority felt that it was not difficult to assess students without test scores. One noted: "[The] biggest opportunity [in test-free admissions] is that a test score was no longer the cloud over the head of an otherwise highly qualified and accomplished student."[105]

Others noted implications for the review process. For example, one respondent noted that being test-free took "the pressure off to not worry about whether our test average would go up or down (even by a few points)" as individuals reviewed applications.[106] While test score averages are no longer part of the *U.S. News & World Report* rankings, they still loom large at selective institutions as a marker of prestige and competitiveness.

Another participant, with almost seventeen years of experience in admissions, noted: "Many readers don't admit this, but they use numbers as shortcuts far too often, so [test-free] requires them to slow down, read the full app, a [*sic*] fully consider a student's achievements and triumphs."[107] The respondent noted how being test-free made their team "slow down" and read the entire application carefully, which could help readers' evaluations. Test-free admissions could also help reduce "positive bias" towards students with stronger test scores but whose accomplishments are less noteworthy.

Efforts to avoid positive bias remind me of Angel Pérez's experience as Vice President of Enrollment Management at Trinity College, a role he held before becoming CEO of NACAC (National Association of College Admissions Counselors). As documented by journalist Paul Tough, Pérez realized that Trinity was admitting rich students who tested well but were academically lackluster once on campus.[108] Their test scores "overpredicted" their actual success. Pérez led the drive to start admitting more students who had lower test scores, but still demonstrated potential. These students often excelled academically, making important contributions to campus life. Their stories speak to the importance of not letting a test score dominate a student's profile. Given the high number of applications that admissions readers review, overrelying on test scores is an all too easy "shortcut."

Gary Clark from UCLA described test-free as "clearer in many ways—for equity and access for less-resourced students, for universities from a training standpoint, and for families and students who are trying to determine if/when they should submit scores. While we were prepared to train our readers to read apps with and without test scores, not having to toggle between two frameworks certainly streamlined that training."[109] According to Clark, staff at UCLA felt that the application "provided more than enough information for us to make an informed decision" without test scores. While admissions officers working at test-optional schools seem comfortable evaluating applications both with and without scores, test-free brings more consistency to the process. Evaluators have to address other inequities that influence the process beyond test scores, but UC's holistic review process is highly sensitive to evaluating student accomplishments in the context of opportunity. Naturally, the College Board, which runs the SAT, is less of a fan.[110] It doesn't have much to worry about. SAT participation is still high, even with test-optional dominating; the SAT or ACT is still required for high school graduation in half of the country.[111] Of course there are still plenty of rich students who take the test multiple times to boost their score, so that's another source of revenue.[112]

WRAPPING IT UP

So there you have it, folks, the ever-evolving debate between test-optional, test-required, and test-free admissions. Beyond data, the debate is shaped by different worldviews and values ascribed to testing. Some see the research and think that reviewers benefit from seeing test scores, so everyone should submit. Others note that the SAT doesn't add much on top of the information provided by the other parts of the application, so the trade-off isn't worth it. While test scores can and should be read in context, some research suggests that wealthier students benefit just as much as low-income students when readers contextualize scores.[113]

If test-optional or test-free admissions was linked with students flunking out, the policy direction would be clearer. However, that doesn't seem to be the case. To quote Yale's dean of admission again, "Students who have been admitted to Yale without test scores have done relatively well in their Yale courses."[114] While the GPAs of non-submitting students are somewhat lower than the GPAs of students with perfect SAT scores, the difference is less notable when one compares non-submitting students with those who scored a 1500.[115]

While the gains in URM student enrollment related to test-optional are often described as modest, some scholars view them as fairly notable; statistical effects linked with test-optional policies exceed those associated with percent plans and holistic review in previous research.[116] How we'll see policies play out after the SCOTUS ruling is a big question, given that most of the research on testing policy was conducted when conventional race-conscious admissions was still legal. Race-conscious admissions has been illegal in California since 1996, so data from UC cohorts admitted through test-free admissions provide insight into how such policies would work in the absence of conventional race-conscious admissions. Altogether, most institutions are making decisions in an era of incomplete and shifting data points. Time will tell how different gambles play out.

Despite claims that test-optional hurts low-income students, the percentage of low-income students remained steady, or even increased, under test-optional policies at elite institutions. Institutions should work to enroll both lower-income students with higher test scores *and* those who might have lower scores but demonstrate talent in other ways. It doesn't need to be an "either-or" decision. Many contributions aren't easily captured through test scores, and non-submitting students bring plenty to the table. Of course there are other reasons unrelated to diversity that lead institutions to adopt test-optional policies. Institutions worried about the impending enrollment cliff (a.k.a. almost everyone) want to encourage more applications, and making test scores optional is certainly one way to do that.

Overall, testing policy is just one piece of the puzzle in supporting equity and access. We still need institutions to step up in other ways to enroll, support, and graduate historically underrepresented populations. That said, both test-optional and test-free admissions have the potential to promote access and broaden the applicant pool.

5

Inequality Beyond Tests

Extracurricular Activities, Letters of Recommendation, and Essays

Standardized tests dominated debates around equity in college admissions for years, in large part due to their complicated and troubling history.[1] Inequality is hard to mask because test scores are easily comparable between groups, versus other parts of the application. Sure, students might have a sense of their peers' activities, but most don't even know what their own letters of recommendation say. Nonetheless, inequality affects other parts of the application besides tests. Families purchase coaching services to help students write (or basically ghostwrite) essays. Not all students have the chance to join a swim team or pick up fencing. Private schools are known for more individualized attention in college counseling, including more personalized letters of recommendation because, hey, paying $50,000 a year should get you something.

Still, these inequities were easier to overlook without more concrete, national data. Until recently, large-scale analyses of nonstandardized components were infeasible for numerous reasons. Even if you could somehow code hundreds of thousands of letters, essays, and activities, consistency is hard to achieve. Getting access to large, national datasets of college applications is understandably difficult, with schools hesitating to turn over anything that could be fodder for a lawsuit.[2] However, thanks to technological developments and the generosity of application platforms, researchers can now analyze large datasets of nonstandardized text from hundreds of thousands or even millions of applications. Yes, tools that summarize product reviews on Amazon and make it possible for OkCupid to match you with someone across the country can be used to study college applications. The Common Application (a.k.a. "Common App") has allowed researchers to access their massive dataset of anonymized applicant data, which includes letters, essays, extracurricular involvement, test scores, GPAs, and demographic information. To note, Common App does not have data about where applicants were ultimately admitted. Common App is the country's largest and most frequently used application platform, so this development has opened the door for research unprecedented in scope, size, and scale. Other key studies on essays and letters have come from researchers collaborating with the UC system.[3]

In this chapter, I'll highlight what we know and don't know about the three key nonstandardized parts of the college application: extracurricular activities, letters of recommendation, and essays. Spoiler alert: There's a lot of inequality. However, the policy implications are sometimes fuzzy, and we don't know a lot about the role that different elements play in admissions review. I'll highlight what we do know, and then make some suggestions about where the field can go from here in light of the SCOTUS ruling.

EXTRACURRICULAR ACTIVITIES: AN UNEQUAL PLAYING FIELD

In theory, anyone can sign up for a club, volunteer, or work a part-time job. However, extracurriculars are influenced by disparities related to time, money, transportation, access, and socialization. The first three relate to family resources: Who can get their child to a 4 p.m. lesson when both parents work? Who has a stay-at-home parent or nanny who can shuttle the kids to activities?[4] Who can dedicate weekends to travel soccer? Let's not forget the cost of registration, equipment, uniforms, summer camps, and private coaching. In our current times, getting on the hamster wheel of youth sports requires starting young. In some contexts, kids are expected to become more serious about a sport by around age seven or eight.[5] Unfortunately, the intense culture around youth sports often leads to injury and burnout, and the costs of activities add up.[6] Right now I'm paying about $2,000 a year for piano lessons, for a kid who's less than enthusiastic about practicing the piano. Ugh, don't remind me.

Access and socialization also affect inequality in activities. By access, I mean issues that shape whether students can join various activities, including historical or contemporary inclusion/exclusion, as well as availability. Regarding historical exclusion, the past affects the present. Swimming is a prime example. In the mid-twentieth century and onward, municipalities nationwide closed public swimming pools rather than integrate; Black individuals were barred from swimming in both public and private pools. In 1971, the Supreme Court ruled that "communities may close their publicly owned recreational facilities rather than comply with court orders to desegregate them," as noted in a *New York Times* article about the ruling.[7] In an interview with NPR, Jeff Wiltse, author of a book on race and the history of swimming pools, explained that "the police and the city officials allowed, and in some cases encouraged, white swimmers to literally beat black swimmers out of the water, as a means of segregating pools, as a means of intimidating them from trying to access pools . . . [at Highland Park pool in Pittsburgh—yes, in the North] young black men . . . tried to access the pool, and if they made it into the water, they were oftentimes beat and dunked and punched in the water. . . . In my book, I have some pictures of black Americans who literally sort of lie still on the ground with bloody heads from being pummeled to the ground, just for trying to access a swimming pool."[8] History matters, and an estimated 64 percent of Black youth cannot swim.[9]

Availability is also a part of access. Offering an activity through a school increases availability. Some private schools facilitate availability by requiring that all students participate in a sport and having a dedicated period for extracurricular participation.[10] Richer communities are more likely to have parents who can pour time and money into supporting or even running their children's activities.[11] Beyond transportation and fees (already a lot), parents are needed to fundraise, coach, and even more. Growing up, I took so many things for granted, in a well-resourced school district with volunteers who coached my Odyssey of the Mind and speech teams.[12] My dad once drove my brother and friends from Ohio to Massachusetts to compete in a debate tournament, showing how parental involvement makes participation at more elite levels possible.[13] Of course, schools vary notably in *what* clubs, organizations, and teams are offered.[14] In a telling sign of inequality, programs like Science Olympiad and debate aren't available at many high schools, but they exist at some rich elementary schools, giving kids an early chance to hone skills.[15]

Another component affecting participation is community-level socialization, which is whether participating in an activity is seen as a normal behavior within a community. Imagine describing travel soccer to someone from the mid-twentieth century. ("So yes, you take your entire weekend and then, yes, you go from New Jersey to Florida to play in a tournament, and yes, these are twelve-year-olds . . .") The experience would seem downright bizarre to someone from the past, but such activities are a normal fixture of suburban communities. Sometimes activities become the norm within certain racial/ethnic groups. What is often referred to as "culture" is really more like a byproduct of cultural socialization. In referring to culture, I don't mean some mystical affinity or innate talent for an activity like piano or spelling. Instead, think of culture as a set of behaviors, norms, and expectations that are seen as normal in one community but unusual in another. Affected by dimensions of access (e.g., historical exclusion or inclusion, availability), cultural socialization works in a feedback loop. If young people achieve success, that success is reinforced by members of the community and community infrastructure, which spurs more participation.[16] You can check the endnotes for the example of spelling bees in South Asian American communities.[17] Socialization and community/peer norms can also affect whether someone feels compelled to "resume pack," picking up as many extracurricular activities as possible to try to stand out in a crowded field.

All right, so extracurricular participation is way more complicated than "anyone can sign up." This inequality is problematic because extracurriculars can shape admission to elite colleges. Many selective institutions will dedicate at least one rating to extracurricular activities. Documents from *SFFA* indicated that Harvard dedicated two ratings to extracurriculars—an extracurricular rating and an athletics rating.[18] Ratings were not determinative of admission, but stronger ratings were linked with a higher rate of admission. Having more extracurricular activities has been linked with a higher likelihood of admission at selective institutions.[19] While admissions officers will tell you that they want quality over quantity, some probably prefer a "high quality, high quantity" combination over a "high quality, low quantity" one. The impact of extracurriculars in the admissions process varies from student to student. Having a strong application isn't enough to get anyone accepted at many highly rejective institutions; it's the baseline to keep someone in the running until institutional priorities take over. In some cases, having unique, standout accomplishments will help an applicant stick out. Activities can serve as a form of triangulation: If a student says that they're passionate about STEM but they're lacking any STEM-related activities, admissions reviewers might raise their eyebrows. On the other hand, having strong STEM-focused extracurriculars can complement a strong STEM transcript.

What can help students? Sports. Being a recruited athlete can open doors. Harvard's expert David Card found that students who received the best athletic rating (generally, recruited athletes) but no other top ratings were admitted at a whopping rate of 88 percent from 2014 to 2019. About 1,340 students fell into this category, meaning that on average, about 235 recruited athletes were admitted each year.[20] Considering that the Harvard first-year class is about 1,600 to 1,700, that's a sizable chunk of the student body. Card's analysis also showed that nonrecruited athletes received considerable preference, all other things held equal, in the admissions process.[21] Who benefited the most from the bump? White students were twice as likely to have a high athletic rating among nonrecruited athletes: 14 percent of White versus 7 percent of Black applicants.[22]

On the whole, preferences for both recruited and nonrecruited athletes disproportionately help White students. When people think of student-athletes, they often think of students of color playing nationally broadcast sports. However, non-revenue-generating sports take up most of the spots in a class. Kirsten Hextrum's *Special Admission: How College Sports Recruitment Favors White Suburban Athletes* (the title says it all) provides a deep dive into the nuances of athletic recruiting and college admissions.[23] A former rower for UC Berkeley, Hextrum documents how opportunities to access rarefied sports are driven through expensive suburban club teams.[24] Colleges form partnerships with suburban coaches, who push them to take their best players. The final result is a system that greatly privileges White, affluent students. To explore this issue further, I investigated athletic rosters at Amherst College and the University of Michigan in the mid-2020s; check the endnotes to learn more.[25]

Hextrum's work disrupts the perception that activities are a level playing field.[26] To examine the issue at a national scale, our CAF Co-LAB team studied a dataset of 5,967,920 applications submitted by 860,003 students who applied to at least one selective (40 percent or lower) institution during the 2018–2019 and 2019–2020 admissions cycles through Common App.[27] Each applicant submitted an average of about seven applications. Students could fill out up to ten activities, choosing from a dropdown menu of the activity category (e.g., Academics, Athletics), timing of involvement (hours per week, weeks per year, years participated, etc.), honors/awards and roles held (open response, up to fifty characters), detailed descriptions of their involvement (open response, up to 150 characters), and whether they planned to continue in college or not.

We used natural language processing techniques to parse through the data, a process which paired human coder interpretive insight with the power of high-speed computing. We developed two constructs to reflect how students described their involvement: *Top-level leadership* reflects various "head honcho" types of leadership roles (e.g., founder, president, CEO), and *honors/awards* refers to the markers of excellence listed by students (first prize, MVP, etc.).[28] White, Asian American, higher SES, and private school students listed the most activities. They were most likely to report top-level leadership positions, as well as honors/awards. They even wrote more about each activity. “Volleyball team assistant” becomes “chief of staff to executive leadership, supporting key strategy, project management, and execution of team goals and priorities.” With some polishing, marching band and Key Club can sound like a case study of Six Sigma.[29]

We saw the most persistent disparities in athletics. White, private school, and more affluent students reported more athletic activities than students from other racial/ethnic and economic backgrounds, as well as public school students. Similarly, White, more affluent, and private school students reported more top-level leadership positions within athletics than their peers. Even when controlling for an array of characteristics, White students reported more athletic activities than students from other racial/ethnic groups. The same trends persisted for top-level leadership roles within athletics. These disparities are concerning because selective institutions are known to favor athletic participation, both for recruited and nonrecruited athletes.[30] I once talked to a director of admissions who said that it’d be easier to get their board to approve special favor for being a descendant of enslaved persons (i.e., reparations) than to get them to walk away from athletic preferences. Priorities![31] In an ideal world, institutions could still have all of the sports teams that they want, and just build teams based on the students already attending.[32] (Insert hysterical laughing from the college athletics industry.) Sometimes the most logical option is truly the most unrealistic one.

While Black, Latinx, Indigenous, and lower-SES students reported fewer activities, they reported similar percentages of top-leadership roles within their activities. Basically, the driving force in the disparities was the overall raw number of activities. White and Asian American students reported more activities overall, and in turn, they had more top-level leadership positions. However, when we examined the *proportion* of activities with a top-level leadership role, the groups looked more similar. For example, the average Black student in the dataset had a top-level leadership role for 14 percent of their activities. Same with the average White student.

Why do differences exist in the raw number of activities that students report? Many affluent students report anything and everything they do, while other students underreport. Affluent students have greater opportunity and more money to try more activities, as well as differential socialization around activity reporting. Altogether, these students are conditioned to see selective college admissions as an arms race, where racking up activities and accolades is the norm. The ethos is an extension of the *concerted cultivation* that upper middle-class and wealthier children experience, a term coined by sociologist Annette Lareau.[33] Such "cultivation" often involves heavy extracurricular involvement from an early age, all with the goal of preparing young people to secure their position in the class hierarchy.

At the same time, many students from historically excluded backgrounds aren't reporting everything that they're doing or giving it the type of "glow-up" that a college concierge would encourage. Activities that students think of as "life" are very much worth reporting, such as caretaking, translating for family members, helping parents navigate paperwork, advocating for a younger sibling, and the like. Students may downplay such experiences, which don't always fit neatly into the traditional reporting form of hours per week. Some colleges are getting better at actively encouraging students to list family and household responsibilities, but these efforts are long overdue.

Excellence is not exclusive to any one group: Students from different racial/ethnic backgrounds report top-level leadership roles at very similar, if not identical, rates. Still, there could be some positive bias toward longer activity lists; admissions readers may forget that shorter lists may be due to less opportunity and fewer resources. A common phrase in admissions circles is that readers like "pointy" involvement, favoring sustained, multiyear involvement reflecting investment and passion, versus more shallow, drive-by involvement. But an activity list with ten total activities, including multiple "pointy" activities and a few less involved ones, may still look more impressive than a list of three or four activities, even if one or two are extra involved. Given these dynamics, in Fall 2023, Lafayette College announced that they would only review the first six activities listed by students. Common App agreed to adjust viewer settings so admissions readers will only see up to six activities instead of the maximum of ten.[34] MIT actually moved in this direction some time ago, and only allows students to list four.[35]

MENTAL HEALTH AND EXTRACURRICULARS

Besides equity, mental health is another reason to consider reducing the number of activities that students can report. A graduate student in my program, Pearl Lo, reflected on the road to get into an Ivy in *Inside Higher Ed*: "Captain of the speech and debate team, Key Club lieutenant governor, Student Government representative, Science Bowl, wrestling team, tae kwon do instructor. These are just six of the 10 activities I listed when filling out the extracurricular involvement section of my college applications back in 2013. We were allowed to list up to 10 on the Common Application platform, and I was determined to max out. During high school, extracurriculars were my favorite part of school because I got to hang out with friends. Still, I sometimes found myself tired, overwhelmed and stressed. I would tell myself, 'I need to stay up all night to practice for the tournament. I need to win the tournament to make it to the state championships. I need to have the strongest application possible to get into a "good" school.' It felt like getting into college would determine the trajectory of the rest of my life, and extracurriculars were a way to shape that future."[36]

While students are free to participate in whatever activities that they wish, lowering the number of activities on the application could reduce some of the pressure to "max out."[37] Seeing as how the favorite extracurricular of many alumni of distinguished schools is lying on the couch and watching Netflix (raises hand), implicitly encouraging students to rack up to ten distinct, impressive activities or accomplishments within three-ish years of high school seems like a lot.[38] Of course there are some students who won't cut back regardless of any changes to the application, but it could help reduce some of the pressure for students. We need students coming to college with energy to burn, versus already feeling burnt out.

Is the heightened interest in early retirement due to the exhaustion that people feel from starting the rat race too early? Cultural critics like Anne Helen Petersen, whose *Buzzfeed* piece "How the Millennials Became the

Burnout Generation" went viral, link millennial burnout to broader global trends like the 2008 financial crisis that obliterated any sense of security or predictability in the workforce. In turn, that instability has sped up the rat race, making more and more young people feel like they have to run faster and faster on the hamster wheel.[39] The impact on academics is bad enough, but the effect on extracurriculars is also worrisome: Too much competition squashes the fun and isn't good for spurring longer-lasting intrinsic motivation. The system isn't serving anyone particularly well, and institutions and application platforms should consider how they could help shift the status quo.

LETTERS OF RECOMMENDATION: WHO BENEFITS?

Let's turn to letters of recommendation. Most selective institutions require one to three letters, including one from a counselor and one or two from teachers, with some exceptions. The UC system does not require letters up front, although some campuses request them later.[40] With Common App, recommenders fill out checkboxes indicating how the applicant fares in relation to their peers, then they upload a letter or complete an open response box. As of the 2023–2024 application season, there was no length cut-off for the Common App letter submission. In this section, some of my comments will apply to both teacher and counselor letters, but in some cases I'll refer specifically to one type of letter.

How much do letters of recommendation matter in admissions? We have fairly limited research on the issue. Letters are the only nonstandardized part of the application not completed by the applicant. Admissions professionals should know that letter quality often varies between public and private school applicants, so a quick, positive-but-not-super-detailed letter should not hurt an otherwise talented public school applicant. People in the field will talk about letters as being a source of triangulation. If the student seems pretty lackluster, a standout letter won't do much. Red flag letters are extra helpful, where a student seems great on paper but the letter says or hints otherwise. If a student claims to be incredibly passionate about STEM through the essay, but none of the recommenders mention these interests, the letter could serve as a sort of a yellow flag; it might depend on the student's school context.

Letters of recommendation are susceptible to inequality through multiple means. Workloads and student-to-counselor ratios differ notably between school contexts.[41] Counselors from private schools can offer more personalization in letters, as well as typically longer letters. In his study of letters of recommendation, sociologist Jonathan Schwarz referred to a "shared language" between counselors at private schools and admissions professionals, where counselors know how to write in ways that catch the attention of evaluators.[42] Many college counselors at private schools previously worked in college admissions themselves, leading to familiarity with what admissions officers are looking for.[43] Relationships matter too. Counselors and teachers at "feeder schools" to elite colleges often know admissions officers in the field, due to work experience and networking.[44] Admission professionals may trust the credibility of the letters written by counselors or teachers whom they know, or who are from schools that they're already familiar with.[45] Also, more often than not, many students at private schools aim for name-brand college attendance. As a result, private school counselors and teachers pick up more experience in how to write the types of letters that will be well-received at selective institutions.

Additionally, college counselors at private schools generally wear one main hat—college counselor. Getting students into top colleges is their foremost responsibility. In contrast, counselors at public schools often wear multiple hats, such as handling discipline, testing, course selection, registration, mental health support, and the like. At a lower-income school, the counselor is basically a social worker, counselor, and jack-of-all-trades rolled into one. Analyzing data from the Common App, Tara Nicola of Common App and Sebastian Munoz-Najar Galvez of Harvard found that public school counselors at large high schools were more likely to reuse text for their students, versus writing a brand new, unique letter for each student.[46] You can hardly blame them, given the crushing workload that too many public school counselors experience. Similar dynamics may affect teachers, who deal with much more than just teaching in underresourced school contexts.

In contrast, many wealthy families, even at private schools, will hire a private college counselor (or, as they like to call themselves, "independent educational consultants") to give their child even more individualized attention and coaching through the process. These consultants can't write letters, but they can help students get the best recommendation possible. Sometimes counselors and teachers will have students submit a "brag" sheet, asking them to list their noteworthy accomplishments and other information that they could use to strengthen a letter. A private college coach can help a student mine gold from—well, let's just say, more common material.

Some distinctions exist between counselor and teacher letters. Counselors compare students to their class (the entire class or a significant portion thereof) while teachers are comparing students to other students they have taught, as well as their current slate of students. Counselor letters may come off as dryer, since students usually develop closer relationships with teachers, especially in public school contexts.[47] In documents submitted during the Harvard trial, counselor letters received lower ratings than teacher letters, perhaps because of the different conditions.[48] At the same time, many of the same inequities that affect counselor letters also affect letters written by teachers. While high-caliber and dedicated teachers can be found at both types of schools, there's a reason, for better or for worse, that private school families pay upwards of $25,000 to $50,000+ a year for private school education. Those who are "full pay" are used to paying the most to get the most bang for their buck, and that includes teachers working to position students to attend elite universities.

Inequality can shape the letters, but what about bias, unconscious or otherwise? Numerous studies point to how bias affects K–12 education. Researchers have documented how counselors have steered qualified Black students away from advanced coursework and discouraged low-income students from applying to four-year institutions.[49] Microaggressions and other forms of racism can occur in classrooms.[50] Having a same-race educator can also matter. Seth Gershenson, professor of Public Policy at American University, and colleagues found that Black teachers were more likely to have high expectations for Black students.[51]

Unfortunately, both the counseling and teaching professions suffer from a lack of diversity. Despite everyone's best intentions, bias can shape letters of recommendation, from the relationships that students build with counselors and teachers to the expectations that educators have of students.[52] Those expectations include the type of student that teachers or counselors think can succeed at a name-brand institution.

Led by Brian Kim, Director of Data Science, Research, and Analytics at Common App, our team examined counselor letters of recommendation in a sample of over 600,000 applications submitted via Common App.[53] We used an NLP technique called topic modeling, where patterns within the text data are clustered together, allowing us to identify key topical themes within letters. Through this process, we discovered what topics were discussed more often by counselors, and whether counselors were more likely to reference key topics for certain groups even when controlling for demographic, academic, and high school–related characteristics. To note, our work only speaks to patterns and relationships between variables within letters. Due to a lack of data on actual application decisions, we couldn't study the actual impact of such letters in the admissions process.

Overall, students from private schools had longer letters and more sentences related to topics like character excellence, intellectual promise, the humanities, extracurricular activities, and athletics. Most Black students had substantially fewer sentences related to topics like character excellence and intellectual promise, although the difference was not apparent when comparing letters written by the same counselor for students with higher test scores (95th percentile or higher on SAT/ACT). White students had significantly more sentences in their letters on athletic involvement than Black, Latinx, and Asian American students, even when comparing letters written by the same counselor at the same school.

Private school students and students living in higher-income communities generally had longer letters. Students who received fee waivers also had longer letters. Their letters tended to focus more on personal qualities, possibly reflecting contextual information about students' backgrounds (e.g., overcoming adversity). At the same time, these low-income students had fewer sentences on academics or extracurricular activities.

Private school students had longer letters with more discussion of personal qualities, but not at the expense of topics like academics or extracurriculars. First-generation students received shorter letters and fewer sentences on numerous topics, even when comparing high-scoring students with similar high school and counselor characteristics. Interestingly, Asian American students had fewer sentences on personal qualities across models, perhaps somehow relating to the personal rating issue from the Harvard case. In a separate study, Kim studied letters written by teachers from Common App, and the endnotes have more on that study.[54]

Raj Chetty and colleagues estimated that after controlling for test scores, about 30 percent of the admissions advantage received by students from the top 1 percent of household incomes is tied to nonacademic traits. Admissions readers glean insights about such traits from reviewing extracurricular activities, letters of recommendation, and other sources.[55] Our team's study on counselor letters provides perspective into how letters may contribute to this nonacademic advantage. First, letters from private school, White, and more affluent students are generally longer and stronger to begin with, due to both students and their letter writers. Second, letters for private school and White students are more likely to touch on athletics and the arts, which are often valued by reviewers.[56] In this way, letters reinforce and reflect inequities shaping extracurricular participation, especially athletics. Letters of recommendation that comment on student accomplishments outside of the classroom may reflect greater familiarity with the student, leading to greater personalization in the letter. In contrast, counselors from large public high schools are more likely to reuse letter text due to overwhelming caseloads.[57] Letters from teachers similarly contribute to the nonacademic advantage accrued to students from the most affluent backgrounds.

Clearly, letters can advantage some students unless admissions systems are sensitive to the influence of a student's environment and background. Recommenders can also use letters to communicate information related to a student's context for opportunity. In these cases, letters have the potential to disrupt and contextualize inequities that affect students' lives. Based on his analysis of letters submitted to UC Berkeley, Rothstein stated: "There is a case for including subjective information like letters in the process in order to make it more visible, at least within systems like Berkeley's that are carefully designed to promote equitable admissions."[58] In other words, letters are most beneficial when the admissions process is geared toward advancing equity, versus letters being read without adequate consideration of factors affecting both advantage and disadvantage.

Let's dive more deeply into Rothstein's work. The UC system does not require letters of recommendation up front. In 2016, UC Berkeley piloted a program where they requested letters for a subsection of students after applications were submitted. Berkeley wanted to know more about who would receive a letter when one was requested, letter quality, and whether letter quality was linked to admissions decisions. They asked Rothstein to study the pilot. He used various text-scraping and NLP tools, allowing him to analyze about ten thousand letters.

Rothstein acknowledges up front that there's something for everyone in his findings, both supporters and opponents of letters. On the downside, students from underrepresented groups (a combination of low-income, URM, and first-generation students) were less likely to get letters to begin with, since Berkeley did not request the letters up front. They also tended to get weaker letters. However, having a letter submitted "modestly improved application outcomes for the average underrepresented student."[59] On the whole, letter inclusion was linked with stronger application scores for both majority-status groups and underrepresented groups; effects were strongest for the latter group. Rothstein noted: "There is no indication that [letter of recommendation] invitations hurt the relative chances of underrepresented applicants, and some evidence that invitations increased these students' enrollment. Ultimately, any impact of the use of letters of recommendation on the diversity of the Berkeley student body seems likely to be small."[60] In follow-up work, Rothstein and collaborators "conclude[d] that soliciting letters of recommendation from a broader pool of applicants would not meaningfully change the composition of admitted undergraduates."[61]

So how to make sense of the findings? Students from underrepresented groups received weaker letters but appeared to benefit modestly from having a letter included. The weaker letters probably reflect issues like high counselor caseloads and unequal access to a rigorous curriculum. Still, the letters had information that helped reviewers understand student accomplishments in the context of opportunities afforded to them. In this way, the letters, even if weaker on average, could still enhance readers' assessments of students. Rothstein doesn't give a clear-cut recommendation on whether letters should stay or go, noting that any impact is probably fairly limited.

For institutions that want to keep letters, a sensible reform would be to have a more standardized letter length or a cap on letter length. Something like three hundred words should be sufficient. Some people chafe at the idea of limiting what a counselor or teacher can say about a student. Still, word limits could reduce the impact of the resource gap between public and private schools. The primary "value-added" contribution of a letter is to offer information not already included by the student, whether it's a red flag or contextual information about the applicant's circumstances. This information can be conveyed in a relatively small amount of space.

Efforts to standardize or limit letter length are definitely worth pursuing, but they are more complicated than just saying "cap it at three hundred," as Brian Kim from Common App kindly explained to me. Currently, Common App allows recommenders to either upload a letter PDF or do direct text entry. At this time, there is no way to enforce a word limit on an uploaded PDF, and any automated way to check for length is currently prone to error. One approach could be to remove the PDF option and just force text entry, but that could be challenging for educators who have workflows built around the old method of writing a letter, converting it to a PDF, and uploading it. Common App has about four hundred partner schools that require letters, and any big change would benefit greatly from their buy-in. So yes, it will take work, but it's a worthwhile endeavor following the SCOTUS ruling.

Of course, besides AI coming to take our jobs and eat us, rapid developments in technology are disrupting all nonstandardized components. Already there's a program that can jazz up the 150-character description of your extracurricular activities. Letters are ripe for AI usage as well, which has pros and cons. Given the rise of AI, putting some sort of cap on letter length makes sense. Letters just need to convey the most critical information.

ESSAYS: AN ONGOING EVOLUTION GIVEN THE SCOTUS RULING AND THE GROWTH OF AI

The last notable part of the application is the essay. Essays received a special shout-out in the SCOTUS majority opinion, with Chief Justice Roberts's comments on how students can still discuss life experiences related to race. He noted that just mentioning race in the essay could not serve as a determinative factor in admissions, not that it did preruling. The ruling noted that experiences linked to one's racial/ethnic identity needed to demonstrate traits or characteristics valued by colleges, such as leadership, creativity, and the like. Some schools added new essay questions specifically asking students to discuss their racial/ethnic identities.[62] More commonly, colleges offered broader questions, such as essay prompts asking students to reflect on their background, life story, or experiences with adversity. Interestingly, in a simulation of admissions conditions preruling by Michael Bastedo and colleagues, writing about grit was not linked with a higher rate of admission, so we'll see how things go.[63]

Given the SCOTUS majority ruling, essays will likely stick around in selective college admissions, although AI is putting things in flux. As noted, Duke no longer gives the essay a numerical rating, but still uses it to inform their understanding of applicants.[64] Right now AI isn't that great at writing essays, but things may change by the time you're reading this book.[65] Of course, essays are vulnerable to inequities that influence other parts of the application. Some people see AI as a tool that can help level the playing field. After all, rich kids have used the human version of AI, the handy college concierge, to polish or even ghostwrite essays for decades. Even without a consultant, having college-educated parents who can give feedback on drafts is a big advantage. It's no surprise that a team based at Stanford University found that patterns related to SES in essays were pervasive. They analyzed a dataset of 240,000 essays submitted to the UC system by 60,000 applicants between 2016 and 2017, and found that essay content and style were correlated with income. Essay content predicted about 16 percent of variation in income, while SAT scores predicted about 12 percent of variation in income.[66]

Troubling, yes. Reason to ax the essay? That's harder to say. Mitchell Stevens of Stanford (also a coauthor of the Stanford paper) did ethnographic work on an admissions office at a selective institution about twenty years ago. At the school he studied, "essays had a negligible role in final decisions."[67] In the Harvard trial, the infamous personal rating included the essay, an often overlooked detail. Could the gap between Whites and Asian Americans on the personal rating be attributed in part to the essay? Quite possibly, given the roles of private school attendance and private college consulting.

Zooming out, a compelling question is how continued inclusion of the essay affects the prospects of first-generation, low-income, and URM students. We likely have a situation similar to the letters of recommendation study by Rothstein. In that study, essays from historically underrepresented groups were weaker when compared to other groups due to disparities in resources but still provided important contextual information for readers. Essays may still be beneficial to these groups due to the important contextual information that they can provide. Any sort of evaluation of essays raises the question of what metrics are used to assess quality and value, which can look very different depending on an institution's priorities.

INEQUALITY IS EVERYWHERE: SHOULD WE RETURN TO REQUIRING THE SAT/ACT?

Clearly, inequality affects nonstandardized parts of the application. Does that mean that institutions should go back to requiring standardized tests? In a press release issued by Harvard upon its return to required testing, Chetty commented: "Critics correctly note that standardized tests are not an unbiased measure of students' qualifications, as students from higher-income families often have greater access to test prep and other resources. But the data reveal that other measures—recommendation letters, extracurriculars, essays—are even more prone to such biases. Considering standardized test scores is likely to make the admissions process at Harvard more meritocratic while increasing socioeconomic diversity."[68]

These comments make standardized tests sound like a breakthrough improvement, maybe discovered on the side when the miraculous COVID-19 vaccines rolled out. The SAT, mRNA: They've been around for a while, but now they're saving lives! Despite getting a makeover in the AOI era, standardized tests are nothing new, and we've had plenty of time to understand their impact on the system.[69] Nonetheless, Harvard Kennedy School professor David Deming, also of Opportunity Insights, practically gushed about the SAT/ACT in the same Harvard press release: "Not everyone can hire an expensive college coach to help them craft a personal essay. But everyone has the chance to ace the SAT or ACT. While some barriers do exist, the widespread availability of the test provides, in my view, the fairest admissions policy for disadvantaged applicants."[70] It's news to me that "everyone has the chance to ace the SAT," and who knew that the SAT/ACT is the "fairest admissions policy for disadvantaged applicants." I'd love to see that last line repeated in a roomful of people who actually work with low-income students.[71] Ironically, Deming's own work undermines the idea that everyone has the chance to ace the SAT, highlighting how disparities stem from cumulative advantage/disadvantage.[72]

Yes, inequality affects all parts of the application. Still, not much is known about how such inequities affect how applicants are evaluated. On the one hand, the Stanford team identified a slightly stronger correlation between income and essay topic than between income and SAT score.[73] At the same time, the authors admit that they don't actually know how essays are evaluated in holistic review, acknowledging: "The present study cannot speak to how admission officers evaluate essays or about the current role of essays in holistic review more generally."[74] Some of the inequities that affect essays, letters, and activities may be offset by the contextual information provided by nonstandardized components when admissions systems are calibrated to consider equity, context, and opportunity. We can think back to the Rothstein study, where the "quality" of letters was lower for students from underrepresented groups, but students who had letters were more likely to be admitted to the UC system.[75] Nonstandardized components also provide opportunities for applicants to discuss their experiences related to race, which is especially pertinent following *SFFA*.

Some might say, well, test scores can be read in context too, so why not require them? While reading test scores in context can help low-income students, it's probably more common for low-income students to be disadvantaged by their test scores than to be advantaged by them: Higher-scoring low-income students are far outnumbered by high-scoring affluent students in the pool, who also benefit when their scores are compared to their peers.[76] This critical point is often overlooked when institutions laud testing as being helpful for low-income students, with less attention given to any downsides. We don't know if the same dynamic applies to nonstandardized components of the application when essays, letters, and activities are read in context, or if things play out differently depending on the component. Still, requiring students to include essays or activities in the application is probably not going to deter anyone from applying to a selective institution. In contrast, test score requirements will discourage some low-income and URM students from applying.

So yes, everything is prone to bias and inequality. Still, how that inequality affects the evaluation process may play out differently for test scores versus other application components. Requiring test scores may not level the playing field in the way that Dartmouth, Chetty, and others hope, especially given the concurrent restrictions on race-conscious admissions.

WRAPPING IT UP

Altogether, inequality in nonstandardized parts of college applications leaves policy makers and educators with plenty to ponder. Inequality clearly influences these parts of the application. For example, our team's work showed that students from private schools received longer letters, and more sentences in their letters related to topics like character excellence, intellectual promise, the humanities, extracurricular activities, and athletics.[77] At the same time, nonstandardized components provide applicants the opportunity to explain their experiences, talents, and goals, while also allowing space for greater explanation of the circumstances and contexts that shape their lives. This dynamic is especially relevant to essays and, to some extent, letters of recommendation.[78] Given the SCOTUS ruling's discussion of how institutions can consider individuals' experiences with race as discussed in the essay, nonstandardized components will play an ongoing important role in helping institutions understand a student's background. Of course, institutions are dependent on students to share information about themselves, and some students may not want to discuss how their lives have been affected by race or inequality. Thus, this indirect avenue may not be enough to prevent major regressions in racial diversity at some institutions.

Regarding extracurricular involvement, while certain groups (e.g., White, affluent, Asian American, and private school students) reported more activities, students across racial/ethnic and economic groups report top-level leadership roles at roughly the same rate. Disparities in extracurricular activity reporting are most pronounced in the raw number of activities, versus the proportion of leadership roles that students hold. Institutions should be aware of how excellence is not the exclusive domain of any one group, and consider how opportunity and resources influence extracurricular participation.

As discussed in chapter 4, inequality in nonstandardized components does not mean that institutions need to return to required testing. Inequality may shape nonstandardized components, but the negative effect of such inequities may be blunted or counterbalanced by information about a student's context that nonstandardized components can provide. The latter phenomenon is dependent on the extent to which admissions offices consider the role of context and environment in their assessments. Further, continuing to require nonstandardized components will not discourage low-income and URM students from applying to selective institutions in the same way that test score requirements might. The field needs more research to help policy makers understand how both disadvantage and privilege are considered in the decision-making process.

We are living in a time of flux that will influence the future of the application and the review process. Given both structural inequality and the growth of AI, institutions and application platforms may consider changes such as encouraging more standardization in letter length, reducing the number of activities that students list, and reconsidering how components are weighed or scored. Altogether, nonstandardized parts of applications will continue to evolve, as stakeholders discern the best way to evaluate applications in a constantly shifting landscape.

6

Implications for Campus Life

How Demographic Changes Affect Students' Lives

While it'll take more time to understand the full impact of the ruling in *Students for Fair Admissions v. Harvard*, enrollment data postruling is discouraging at many institutions. After the first admissions cycle post-*SFFA*, we saw notable drops in Black enrollment at schools like MIT, Amherst, Tufts, Brown, Columbia, Boston University, and others.[1] Latinx enrollment also dropped at schools like Amherst, Caltech, Wellesley, Brown, and MIT.[2] At Amherst, Black enrollment dropped from 11 percent in 2023 to just 3 percent of the first-year class in 2024.[3] Things weren't all sunshine and roses even before the ruling. Now the situation is worse at many campuses, with URM students experiencing a higher level of marginalization, tokenization, and isolation.

Besides the impact of *SFFA* on admissions, sweeping changes in policy affect the everyday lives of students. In this chapter, I discuss implications for the campus climate for diversity, and how universities should respond. I'll also discuss the importance of efforts like working to diversify the professoriate, as well as supporting entities like racial/ethnic student organizations and cultural centers. Unfortunately, some institutions are pulling back support for key initiatives because of the ongoing movement to squelch diversity, equity, and inclusion in higher education. While we live in a climate of fear and intimidation, we must push back against *repressive legalism* to advance policies needed to support historically underserved populations.[4] Finally, I will remind institutions of their responsibility to guarantee nondiscriminatory environments under Title VI of the Civil Rights Act.

AFTER THE RULING: FROM ALREADY UNDERREPRESENTED TO EVEN MORE UNDERREPRESENTED

Even though university campuses weren't beacons of racial harmony before the SCOTUS ruling, many students still benefited from the rich learning and community linked to diversity: the late-night conversations in the residence halls, the vibrant back-and-forth of a class discussion done well, and so on. While I experienced a difficult campus climate during college, I still have many good memories from the diversity that did exist on campus: an elaborately choreographed Diwali performance where Black fraternity members danced with South Asian American students, late nights spent collaborating with other ethnic student organizations, and alternative spring break trips that helped bridge campus divides. Antar Tichvakunda, Assistant Professor of Education at the University of California, Santa Barbara, reminds us that Black joy is real and critical to students' experiences, Black and otherwise.[5] While Black students often face incredible challenges on campus, their recreation and celebration need to be encouraged and supported as part of a broader call to human flourishing. As an Asian American, some of the best parts of my college experience came from witnessing and benefiting from that joy, which could not be suppressed even on a campus with literal monuments to exclusion.[6]

Things weren't always great in college, but they would've been even worse without the tool of race-conscious admissions to help support the enrollment of students of color.[7] We experienced some of the rich learning that can come from diversity, as well as the growing pains and associated conflict.[8] My current employer, the University of Maryland, College Park (UMD), has benefited tremendously from intentional efforts to attract a racially diverse student body. In *Race on Campus*, I wrote about how one thing I cherish at UMD is the common occurrence of seeing students casually interact across race in campus spaces. As a professor, my classes are richer when students from different backgrounds share their experiences and perspectives. It's incredibly rewarding to see lightbulbs go off in students' heads when they learn from each other's lives. Still, while UMD can pat itself on the back for having the highest percentage of Black students in the Big Ten, the bar is fairly low there.[9] While Black students usually make up about 10 to 13 percent of the student body at UMD, a relatively high number among state flagship institutions, Black individuals make up over 30 percent of Maryland residents.[10]

Numerical diversity in the student body is a necessary precondition for interracial engagement, although it's not the only important factor.[11] To state the obvious, you can't have friends of different races if there aren't people of other races to befriend. As noted by sociologists Peter Blau and Joseph Schwartz, "we are obviously not free to become friends if there are no opportunities for such friendships in our surroundings."[12] I saw this reality play out in my first book, where I tell the story of a campus religious organization, InterVarsity Christian Fellowship (IVCF) at "California University" (CU, pseudonym).[13] During the 1990s, IVCF at CU transformed from a predominantly White community to one that was more racially diverse, shifting from a norm of colorblindness to talking frankly about race.[14] Over time, the organization attracted more Black and Latinx students, making IVCF the only Christian campus fellowship at CU that wasn't almost all White or all Asian American in makeup. Rich interracial friendships were common within the community.

Over time, it became more challenging for IVCF to live out its values around diversity. As the Black student population at CU dropped starkly following Prop 209, it became harder and harder to attract Black students to the group. First, there were just fewer Black students on campus overall. Second, Black students at CU increasingly wanted to spend more time in same-race environments outside of class, which is understandable given the incredible strain of being an extreme demographic minority on campus. Eventually IVCF regained some of its footing, and started prioritizing addressing race and racial diversity more directly again. Still, it was harder to foster interracial friendships (beyond those between Whites and Asian Americans) in the community due to the literal lack of Black, and to some extent, Latinx students, both on campus and within IVCF.[15]

I studied IVCF at CU from 2007 to 2009, a good sixteen years before the *SFFA* ruling came out. The study feels more relevant to me now than it did during much of the 2010s. Part of me wishes that I had saved the title (*When Diversity Drops*) for the book you're reading now. Postruling, campuses that already struggled to attract and retain URM students will struggle even more. When campuses become less diverse, we expect that URM students will need to spend more time outside of the classroom recharging with same-race peers. The need is completely understandable, but could affect the overall levels of cross-racial interaction on campus. Greater demographic diversity is linked with more cross-racial interaction, meaning that the inverse is also true: Less diversity, less engagement across race.[16] This dynamic is the byproduct of structural forces and not the fault of any Black or Brown student, although they'll inevitably be blamed.

In the curricular realm, environments that already struggled to attract diversity before the SCOTUS ruling (e.g., STEM fields, schools of business, honors colleges, Greek life, etc.) will also struggle when campuses lose diversity. Some campuses are abandoning intentional efforts to foster racial/ethnic diversity and a positive climate for all students, despite the ruling's focus on admissions.[17] Thanks to intimidation from the Trump administration and anti-diversity legislation in many states, programs and offices dedicated to serving marginalized groups face budget cuts or even elimination. In these challenging times, it is vital for campus leadership to clearly communicate institutional commitments to fostering environments where all students can flourish.

Just because admissions readers may not see racial/ethnic demographic data at the time of review doesn't mean that campuses need to embrace a colorblind approach to policy and programs. Using demographic data to diagnose disparities in college access and completion is both necessary and legal. Educators also need to be aware of how supposedly "race-neutral" policies can stifle opportunity for historically underrepresented groups; we'll discuss some examples later in this chapter. Following the SCOTUS ruling, some policies will use markers of social class or income to determine eligibility, like first-generation status. While these designations are appropriate for programs designed specifically for these populations, it's important for educators to consider both race and class in policy design; the two aren't interchangeable.

SHIFTS IN DEMOGRAPHY: THE DONUT HOLE CAMPUS AND THE (EVEN MORE) MISSING MIDDLE

As the story of IVCF shows, macro-level policy decisions trickle down to affect students' lives: who they might meet, befriend, and even marry. Beyond the numbers, there are numerous ramifications for the campus experience. Notable drops in Black student enrollment following *SFFA* will make the campus even more of an isolating place for Black students. I anticipate specific drops in middle-class Black student enrollment, as well as possible drops in enrollment for Black students from upper-income backgrounds. These students may have benefited under conventional race-conscious admissions but are less likely to benefit from class-conscious policies. Some think that under race-conscious admissions policies, "all of the Black kids at Harvard/Stanford/etc. were rich," which is a real myth.[18] Hands down, Black students are notably less likely to come from wealthy backgrounds than White students at selective/rejective college campuses; check the endnotes for a recap from *Race on Campus*.[19] Also, tangible differences often exist between what it means to be a "middle-income" White student versus a "middle-income" Black student due to the racial wealth gap.[20] Part of the drop in middle-class Black student enrollment may also come from some students who are admitted but choose to attend another institution that they view as being more supportive.[21]

Losing some middle-class and upper middle-class Black students will be a real loss for intergroup relations at historically White institutions; these students often serve as a "bridge" between different racial and economic groups on campus. A precondition for healthy interracial interaction is something called *relative equal status*.[22] Basically, power differentials between groups make it harder to cross racial or economic boundaries. People assume that students share equal status because they all have campus ID cards, but inequality by race, class, and other categories is pervasive.[23] Still, surmounting the distance that exists between different groups can be challenging, such as the divides between Black and White students, or the gap between wealthy versus low-income students. Such divides are harder to cross when economic divides overlap with racial divides, and vice versa. More social distance (it's not just a COVID term) exists between a low-income Black student and a rich White student than between a Black student and a White student who come from similar economic backgrounds.[24] Of course, not all students of any group have the same experience; I'm painting in very broad brushstrokes here.

Middle-class Black, Latinx, and Indigenous students often help bridge divides between groups on campus, serving as "in-between" groups. Think of our scenario of a lower-SES Black student and a rich White student. That's a lot of social distance, by both race and class, making it harder for interracial interaction to happen. Let's add a middle-class Black student and an upper middle-class Black student to the mix, as well as a lower- or moderate-income White student. Here we're trying to facilitate relative equal status by adding some commonality across social class, even when difference exists due to race. Now we potentially have more opportunities for students to engage across racial/ethnic lines. Without middle-class and even affluent URM students, the gap existing between lower-SES URM students and more affluent majority-status (e.g., White and sometimes Asian American) students grows: We are missing our in-between groups. That doesn't mean that lower-SES students of color don't engage across race and class at all, but peers who share a racial/ethnic identity can facilitate connections between groups. Reflecting this dynamic, middle-and upper-income Black students have the highest rates of cross-racial interaction on college campuses.[25] Other groups can help bridge racial divides. For example, lower- and moderate-income White students often have more precollege interracial interaction than affluent White students. The former are more likely to attend racially diverse high schools, which leads to more precollege experience interacting across race. In turn, precollege engagement with racial diversity is linked with higher cross-racial interaction during college.[26]

With the SCOTUS ruling in *SFFA*, some selective institutions will become like donuts, with growing social distance (i.e., the hole of the donut) between groups with more privilege and students from lower socioeconomic backgrounds, especially low-income URM students.[27] This issue already existed preruling due to widening economic inequality, and will probably get worse. Increasingly, name-brand institutions are mostly made up of full-pay, affluent students (mostly White and, to some extent, Asian American) and to a lesser extent, low-income students who receive need-based financial aid, with less representation from groups in between: the missing middle. Following the SCOTUS ruling, the gap between these two groups may widen if we see drops in in-between groups like middle-class Black students, who have traditionally helped bridge racial *and* economic divides on campus.

Economic background also affects how White students engage, or don't engage, across race. The dividing lines on campus are not just by race; they're reinforced by class. When White student populations are disproportionately made up of recruited athletes, legacies, and full-pay students, it becomes harder to cross racial/ethnic lines because of the larger social distance/donut hole between racial/ethnic groups. Reflecting this dynamic, research indicates that it's not just White students, but wealthy White students that have less diverse friendship groups.[28] Due to K–12 and residential segregation, they're less likely to have extensive precollege experience interacting across racial/ethnic lines.[29] On campus, they often insulate themselves with peers of similar racial and economic backgrounds, as well as communities like historically White Greek life.[30] Unless campuses act more intentionally to attract middle and working-class students from all racial/ethnic backgrounds, expect to see these trends continue and even get worse.

SHORTCHANGING STUDENTS: IMPLICATIONS FOR THE EDUCATIONAL BENEFITS OF DIVERSITY

Even prior to the SCOTUS ruling, college campuses weren't known for racial harmony. The decade preceding the ruling was known for a wave of campus activism that went viral on social media. A pivotal moment came in 2015, when Jonathan Butler at the University of Missouri went on a hunger strike to protest the racism he and others experienced at Mizzou (the University of Missouri). The hunger strike launched the #ConcernedStudent1950 movement, commemorating the first year Black students could attend the institution.[31] Headline-making protests at Yale and others followed, alongside national tensions surrounding the first election of Donald Trump. College communities like Charlottesville, Virginia had to grapple with White supremacists marching around town. With the horrific murder of George Floyd, thousands marched to protest police brutality, and students organized against the militarization of campus police. As I write these pages, campuses are grappling with conflict and tensions related to Israel and Palestine, with the unprecedented resignations of presidents at multiple Ivy League institutions.

Altogether, these incidents spurred national debates around free speech, campus climate, safety, micro-/macroaggressions, and the right to a nondiscriminatory climate. Many of them occurred when campuses were still using conventional race-conscious admissions. Does that mean that such policies failed to bring about the benefits of diversity that social scientists have repeatedly documented, including healthier intergroup relations, a more positive campus climate, and reductions in prejudice?[32] No, but two things are true. Students gain tremendous benefits from the racial/ethnic diversity that resulted from race-conscious admissions. At the same time, college campuses are rife with inequality, and students are well positioned to challenge it. The presence of conflict on campus, while not always ideal, can reflect how diversity is contributing to a more complex environment for learning. After all, people of color can't complain about racial injustices on college campuses when they aren't allowed to attend in the first place. Some might long for the more harmonious "good ol' days" when people of color "knew their place," but those days are nothing to yearn for. Sure, maybe things feel superficially harmonious when everyone has the same skin color. Growing pains related to intergroup relations can be part of a necessary struggle, albeit one where racially minoritized students bear a disproportionate share of the burden to educate their peers. Of course, conflict can spiral out of control, especially when institutions neglect their responsibility to ensure nondiscriminatory learning environments.

So what does the SCOTUS ruling mean for the educational benefits of diversity? Likely, many students will miss out on much of the richness that can come from engaging across racial/ethnic lines, both inside and outside the classroom. In the first year post–SCOTUS ruling, some of the drops in Black student enrollment in particular are stark and troubling. Will there still be some positive interactions, community, and interracial engagement? Yes. But without a doubt, students will be missing out tremendously. URM students will have to bear an even larger amount of the burden and may experience greater isolation in the classroom, possibly making them need to spend more time with same-race peers outside the classroom.[33] These developments are especially worrisome because of concurrent cuts to support for students of color, a major threat to student well-being.[34]

TITLE VI AND WHAT INSTITUTIONS NEED TO DO TO SUPPORT STUDENTS

The SCOTUS ruling is not the only legal mandate that institutions need to address. Institutions that receive federal funds (i.e., almost everyone) are still fully accountable to Title VI of the Civil Rights Act, which declares that institutions are obligated to uphold nondiscriminatory environments. Title VI reads: "No person in the United States shall, on the ground of race, color, or national origin, be excluded from participation in, be denied the benefits of, or be subjected to discrimination under any program or activity receiving Federal financial assistance."[35] According to the Office of Civil Rights of the US Department of Education, which is charged with enforcing Title VI, "the existence of a racially hostile environment that is created, encouraged, accepted, tolerated or left uncorrected by a recipient" constitutes a violation of Title VI.[36] If an individual or institution has knowledge of the hostile environment and does not act to correct it, a violation has occurred. As noted by Jonathan Feingold, Associate Professor at Boston University School of Law: "In short, Title VI mandates that all covered universities take affirmative measures to prevent racially hostile environments. Failure to do so violates students' civil rights and exposes the university to legal liability and the potential loss of federal funding."[37]

In the Harvard case, SFFA used Title VI in ways that arguably depart from the original intentions of the Civil Rights Act. Title VI has also been invoked by executive orders that seek to censor and ban the teaching of "inherently divisive concepts," which is an overly broad cudgel against material that addresses America's complex and sometimes disturbing history.[38] The use of Title VI to roll back civil rights and opportunity is a travesty. Another important aspect of Title VI is the concept of disparate impact. Disparate impact occurs when a group is being harmed (and in particular, disproportionately harmed) by a policy without an adequate justification for the harm enacted.[39] Importantly, disparate impact pertains to the consequences of what a university does or doesn't do, as opposed to its intentions or motivations. A group can be disproportionately harmed by a policy regardless of whether or not there are actors plotting away with nefarious intentions. In the realm of admissions, numerous policies operate under the guise of so-called race neutrality, but have a disproportionately negative effect on access for historically underrepresented populations. These policies include legacy admissions and out-of-state recruitment.[40] How and why these policies have been allowed to go on for so long is bewildering.

Institutions need to show that they are taking appropriate steps to counter a negative climate and facilitate nondiscriminatory learning environments. Unfortunately, efforts to aggressively to gut policies, offices, and initiatives that support diversity, equity, and inclusion are alive and well.[41] Yes, I'm going to spell the words "diversity, equity and inclusion" out over and over again. While the "DEI" acronym is convenient, it's too easy to mischaracterize something when it's in a handy three-letter acronym. Let's not forget that behind the letters are concepts that are critical to education, the workforce, and society at large. Like any other endeavor, diversity, equity, and inclusion efforts are at times executed imperfectly. However, we cannot forget that when done well, they are vital to supporting institutional missions and goals. Unfortunately, support is being stripped for diversity, equity, and inclusion work writ large, with catastrophic consequences for students, faculty, and staff. With repressive legalism running rampant, we are truly living in challenging times.

As noted, the Trump administration has added to the confusion by referencing *SFFA* to argue that institutions need to turn away from diversity, equity, and inclusion efforts. On the contrary, these efforts remain both legal and necessary. As noted by Art Coleman of EducationCounsel, the argument advanced in the Trump administration's "Dear Colleague" letter is flawed "not only because it again drapes the broad net of 'illegal' over all diversity, equity and inclusion efforts, but also because it fails to recognize that such interests have grounded postsecondary and school district missions for decades, often with the explicit endorsement of federal law."[42] Efforts to address race in the classroom and in programming aligned with institutional missions and goals remain protected by the First Amendment.

I now turn to some of the initiatives that have been adopted to foster supportive, nondiscriminatory learning environments within higher education, including in states that already banned or restricted race-conscious admissions prior to the SCOTUS ruling. This list is not exhaustive; I highlight these examples to show how institutions cannot shy away from addressing race despite the restrictions on race-conscious admissions. I'll also speak to some of the challenges of supporting these programs. While we live in dire times, let's not forget that political currents can and do change. I deeply hope that we'll see the restoration of programs and services that have been cut. Within the academic realm, key initiatives include working to attract and retain a diverse faculty, supporting and expanding Ethnic Studies curriculum and programs, and investing in infrastructure within colleges to advance a positive climate.

Diversifying the Professoriate: More Important Than Ever

The SCOTUS ruling itself has no direct impact on faculty recruitment and hiring, although some may overread it and argue otherwise. Institutions can and should continue to act proactively to diversify the professoriate given their institutional mission and goals. Faculty from historically underrepresented backgrounds, including faculty of color, are vital to fostering scholarship and teaching linked to discovery and community-based application of learning.[43] They often serve as "possibility models" to students of all backgrounds, reinforcing the idea that knowledge and expertise are not the exclusive domain of any one group. Their presence is vital to retaining and graduating students of color, which continues to be a pressing need following the SCOTUS ruling.[44]

California has not been able to consider race in hiring/employment practices since 1996. Since then, California institutions have linked hiring initiatives to curricular needs and priorities. One approach is cluster hiring of faculty around a key research priority. Thematic cluster hiring supports multiple goals, including interdisciplinary collaboration, building community across campus, and fostering innovative scholarship. Thematic cluster hires do not mean that the faculty have to be from a particular race/ethnicity group to be hired. Job postings, like all faculty job postings, are open to everyone; the priority is hiring people whose work will advance institutional goals and priorities. One example is the Black Thriving Initiative Faculty Cluster Hiring Program at the University of California, Irvine.[45] One round of hiring focused on disparities related to environmental health, resulting in an interdisciplinary group of faculty in fields ranging from Anthropology to Civil and Environmental Engineering. Other hiring clusters have pertained to infrastructure equity ("comprises the fields of planning, policy, engineering, environmental science and law to address social, environmental and racial disparities in infrastructure planning, design and implementation") and poetic justice, which aims to bring together scholars from fields like "art, business, African American Studies and Criminology, Law, and Society."[46] For several years, the Anti-Racism Hiring Initiative at the University of Michigan coexisted with the state's ban on race-conscious admissions. The program doesn't exist anymore, but that's because of political posturing and not legal requirements.[47]

California has also used the UC Presidential Postdoctoral Fellowship (UC PPF) to recruit talented faculty. When the program started in 1984, the goal was to "encourage outstanding women and minority Ph.D. recipients to pursue academic careers at the University of California."[48] In more recent times, the program provides postdoctoral fellowships and support to "outstanding scholars in all fields whose research, teaching, and service will contribute to diversity and equal opportunity at the UC." UC PPF had no problem rejecting me when I applied many years ago, but it's still a great program. UC PPF recipients are truly a diverse group, with a number of Asian American recipients, given that Asian Americans are underrepresented within sectors of the professoriate.

In states without restrictions on race-conscious hiring, as well as private institutions, efforts to recruit talented faculty have included initiatives to encourage departments and units to hire faculty from historically underrepresented backgrounds, such as financial incentives and/or matching funds from the provost's office, fellowship programs geared towards historically underrepresented groups, and targeted opportunity hire programs. Such initiatives can also be tied to curricular needs, similar to cluster hires in California. Altogether, these programs are a critical way to expand opportunity in hiring, but sometimes are underutilized by different sectors of campus. Sometimes stigma about proactively hiring faculty from different backgrounds can come from the "old boys' club" that still exists within departments.[49] Academic leadership from provosts and deans is important to encourage units to recruit faculty from a diverse range of backgrounds.

Regardless of the institutional context, institutions should utilize practices that seek to mitigate bias in hiring. The pathway to the professoriate is overly clubby or chummy at times. Faculty often rely on shortcuts to winnow down overwhelmingly large applicant pools. Sometimes talented applicants, including those from historically underrepresented backgrounds, can get overlooked due to reasons like graduating from a less prestigious institution or the adviser's reputation (or lack thereof).

Practices like evaluating applicants more systematically, reaching out to potential candidates from a wide array of backgrounds, and other approaches can help expand opportunity.[50]

Supporting and Expanding Ethnic Studies and Related Curricula

Another measure that institutions should utilize to build welcoming environments is adopting or expanding courses in Ethnic Studies and related content advancing knowledge and inquiry around communities of color. The field of Ethnic Studies has a rich tradition of breaking down barriers between the university and community, encouraging community engagement that's right in line with the civic purpose of higher education. Numerous Ethnic Studies programs and courses are hosted in states that already restricted race-conscious admissions prior to the SCOTUS ruling. Importantly, even the January 21, 2025 executive order "does not require universities, departments, or individual academics to alter the courses they offer and teach, or censor classroom discussion about racism, gender identity, or other topics disfavored by the Trump administration."[51]

In addition to supporting Ethnic Studies–related programs and departments, some institutions host centers that foster research and programming. Such centers can be vibrant hubs for intellectual collaboration, as well as community-based partnerships, with students and faculty reaping the benefits. Ethnic Studies courses provide students the opportunity to learn about historical and contemporary issues affecting their own communities, as well as other communities. In the K–12 arena, studies have linked taking Ethnic Studies courses with "surprisingly large effects" on outcomes such as increased attendance, GPA, and credits earned.[52] These findings are unsurprising given research that indicates that learning is especially effective when grounded in the learner's experience.[53] Students of any race/ethnicity can benefit greatly from taking courses related to Ethnic Studies, communities of color, and other related issues. I have had highly meaningful experiences teaching Asian American Studies courses at UMD to classes made up of students of different races/ethnicities; such classes provide opportunities for both intragroup and intergroup learning.

Some say that Ethnic Studies courses foster groupthink and stifle dissent. Like any area of study, courses related to communities of color and diversity can be taught well or taught poorly. To note, numerous studies have found generally positive or neutral effects linked with coursework related to diversity; such courses are linked to outcomes like greater interest in ideas and more effortful thinking for students of all backgrounds.[54] Most of us have endured a bad math or English course along the way, but does that mean that we should stop teaching those subjects? The same goes for Ethnic Studies. I've heard numerous positive testimonials from students who have taken these courses, and have never heard a complaint about brainwashing. Trust me, if there's a complaint, faculty will hear it. Students sometimes complain that professors are assigning too much reading or giving too many reading check quizzes, which isn't unique to Ethnic Studies. (Professors actually wanting you to do the reading—what a shocker.) If there are professors who are being overly political or fostering a repressive climate, which can happen in subjects besides Ethnic Studies, these instances should be dealt with on a case-by-case basis, rather than taking a sledgehammer to Ethnic Studies and diversity-related coursework altogether.[55] The sledgehammer approach sounds more repressive and politicized to me than any Ethnic Studies class I've ever taken.

Advancing Equity and Excellence Within Academic Units

In wake of the SCOTUS ruling, institutions must remain committed to fostering healthy environments within specific schools, colleges, and academic departments. Addressing the "microclimates" of the institution is vital to supporting a nondiscriminatory environment. Diversity in the classroom is relevant to learning and retention. A study analyzing 11,868 students from twenty institutions found that the proportion of URM students within a class is linked with students receiving higher grades in STEM coursework, both for students in general but particularly for URM and first-generation students.[56] The climate that students experience in classroom and laboratory settings is a key part of the student experience. Schools, departments, and units should consider adopting mechanisms for bias reporting and mediation, climate assessments, faculty needs, ombudspersonship, student-facing programming, admissions support, and strategic planning. Investing in centers and programs that support students from historically underrepresented backgrounds within particular fields of study (e.g., STEM, business, and others) is also important. Oftentimes these centers and programs provide vital support and mentoring for racially minoritized and low-income students, serving as a haven within schools and colleges.

One important issue for leaders within academic units is the need to scrutinize policies that appear "neutral" on the surface but have negative ramifications for opportunity. For example, limited enrollment programs and majors, usually found within STEM and business departments and colleges, often utilize restrictive admissions criteria due to high demand. The same goes for transfer policies into such majors, whether transferring from another major at the institution or transferring from a community college. For example, one institution we studied required a 3.65 to transfer into computer science from a community college and an A- or higher in two required prerequisite courses. The policy penalized students who could do well in the major but who ended up with a 3.5, for example. At face value, such policies seem "fair" because they apply to everyone. Administrators will shrug their shoulders and say that they have no choice, and that high GPA requirements for transfers are just an efficient way to give everyone a fair shake.

However, such approaches don't necessarily facilitate degree attainment in science, and restrictive requirements for high-demand majors have a disproportionately negative impact on historically underrepresented populations. Zachary Bleemer and Aashish Mehta, economists at Princeton and the University of California, Santa Barbara, respectively, found that such requirements resulted in a 20 percent reduction in URM enrollment in limited enrollment majors (e.g., STEM, business).[57] They explain how limiting access to certain majors is inefficient for both students and society at large: "We find evidence against the hypotheses that major restrictions improve the signal or human capital value of restricted majors . . . improve match quality by allocating majors toward students with comparative advantages in the field, or improve educational attainment among the students who are excluded from restricted majors due to their low grades. Instead, major restrictions are likely to generate new inefficiencies by disproportionately reducing aggregate science major attainment . . . allocating majors away from interested and academically-promising students with limited precollege educational opportunity, a group who are likely to receive above-average returns from lucrative college major attainment."[58] In other words, restrictive major policies aren't improving the caliber of students allowed to go into business or STEM. Instead, they work as a gatekeeper, keeping out students who could benefit from being able to major in a field, while limiting societal benefits. Identifying and addressing policies that appear race-neutral on the surface, but have a disparate negative impact on certain populations, is an important way to help units support a positive climate for all students.

Another issue to consider is how leadership roles within academic units related to diversity, equity, and inclusion are often held by individuals who hold staff or nontenure lines, sometimes due to the lack of faculty with expertise on such issues. While these individuals bring tremendous assets to their roles, they may be limited in their ability to advocate for change among faculty due to their differential status. They also lack job security, which is concerning given the sensitivity of equity issues. However, just because an individual has tenure doesn't mean that they're well positioned to hold a leadership role related to diversity and inclusion. Greater success may come from units that are able to recruit both tenured and nontenured individuals into an office to provide collaborative and strategic leadership.

The impact of anti-diversity legislation on staff infrastructure is playing out differently around the country. During the Florida crackdown on diversity, equity, and inclusion, colleges at the University of Florida (UF) initially retained senior-level leadership within academic units, but changed individuals' job titles.[59] Robert Thomas was formerly Assistant Dean for Diversity, Equity, and Inclusion in the UF Warrington College of Business. He holds the same position at Indiana University's Kelley School of Business at the Associate Dean level. At first, he kept the same title except with "Belonging" tacked onto the end. Now he's Associate Dean for Access, Empowerment, and Social Impact, as of 2025 at least. Kudos to Indiana for a smart hire. Thomas commented: "The activities that are performed, the inclusiveness, the attempt to increase success rates for all students—that work needs to happen regardless of what title you associate with it."[60]

In other words, what the far right likes to vilify as boogeyman "DEI" work is just sensible, necessary work aimed at helping higher education work for all students. In too many states, educators have to walk a fine line between doing their work and explaining to politicians that what they're doing is, well, necessary. In some cases, it means assuring outsiders that you aren't doing *those* kinds of terrible things, the ones that no one is doing anyway. Seriously, what do they think is going on, loyalty oaths? It also means explaining that you're working on worthy endeavors like helping students navigate the institution so they can succeed academically. How radical is that? In some states, institutions have been able to restructure programs in ways that allow much-needed activities to continue while avoiding the ire of the legislature. Unfortunately, things got worse at UF, with the firing of thirteen diversity-related roles and the ending of fifteen administrative appointments for faculty.[61] Individuals working in diversity and equity-related roles have been fired in other states as well. It's incredibly disappointing to see institutions being excessively aggressive in their efforts to appease state legislators. The need for savvy educators, students, and lawmakers who will push back against counterproductive legislation is necessary now more than ever before.

THE ROLE OF STUDENT AFFAIRS IN ADVANCING NONDISCRIMINATORY ENVIRONMENTS

Within the realm of student affairs, key initiatives to support nondiscriminatory environments include support for cultural centers, racial/ethnic and cultural student organizations, residence life initiatives such as halls or buildings that highlight different communities, and overall infrastructure for advancing a positive climate. Once again, this list is nonexhaustive; I highlight programs and structures that will likely attract questions following the SCOTUS ruling. Importantly, they all exist in states that already banned race-conscious admissions prior to the ruling. To note, depending on a campus's organizational structure, these initiatives may or may not fall under the purview of student affairs. Regardless, they often serve to spur collaboration between student affairs and academic affairs, supporting institutional missions to advance student learning outside of the classroom.

Cultural Centers: A Home Away from Home

Cultural centers are open to all members of the university community. While cultural centers can highlight a particular racial/ethnic group, the cultural center model is also used for centers that support populations on campus like women, veterans, and students with disabilities. Cultural centers play a vital role by bringing students, faculty, and staff together, spurring dialogue and intergenerational support.[62] Staff at cultural centers often serve as institutional agents, helping students navigate university bureaucracy. I've heard students describe staff at the cultural center as reminding them of family, who go above and beyond the call of duty to help them thrive. Staff at cultural centers often help students adjust to campus, process culture shock, and persist.

Just because a cultural center exists at a campus doesn't mean that it's adequately funded. Our research team studied one campus where the cultural centers had difficulty retaining staff due to low pay and a lack of institutional support. Given the heightened needs of URM students following the SCOTUS ruling, it's crucial that cultural centers are well resourced. Race/ethnicity-themed cultural centers are a common fixture within states that already banned or restricted race-conscious admissions prior to the SCOTUS ruling, such as public institutions in California, Michigan, Washington, Arizona, Oklahoma, and others. Fingers crossed that they'll all survive. At UF, the Center for Inclusive Engagement and Multicultural Engagement closed, and will reportedly reopen as "The Office of Community and Belonging."[63]

In the years to come, cultural centers will experience continued pushback, whether due to state laws hostile to diversity, equity, and inclusion, false assumptions that the centers promote campus balkanization, or some combination thereof. In the political arena, protecting these spaces that are critical to student learning, community, and retention is a vital priority. University leadership must commit to harnessing their political and social capital to defend these centers, which play an increasingly vital role in the campus environment following the SCOTUS ruling.

Refueling and Retaining Students: Racial/Ethnic and Cultural Student Organizations

Student organizations supporting different racial/ethnic, ethno-religious, or cultural communities remain completely legal following *SFFA*. These organizations generally remain protected as of mid-2025 despite the Trump administration's attacks on diversity. Sadly, in 2025, West Point shut down student organizations related to supporting women, students of color, and LGBTQ+ students.[64] This action was a military academy–specific decision and is unrelated to *SFFA*; the academies also pulled Maya Angelou from the library, which seems to be a weird form of virtue (or lack thereof?) signaling. Ethnic student organizations play a vital role in advancing a more positive and inclusive climate. A false perception exists that these groups promote division and so-called self-segregation. On the contrary, involvement in such organizations has been linked with higher cross-racial interaction in the research, both for students generally and more specifically for Black and Latinx students.[65] These groups play an important role in helping recharge racially minoritized students, who spend much of their time crossing racial/ethnic lines, an activity that can be draining.[66] Time spent in communities with a higher presence of same-race peers plays an important role in helping students keep engaging across race in other spheres of campus life.

One study found that participating in organizations addressing the needs of Black students on campus was linked with a higher sense of belonging at the institution, showing how racial/cultural organizations can promote a greater sense of connection to the overall institution.[67] Indeed, these organizations can serve as bridges to the greater institution, facilitating connections to other parts of campus. While an organization advancing awareness around a particular demographic group will naturally attract students from that group, these student organizations can also foster interracial friendships and interaction across race. For example, in her book *Black Space: Negotiating Race, Diversity, and Belonging in the Ivory Tower*, Sherry Deckman, Associate Professor of Education at Lehman College, documented the stories behind Kuumba, Harvard's gospel choir that serves as a haven and support network for Black students while maintaining a racially diverse membership and promoting interracial friendship.[68] The choir is open to any student, or at least anyone who can sing on key. Post-*SFFA*, we can only hope that Kuumba will be able to sustain that diversity while continuing to be a special congregating place for Black students at Harvard. Of note, racial/ethnic and cultural awareness student organizations continue to exist at institutions in states that banned race-conscious admissions prior to the SCOTUS ruling. They provide spaces where students can build community with students who share common interests or backgrounds, or who simply want to learn more about the experiences of a particular population.

Unfortunately, some institutions affected by anti-diversity legislation are restricting the activities of these organizations. At the University of Missouri, the Legion of Black Collegians was told that they had to change the name of their yearly "Welcome Black BBQ" or else face cancellation.[69] At the University of Alabama (UA), the Black Student Union and a Safe Zone group supporting LGBTQ+ students were forced to vacate their offices in the flagship student center.[70] Student organizations seeking to support and celebrate communities of color face extra challenges in states hostile to diversity initiatives. Still, their right to assemble is still protected, and they contribute greatly to the campus community. Once again, university administrations must demonstrate leadership by broadcasting their commitments to supporting these organizations, especially in states where diversity, equity, and inclusion efforts are being attacked.

Racial/Ethnic Community–Themed Living Learning Programs

African American Theme Program. The Asian Pacific American Theme House. Native American Theme Program. Chicanx/Latinx Living Learning Community. Native Hawaiian and Pacific Islander Pilot Program. Casa Magdalena Mora Theme Program. African Diaspora Theme Hall.[71] These communities supported by residence life don't shy away from naming and addressing race, ethnicity, and indigeneity. What else do they have in common? They all exist in a state (California) where race-conscious admissions has been banned since 1996. These theme halls or houses are a type of living-learning community (LLC) that can gather students among common interests, spurring learning outside the classroom. LLCs are popular at many institutions, with themes ranging from the arts to cybersecurity.[72]

LLCs that highlight a particular community are a unique way to build support and community for students from different backgrounds. Students from any background are free to apply as long as they are interested in diving deeper into the issues highlighted by the LLC. At times LLCs are combined with an academic seminar. They often incorporate community service and civic involvement, as well as events and programming to help students engage with compelling topics outside of the classroom. Given the frequent and purposeful programming that brings residents together, racial/ethnic or community-themed LLCs can be a powerful way to support retention, community-building, and learning for students from different backgrounds.

Infrastructure for Supporting Diversity, Equity, and Inclusion Throughout Institutions

As mentioned earlier, I'm taking the cumbersome but necessary approach of spelling out "diversity, equity, and inclusion" instead of abbreviating it. Hopefully, taking the time to say the actual words can remind people of why these offices exist. They're dedicated to concepts that had widespread, bipartisan support not that long ago.[73] Offices dedicated to promoting diversity, equity, and inclusion offer a wide array of services and support, from campus traditions in multicultural student programming to programs like intergroup dialogue to antibias training and education. These offices and staff play a vital role in community building for students from historically underrepresented backgrounds, fostering a sense of belonging crucial to retaining students. Diversity, equity, and inclusion–related offices, units, and staff are at the front lines of helping support institutional obligations to Title VI, creating space for students to access the resources needed to thrive in higher education. They serve the entire campus, providing vital support and bridge-building efforts to help institutions understand the essential role of diversity, the necessity of inclusion, and the call to equity—all of which are essential for fostering positive learning environments. Are they perfect? Of course not, and what is, in higher education? Still, any flaws are better treated by reform, versus mass elimination.

Units supporting diversity play an especially important role post-*SFFA*, but their very existence is being threatened in a growing number of states. A need exists for philanthropic dollars to help fill some of the gap in states that ban the use of state funds for diversity-related work but do not prohibit the use of donor funds. Understanding the demarcations outlined in laws feels like threading the eye of a needle. For example, in Alabama under SB129 (Senate Bill 129), institutions are not allowed to "apply for or accept a grant, federal funding, or private funding, for the purpose of compelling assent to any divisive concept or any other purpose prohibited in this act."[74] At the same time, the bill explicitly states that faculty and student organizations can still host diversity and equity-related events and discussions, as long as state funds are not used.[75] Yes, it's confusing, and people naturally disagree on what constitutes a divisive concept.[76] In the current regime of intimidation and repressive legalism, institutions bear the burden of showing how they are steering clear of the so-called divisive concepts highlighted in the legislation. Concurrently, private funders need to help fill gaps left by the abandonment of support for the bread-and-butter acts that make up most of diversity, equity, and inclusion work on campuses: your basic community-building activities, leadership retreats, and lunch and learns. To quote Chris Cooper, professor at the University of Cincinnati: "It is worth noting that most DEI initiatives and offices on campus offer noncontroversial services like tutoring, mental health counseling and accessibility services like sign language interpreters."[77] Why these activities are so threatening to some people, I have no idea, but it says a lot that they are.

Campuses must make sure that students from historically underrepresented backgrounds are well served by all parts of campus, and not just units and centers that have an explicit focus on diversity, race, or multiculturalism. This imperative is even more pressing in states where offices related to diversity, equity, and inclusion have been restricted or eliminated. All too often, "diversity work" has been seen as the main responsibility of offices like multicultural student life or cultural centers. Oftentimes, offices such as advising, career centers, and others have operated under more colorblind norms, taking a generic "all students matter" approach, versus proactively recognizing barriers to access and equity. For example, advising is one area with tremendous implications for racially minoritized, first-generation, and low-income students. However, over the years, professional development for advisors has not recognized key issues affecting students from low-income backgrounds, resulting in many students not getting the support that they need. Especially in times when diversity, equity, and inclusion are under attack, it is paramount for all units that work to support students to recognize the need to proactively serve students from historically underrepresented groups.

WRAPPING IT UP

College is a pivotal time for students to experience the educational benefits of engaging in a racially diverse student body, and the *SFFA* ruling will likely constrain such opportunities. Changes in admissions policy can affect who can be a potential roommate, friend, lab mate, or life partner. Drops in Black, Latinx, and Indigenous enrollment will limit the ability of institutions to facilitate positive intergroup relations. Declines in middle-class and moderate-income Black student enrollment may affect campus dynamics, because these students often help bridge campus divides by supporting interaction between racial/ethnic groups. Institutions should be sensitive to shifts in campus climate.

While institutions have to comply with the *SFFA* ruling, the responsibility to foster nondiscriminatory environments remains. Numerous options remain for institutions wishing to foster a positive climate for students, including but not limited to support for racial/ethnic student organizations, cultural centers, and Ethnic Studies units. Addressing policies that appear race-neutral on the surface, but that negatively affect opportunity for students of color and low-income students, is also needed. Institutions must remember the civil rights spirit of Title VI, and their responsibility to challenge discrimination. The ruling in *SFFA* is a blow, but institutions must stand up to repressive legalism. Higher education cannot be passive, especially in these perilous times.

7

We Won't Go Back

Reimagining Admissions in an Era of Repressive Legalism

The 2023 SCOTUS ruling in *SFFA v. Harvard/UNC* took away one of the most critical tools needed to expand racial equity in higher education: the ability to consider demographic data around race/ethnicity to inform understanding of who a student is, their context for opportunity, and potential contributions. Things got even worse in the mid-2020s, when the executive branch of government launched an all-out war on diversity, equity, and inclusion.

Yes, things are dire, but we can't forget the facts that still exist despite the chaos. The ruling in *SFFA*, unfortunate as it is, left the door open for campuses to consider the role of race in students' lives, experiences, and identity as shared by the student in the application. The ruling in *SFFA* isn't a particularly colorblind one that completely denies the relevance of race to students' lives, nor does it remove the ability of institutions to advance their missions related to diversity. Further, campuses have the continued ability to directly consider social class, including but not limited to family income, household assets, parental education, wealth, neighborhood conditions, school context, and the like.

Still, even economic diversity is an uphill battle. We can't just wave a magic wand and hope that suddenly a rush of low-income students will enroll. No magic wands, or even big pots of money (although they're helpful), can magically level the uneven playing field that cuts across race and class. Combining practices linked to incremental change will hopefully help preserve a certain level of diversity following the SCOTUS ruling. Such practices include considering contextualized GPA, direct admissions and scholarship offers, test-optional or test-free admissions, aggressive investments in need-based financial aid, support for student needs beyond tuition, and culturally responsive outreach. Only time will tell how successful institutions will be.

The most meaningful change requires true institutional transformation to dismantle structures that have perpetuated privilege for far too long. The transformation at UC Davis School of Medicine, where URM enrollment grew from 8 percent of the student body in 2000 to an impressive 52 percent by 2020, shows us what's possible, as well as the significant investments needed to get there.[1] Transformation requires making tremendous investments in need-based financial aid, deemphasizing or eliminating standardized tests, and interrogating selective higher education's obsession with prestige. Institutions need to prioritize partnerships with local communities over relationships with corporate recruiters and consider how pathways for students can respond to the most pressing needs of society. Hiring faculty to respond to key curricular needs linked to institutional missions is also crucial. State institutions need to recommit to expanding access for historically excluded populations within the state, instead of bypassing residents for wealthier out-of-state students. Real change requires challenging the outsize role of athletics and calibrating the evaluation of students around goals like social mobility and opportunity. Finally, it requires putting structures in place that help students thrive and graduate.

Some schools may enact certain reforms, but will balk at things like dropping or even scaling back athletic preferences. Others will make numerous changes, but might find that there's still no substitute for conventional race-conscious admissions. Combining incremental "race-neutral" approaches may not be enough to prevent major regressions in racial/ethnic diversity at some institutions. As institutions assess the damage from the ruling, they need to consider remaining legal options for defending the ability to consider race in admissions in a holistic, nonformulaic fashion. As discussed in chapter 2, these approaches include justifying programs due to institution-specific discrimination and obligations under Title VI, among others.[2] General counsels may balk at the risk involved, but it's time for bold and courageous leadership.

We have to remember that race-conscious admissions has gone through noteworthy shifts before. First, due to the ruling in *Regents of the University of California v. Bakke*, institutions phased out allocating seats for certain groups and shifted to race-conscious holistic review. Harvard's program was held as an exemplar. After *Gratz v. Bollinger*, large public institutions moved away from automatically assigning points to applicants from historically underrepresented backgrounds. Now policies are going through another evolution after *SFFA*, with the loss of being able to consider demographic data on race/ethnicity. Institutions can still recognize the relevance of race in a student's life as discussed by the student, and how it relates to traits and experiences valued by institutions. The shift to "race-aware if chosen by the applicant" admissions is less than ideal, but one that we have to live with unless higher education institutions seek out other legal defenses for race-conscious admissions. Race-conscious admissions is restricted, but not dead.

Too often, the law, legalese, and threats of litigation are used to intimidate institutions, individuals, and communities out of exercising their rights. We live in a political environment rife with repressive legalism, with relentless attacks on diversity, equity, and inclusion. These movements want institutions to pull back out of fear and negative media attention. The SCOTUS majority ruling was devastating, don't get me wrong. However, it didn't say that students must censor themselves on race. It didn't say that institutions can't request applicant data around race/ethnicity. It didn't say that institutions can't highlight race or culture when designing outreach programs open to all students. SFFA and company want the outcome of the ruling to be even worse than it already is, and they're working overtime to widen the damage. Let's not do them any favors.

For those of us who care deeply about higher education, it's our job to push back. We have to do so on multiple fronts, from making sure that institutions are investing heavily in outreach to refusing to be silent about the reality of race in students' lives. We have to defend the ability of schools to use race-neutral policies that advance diversity like the one used at Thomas Jefferson High School for Science and Technology (TJ), where most seats are assigned through a percent plan.[3] Yes, in this day and age, even race-neutral policies typically popular with conservatives need defending, given the aggressive tactics of the far right. To my fellow Asian Americans being recruited to challenge race-neutral policies, don't buy into a movement that's trying to restrict opportunity for low-income students.

TESTING POLICY: A CONTINUING DEBATE

The SCOTUS ruling overlapped with a tremendous shift in the admissions community: Over two thousand institutions went test-optional or test-free during the pandemic.[4] The air is filled with mixed messages about testing. Schools bringing back test requirements now hail the SAT/ACT as a wondrous tool that will somehow level the playing field. Still, even Yale acknowledged that requiring the SAT/ACT for years "likely discouraged some promising students from underrepresented backgrounds from applying."[5] In chapter 4, I highlighted how decision-making around testing policy is a pretty gray area. Yes, SAT/ACT scores can predict measures of college success, but so can measures like contextualized GPA, which outperforms standardized tests in some studies.[6] Some are convinced that they need test scores to make admissions decisions; others are confident that they can admit strong cohorts without scores. There are different trade-offs to consider. Elite institutions argue that test scores can help identify higher-scoring lower-income students who won't submit scores under test-optional admissions. Others recognize that (1) under test-optional, institutions are admitting just as many lower-income students if not more; (2) in general, students admitted via test-optional at elite schools are doing fine in college, and B+ GPAs are not the end of the world; (3) even if evaluating test scores in context benefits low-income students, it also benefits richer students, and perhaps disproportionately so; (4) those same lower-income students may not apply if test scores are required; and (5) the same goes for some URM students. All said, there's a lot to consider.

Test-required policies may help lower-SES students with higher test scores whose essays, letters of recommendation, extracurricular activities, or grades are weaker when viewed by dominant standards. Test-optional policies benefit lower-SES students who stand out more because of accomplishments demonstrated through grades, essays, letters, or activities. Institutions shouldn't limit themselves to one "type" (apologies for talking in gross generalizations here) of lower-SES student. If test-optional policies appear to be more effective at enrolling the latter group, why not provide more guidance via outreach and websites to get the former group to submit test scores?

I'm not saying that the issue is an easy fix. Still, it makes sense to try to think outside of the box and maximize opportunities to enroll as many lower and moderate-income students as possible: both those who are a little more likely to work at McKinsey *and* those whose talents, traits, and potential are less reflected in their test scores. Even if required score submission helps identify some talented low-income students, implications for racial/ethnic diversity are unclear. Race and class aren't interchangeable in admissions, and policies seeking to boost low-income student enrollment generally don't do the same for racial/ethnic diversity.[7] Required score submission without race-conscious admissions is a very different thing from required score submission paired with the ability to consider race more directly.

Once again, only time will tell what happens when schools return to required testing. In the end, test scores seem more like a "want" than a "need" in selective college admissions, both at the moderately selective and highly selective levels. Some note that the benefits of test-optional are most pronounced in the moderately selective sector, and that test scores are more helpful at the most elite level of institutions.[8] Still, I would argue that the most elite, highly rejective schools don't *need* test scores to admit fantastic applicants. Want, yes; need, no.[9]

The benefits of test-optional policies seem modest at first, but are notable in comparison to options like percent plans, as discussed in chapter 4. Given the restrictions of the SCOTUS ruling, we need all of the help we can get. We should also consider lessons from our friends in the UC system who have not been able to consider race in admissions for decades. So far they seem to be happy with test-free admissions.[10] Yes, it's more than possible to evaluate applications without test scores, even in schools that have some of the largest applicant pools in the country.

NAME-BRAND HIGHER EDUCATION: WHO "DESERVES" A SEAT AT THE TABLE?

The test score debate is part of the broader conversation about who "deserves" a coveted seat at a name-brand institution. For years I, like many college presidents, threw around the term "best and brightest" to describe students who attended these schools. Yes, there are donor kids (sigh), but in my heart of hearts, I really thought that it was true for the most part.[11] These days, I'm less enthusiastic about the idea that name-brand admissions somehow identifies the "best and brightest," or that anyone really "deserves" a seat. For most students at these institutions, the more appropriate alliterative term is "pay to play," or more specifically, "pay to play among the broader pool of talented students."[12]

Race is threaded throughout these dynamics. Don't get me wrong, many White and Asian American students *do* get left behind. Still, the students who benefit in the selective admissions rat race are disproportionately more likely to be White and Asian American.[13] Yes, people are talented, but the ability to pay a hefty tuition bill is a particularly favored talent at many esteemed institutions, and that ability is shaped by both race and class. The advantages start in the early years, when parents leverage their finances to live in school districts with the highest school ratings, which are shaped by residential and school segregation.[14] The next step is to engage in the resource-intensive "cultivation" of children through lessons and activities. Raising children in the twenty-first-century rat race requires major investments of money, time, and attention. During high school, the intensity heightens as students polish their resumes and test scores in hopes of getting a spot at a top institution. In many states, securing a spot at the state flagship is an increasingly difficult task. Then there's the application process itself, where money simply gets you more, including the ability to file more applications, visit more schools, and hire a college concierge. Yes, there are fee waivers and support for low-income students, but they're notably underrepresented in the competitive college application pool.[15]

Colleges reward students and families for being rich, or at least upper middle-class: groups that are disproportionately White and, to some extent, Asian American. It's a plain and ugly truth. Being at a predominantly White, private high school often means more visits from colleges, both elite privates and out-of-state publics.[16] Coming from a more affluent background means not getting rejected because the institution can't afford to pay your financial need.[17] It puts you in the position of having a school counselor who might write you a longer letter. At private school, that letter would probably have more sentences about your character excellence, intellectual promise, athletic prowess, and love for the humanities.[18] Best and brightest? Among those who can pay.

For affluent students, from the upper middle-class to the flat-out filthy rich, most of these privileges are invisible. Until you see more of the world, it's easy to assume that everyone has it more or less like you. The behind-the-scenes work to cultivate opportunity is usually invisible to children, who aren't making choices about mortgage payments or school ratings. Parents choose what activities a family can afford, or whether a parent should leave the workforce so they can spend even more time cultivating their children. A young person from an affluent family might have a vague awareness that some families have less money. Still, there's always someone richer too, and thanks to social media, it's easy to feel average. The sociopolitical and historical dynamics that explain structural inequality in K–12 education and residential segregation are often invisible to young people and their families. These truths are uncomfortable for many—so uncomfortable that it's getting harder to teach about the reality of race in this country. What *is* visible is the hard work that individual students put in to succeed, the late nights spent cramming for tests or endless practices to become a better athlete/debater/Science Olympian. When someone reaches college and is told that they're "the best and brightest," it's easy to nod in agreement.

Beyond hard work, landing at a prestigious college is equally, if not more, a byproduct of being able to afford a ticket for the "pay to play" lottery of admissions. The cost is often invisible to the actual participants, despite being tremendous. Back in the 1990s, it was easier to have your ticket pulled. Today, because of population trends, economic forces, and other factors, there are considerably more students who can buy a ticket in the pay-to-play lotto. Yes, it's unfair that some people can basically do the equivalent of buying more tickets by applying early decision or being a recruited athlete. Still, things are even more unfair for those who don't even get to play in the first place.

REMEMBERING VALUES AND THE CONTINUED NEED TO CONSIDER RACE

What needs to happen to make admissions more equitable, especially in an era without conventional race-conscious admissions? First, we need to realize whom name-brand schools serve in the current day and age: in most cases, decently strong and fairly bright students (let's hope) among those who can pay for attendance as well as the cost of all the experiences that got them admitted. We should be over the facade that the schools with the lowest admit rates really are "the best," recognizing that these schools have to reject thousands of students who could succeed. Also, many with strong potential never even apply. The admissions process is not a magical Sorting Hat of destiny, but a bunch of well-intentioned but imperfect people trying their best while being shaped by implicit bias, an imbalanced applicant pool, and pressures from enrollment management. Whew, that's a lot. When it comes to the question of who "deserves" to attend a high-profile institution, sociologist Natasha Warikoo of Tufts University explains: "No one *deserves* to be selected. This means that 'merit' is inherently situational—it depends on what would benefit a particular society in a particular moment in time, and those needs are not static. . . . Admission to a selective college, unlike awards, is about university goals, rather than certification of individual worthiness, as many believe."[19]

So what should those goals be and who should be admitted? What criteria should be used to select students and what interests do we prioritize? We often hear that college matters for equipping people who will serve society, preparing students for a diverse democracy, cultivating civic mindedness, and giving back to the common good. Arguments that test scores are valuable because they predict who will work at a top firm seem pretty distant from those goals. Do we want to be driven by prestige, money, and reproduction of the status quo, or can we think bigger? Regardless of whether admissions criteria are more aligned with the goals of McKinsey or advancing the common good, you can still select a class of outstanding students. Still, something is undeniably lost when priorities for selection are driven by prestige. Schools requiring test scores are quick to say test scores aren't the only factor for decision-making. Still, it's too easy for someone's higher score to be rewarded, and for a lower score to take someone out of the running. By bringing back test score requirements, maybe schools are just being more transparent about how they *are* driven by power and prestige. After all, the most respected post-college outcome at elite schools *is* working at a top firm.[20] Still, can't we aspire to something more?

Of course, test-optional and test-free schools aren't immune to market forces that reward affluent students. As noted by scholars like Warikoo and the late, great Lani Guinier, selection criteria should be driven by societal priorities: the responsibility that institutions have to contribute to societal leadership, a diverse democracy, and the common good.[21] In such a system, students are selected in significant part due to their potential to respond to critical societal needs and challenges, versus an overemphasis on "individual effort," which is often a byproduct of a family's financial means. While considering societal priorities in admissions includes recognizing students committed to improving their communities through service and activism, affluent American high schoolers have shown time and time again that if you hang a hoop, they'll jump through it. If you change the incentives, you change the game.[22] It's not enough to say that you'll reward community service, and then service becomes the new arms race. Part of responding to societal needs includes giving considerable preference to low- and some middle-income students. It also includes paying attention to the overrepresentation of students from the top 1 percent—and not even just the top 1 percent, but really the top 0.1 percent—in name-brand higher education. Given that much of the advantage heaped upon these students works through legacy and athletic preferences, eliminating both are much-needed steps toward building a better system.

Finally, we can't respond to some of the most entrenched needs within society without taking race into account. If colleges are brave enough to show leadership, admissions policy should also include efforts to address an institution's specific history of racial discrimination by considering race as a factor among many in admissions, an option that has yet to be tested in the courts.[23] You don't have to hunt much to see how institutions have played a role in fostering exclusion, be it active or passive. The option is still on the table. We can't respond to the most pressing of societal needs if we don't support the advancement of Black, Latinx, and Indigenous students in this country, including access to the credentials and networks that pave the way for societal leadership.

SHIFTING THE MINDSET TO ABUNDANCE

Very little of the status quo will change unless we can shift our mindset on higher education from scarcity to abundance. I know, the idea of bringing abundance into a conversation about college admissions seems absurd when some admit rates are so low. Still, there are many schools beyond the household names where students can get a strong education. Only a relatively small slice of the higher education spectrum admits fewer than half of their applicants, but tiny acceptance rates are more related to prestige than actual educational quality. In the frenzy of trying to secure a spot at a name-brand institution, many miss the importance of looking for a school that pays attention to undergraduate education, and dare I say, teaching. Unfortunately, high-quality teaching is not something to take for granted in academia. You want a school that actually cares about talent development, and not just reputation.

Yes, these schools exist, and sometimes it feels like there's almost an inverse relationship between selectivity and a commitment to undergraduate education. My first teaching gig was at Miami University in my home state of Ohio, a place known for strong undergraduate teaching.[24] My brother went there many years ago, as did others like former Speaker of the House Paul Ryan and President Biden's head speechwriter Vinay Reddy.[25] For the 2023–2024 admissions cycle, Miami admitted over 80 percent of applicants.[26] Worried about getting into your state flagship as a STEM major? Consider a STEM-oriented school dedicated to supporting undergraduate student development versus a "sink or swim" environment. Places like Rensselaer Polytechnic, Rochester Institute of Technology, and Rose-Hulman are well respected in industry and have admit rates over 50 percent; at the time of writing, Rose-Hulman's was 77 percent. Rankings be damned, but it's *U.S. News & World Report*'s top-ranked program for undergraduate engineering education.[27]

One caveat is that some historically White schools known for high-quality undergraduate education with relatively high acceptance rates are also known for their lack of diversity. The forty-four institution collective that brands itself as *The Colleges That Change Lives*, I'm looking at you, or at least a good chunk of you.[28] I taught at Miami, and while it's a great school, it can be a difficult place for many students and faculty of color. These schools are going to suffer without conventional race-conscious admissions. They still have a lot to offer, but need to keep working to strengthen campus climate, access, and retention.

Additionally, the sticker price for so many private institutions that value teaching, even those without high name recognition, is high. Because of that, increasing state funding for higher education is essential in order to expand access to public institutions, and take some of the pressure off of the private sector. In general, state flagships have the highest name recognition, familiarity, and proximity for in-state students, so ensuring access for first-generation, low-income, and URM in-state students is especially critical. Admission to the state flagship should be more predictable for in-state students with strong academic track records; it shouldn't take a percent plan to bring a greater sense of consistency to admissions. Access is threatened when publics decide to fill a third or more of the class with nonresidents, despite high in-state demand. Given the legacy of exclusion surrounding many of these institutions, state flagships have a special responsibility to do everything they can to maximize in-state access. Still, they aren't going to reverse course without pressure from the public and state legislatures. Instead of harping on diversity, legislators should prioritize this issue, striking agreements to increase funding in return for expanding seats for in-state students. To my fellow Asian Americans, this issue is a good one to target, versus trying to sue the Ivies.

Advancing abundance in higher education also means investing more in the institutions that educate the most students. These include state comprehensive regional institutions that are doing the heavy lifting involved in the public land grant mission, minority-serving institutions, and community colleges. MacKenzie Scott got it right when she decided to pour money into HBCUs instead of slapping her name all over buildings at her alma mater.[29] Public higher education, from state flagships to community colleges, has a special opportunity to facilitate access, retention, and graduation for historically excluded and underrepresented students.

When nonprofit institutions fall short in reaching these populations, actors with less than benign interests step in to fill the gap. In his article published in *The Sociology of Education*, "The Anti-Affirmative Action Avalanche: The Rise of Underrepresented Minority Enrollment at For-Profit Institutions," scholar David Mickey-Pabello analyzed IPEDS data from 1991 to 2006. He concluded that "a small group of for-profit institutions with very large enrollments became a destination for underrepresented minority students in the wake of affirmative action bans."[30] Latinx and Black students are already three times more likely to attend a for-profit institution than their White peers.[31] Many of these for-profit institutions are known for using predatory recruitment tactics, and in particular, many Black students have left for-profits with high amounts of debt but no diploma.[32] This issue is of particular concern following *SFFA*, and we need to make sure that nonprofit institutions don't drop the ball on access.

CLOSING THOUGHTS: WE CAN'T GO BACK, WE WON'T GO BACK

The current system doesn't serve anyone well, from an equity perspective or a mental health perspective. We have options. We can stick with the status quo, continuing the relentless optimization that the rat race demands. We can keep pressuring young people to be hyperconscious about how they present and package themselves as they try to attract the attention of an admissions reader. It's bad enough that social media pushes them into this type of performativity at earlier and earlier ages; it's even worse that it feels like an almost required part of getting into a name-brand college. We can make young people pack on the most challenging courses even earlier, even though curricular rigor during high school is a weaker predictor of college outcomes than one might think, and many students could benefit from slowing down a bit.[33] With all of these courses being taken for college credit during high school, what's the point of high school? Maybe the next step will be just to jump from junior high to college. We've painted ourselves into a corner. When everyone is a superstar, accomplishments become unexceptional, which makes students feel like they have to go to even greater lengths to distinguish themselves. Rinse and repeat, and it becomes harder and harder to step off the hamster wheel.

A "winner takes all" system based on a hyperindividualistic framing of merit is making us miserable. Another option is to take a deep breath and question whether the relentless optimization is worth it. On this path, it's critical to remember that educational quality and support for students is more important than prestige. Government and philanthropy should collaborate to encourage institutions to invest in high-quality teaching, so more schools can be known for talent development instead of racking up student debt. Beyond the name on the bumper sticker, the priority should be on how students actually grow during college, both inside and outside the classroom. Such growth comes not just from student effort, but also from an institution's commitment to fostering an environment where all students can thrive. In this realm of thinking, helping students reach their potential is not a matter of individualistic hyperoptimization, but instead part of our public responsibility to invest in the sectors of higher education that have been traditionally underfunded and underresourced due to societal inequality and institutionalized racism. "DEI" needs to be more than just a corporate catchphrase or a boogeyman to attack, but a call to remember that the actual words behind the acronym—diversity, equity, and inclusion—play a pivotal role in making higher education invigorating, exciting, and accessible.

We have to revisit the very purpose of higher education, and how our values influence the type of institutions that we build and the admissions criteria that we use. What is our responsibility to the nation? Are we looking to educate corporate warriors who help the rich get richer, or do we have a baseline responsibility to foster an educated citizenry that can help society flourish? Higher education should work to disrupt societal inequality, not perpetuate it. We will always live with the vestiges of racial discrimination that have been present throughout the history of our country. The question now is how higher education will act to build a better future, while not forgetting the past that still shapes us.

Some politicians are literally trying to make us go back to a time when we couldn't learn, teach, or talk honestly about race. Still, we have to remember that race still matters in students' lives, a point recognized even by the conservative SCOTUS majority. It still matters for higher education and society. It matters for the ability of higher education to respond effectively to society's most pressing needs, working to fulfill institutional missions that seek to contribute to the flourishing of humankind. The SCOTUS majority ruling in *SFFA v. Harvard/UNC* is one turning point in the journey to build a more just and equitable educational system, but it's not the last word. Once again, the toolkit that institutions can use to attract, enroll, and graduate historically excluded populations has been restricted, but not obliterated. Higher education needs to think outside the box by experimenting with new methods, investing boldly in outreach and financial aid, and considering innovative legal options.

I end this book with a call to hope. Yes, these are challenging times to hold on to hope, but what other option do we have?[34] While the ruling in

SFFA is far from ideal, it still leaves us with room to recognize the reality of race in students' lives. There may be a crackdown on diversity, but the right of institutions to define their missions and pursue their goals is still there. We need to find new ways to do our work, but we have to stay the course. The path ahead isn't always clear, but as law faculty Charles Lawrence III and Mari Matsuda wrote almost thirty years ago in their seminal volume on affirmative action, "we won't go back."[35] That message is more essential now than ever, given the political currents of the country and relentless attacks on civil rights. The message of refusing to go back, and not forgetting those who fought the good fight before us, is as powerful and necessary as ever.

Notes

Introduction

1. "Q&A: Undergraduate Admissions in the Wake of Supreme Court Ruling," *MIT News*, August 21, 2024, https://news.mit.edu/2024/qa-undergraduate-admissions-in-wake-of-supreme-court-ruling-0821.
2. Anemona Hartcollis and Stephanie Saul, "Black Enrollment and Affirmative Action: The Impact on Amherst, Tufts, and UVA," *New York Times*, August 30, 2024, https://www.nytimes.com/2024/08/30/us/black-enrollment-affirmative-action-amherst-tufts-uva.html; Johns Hopkins University, "Johns Hopkins' Demographic Makeup Following SCOTUS Ruling," *Hub*, September 19, 2024, https://hub.jhu.edu/2024/09/19/johns-hopkins-demographic-makeup-scotus-ruling/.
3. Johns Hopkins University, "Johns Hopkins' Demographic Makeup"; Hartcollis and Saul, "Black Enrollment."
4. James Murphy (@James_S_Murphy), "Colleges that did not report disaggregated data on race/ethnicity in their profile," September 25, 2024, X (website), https://x.com/James_S_Murphy/status/1838924939945980028.
5. Aatish Bhatia, "Colleges Are Reporting Post-Affirmative Action Data. Be Careful Interpreting It," *New York Times*, September 27, 2024, https://www.nytimes.com/2024/09/27/upshot/colleges-affirmative-action-race.html.
6. Ira Katznelson, *When Affirmative Action Was White: An Untold History of Racial Inequality in Twentieth-Century America* (W. W. Norton & Company, 2005); Fidan Ana Kurtulus, "Affirmative Action and the Occupational Advancement of Minorities and Women During 1973–2003," *Industrial Relations: A Journal of Economy and Society* 51, no. 2 (2012): 213–46; Julie J. Park, "Asian Americans and the Benefits of Campus Diversity: What the Research Says" (National Commission on Asian American and Pacific Islander Research in Education, 2012).
7. Kalli Holloway, "Inside the Cynical Campaign to Claim Affirmative Action Hurts Asian Americans," *The Nation,* August 9, 2023, https://www.thenation.com/article/society/affirmative-action-asian-americans/.

8. Kirin Gupta, Bernadette N. Lim, and Eva Shang, "Left Unheard in the Debate," *The Harvard Crimson*, May 12, 2014, https://www.thecrimson.com/article/2014/5/12/left-unheard-in-the-debate/.
9. Julie J. Park, "The White Admissions Advantage: How Affirmative Action Impacts College Admissions," *HuffPost*, March 25, 2015, https://www.huffpost.com/entry/the-white-admissions-adva_b_6932670.
10. In general, for brevity I will refer to *SFFA v. Harvard*, as SCOTUS noted that the ruling encompasses the UNC case as well.
11. Kimberly West-Faulcon, "Affirmative Action After *SFFA v. Harvard*: The Other Defenses," *Syracuse Law Review* 74 (2024).
12. See for example Christopher Bennett, Brent Evans, and Christopher Marsicano, "Taken for Granted? Effects of Loan-Reduction Initiatives on Student Borrowing, Admission Metrics, and Campus Diversity," *Research in Higher Education* 62 (2021): 569–99.
13. Benjamin Eidelson and Deborah Hellman, "Unreflective Disequilibrium: Race-Conscious Admissions After SFFA," *American Journal of Law and Equality* 4 (2024): 295–325. We'll discuss more in chapter 2.
14. Liliana M. Garces, Brianna Davis Johnson, Evelyn Ambriz, and Dwuana Bradley, "Repressive Legalism: How Postsecondary Administrators' Responses to On-campus Hate Speech Undermine a Focus on Inclusion," *American Educational Research Journal* 58, no. 5 (2021): 1032–69.
15. See David Card, "Report of David Card, Ph.D. *Students for Fair Admissions, Inc. v. Harvard*," website of Harvard University, December 17, 2017, https://projects.iq.harvard.edu/files/diverse-education/files/expert_report_-_2017-12-15_dr._david_card_expert_report_updated_confid_desigs_redacted.pdf, 83: "As shown in Exhibit 27, a regression that includes only the variables for racial categories has a tiny Pseudo R-Squared value—just 0.002. That means that race alone explains almost nothing about admissions outcomes. For comparison's sake, the profile ratings collectively explain a much larger proportion of the variability in admissions outcomes (Pseudo R-Squared value of 0.33). School support ratings and alumni interview ratings have Pseudo R-Squared values of 0.19 and 0.13, respectively. Even contextual factors . . . such as College Board high school and neighborhood variables, parental occupation, and intended career—explain more about admissions decisions than race."
16. Over the years, I've had the pleasure of hearing Art Coleman of EducationCounsel comment how the issue taken up by SCOTUS is race-conscious admissions and not affirmative action. In other words, race-conscious admissions prior to SCOTUS included knowing an applicant's race and allowing that knowledge to inform the reader's assessment of the applicant's context for opportunity and potential contributions to campus. However, such knowledge did not necessarily mean that an institution would act affirmatively in favor of an applicant from a historically underrepresented background. Imagine a Venn diagram where both overlap and distinctions between the two concepts exist. Affirmative action encompasses a more expansive set of policies than what we see in higher education.
17. Card, "Report of David Card," 43–44, 48, 50.
18. Card, "Report of David Card," 57.
19. Card, "Report of David Card," 54, 57–58. The omission of ALDC applicants was already puzzling, but I'm amazed that Arcidiacono also excluded early action applicants from

his baseline analysis, given that so many students apply early action. There's nothing to lose since the decision is nonbinding. To my knowledge, the data came from years when Harvard did not use "restrictive early action," where students can only apply early to one private institution.

20. Daniel Golden, ProPublica, and Kunal Purohit, "The Newest College Admissions Ploy: Paying to Make Your Teen a 'Peer-Reviewed' Author," *ProPublica*, May 18, 2023, https://www.propublica.org/article/college-high-school-research-peer-review-publications. The investigation was also supported by the Chronicle of Higher Education. Also see Kirsten Hextrum, *Special Admission: How College Sports Recruitment Favors White Suburban Athletes* (Rutgers University Press, 2021); Uma Mazyck Jayakumar and Scott E. Page, "Cultural Capital and Opportunities for Exceptionalism: Bias in University Admissions," *The Journal of Higher Education* 92, no. 7 (2021): 1109–39.
21. Ozan Jaquette, "State University No More: Out-of-State Enrollment and the Growing Exclusion of High-Achieving, Low-Income Students at Public Flagship Universities," Jack Kent Cooke Foundation, 2017, https://www.jkcf.org/research/state-university-no-more-out-of-state-enrollment-and-the-growing-exclusion-of-high-achieving-low-income-students-at-public-flagship-universities/; Karina G. Salazar, "Recruitment Redlining by Public Research Universities in the Los Angeles and Dallas Metropolitan Areas," *The Journal of Higher Education* 93, no. 4 (2022): 585–621.
22. For more on how race and class are not interchangeable in admissions, see Zachary Mabel, Michael D. Hurwitz, Jessica Howell, and Greg Perfetto, "Can Standardizing Applicant High School and Neighborhood Information Help to Diversify Selective Colleges?," *Educational Evaluation and Policy Analysis* 44, no. 3 (2022): 505–31; Christopher Bennett, Brent Evans, and Christopher Marsicano, "Taken for Granted? Effects of Loan-Reduction Initiatives on Student Borrowing, Admission Metrics, and Campus Diversity," *Research in Higher Education* 62 (2021): 569–99.
23. A. J. Alvero, Sonia Giebel, Ben Gebre-Medhin, Anthony Lising Antonio, Mitchell L. Stevens, and Benjamin W. Domingue, "Essay Content and Style are Strongly Related to Household Income and SAT Scores: Evidence from 60,000 Undergraduate Applications," *Science Advances* 7, no. 42 (2021): eabi9031; Julie J. Park, Brian Heseung Kim, Nancy Wong, Jia Zheng, Stephanie Breen, Pearl Lo, Dominique J. Baker, Kelly Ochs Rosinger, Mike Hoa Nguyen, and OiYan Poon, "Inequality Beyond Standardized Tests: Trends in Extracurricular Activity Reporting in College Applications across Race and Class," EdWorkingPaper (23-749), 2023, https://doi.org/10.26300/jkcy-x822.
24. Eddie Comeaux, Thandeka K. Chapman, and Frances Contreras, "The College Access and Choice Processes of High-Achieving African American Students," *American Educational Research Journal* 57, no. 1 (2020): 411–39.
25. Julie J. Park, Nicholas Bowman, Nida Denson, and Kevin Eagan, "Race and Class Beyond Enrollment: The Link Between Socioeconomic Diversity and Cross-Racial Interaction," *The Journal of Higher Education* 90, no. 5 (2019): 665–89.
26. Garces et al., "Repressive Legalism."
27. Lani Guinier, *The Tyranny of the Meritocracy: Democratizing Higher Education in America* (Beacon Press, 2016); Natasha Warikoo, *Is Affirmative Action Fair?: The Myth of Equity in College Admissions* (John Wiley & Sons, 2022).

28. David Mickey-Pabello, "The Anti-Affirmative Action Avalanche: The Rise of Underrepresented Minority Enrollment at For-Profit Institutions," *Sociology of Education* 97, no. 1 (2024): 37–57.
29. As many know, the Bill & Melinda Gates Foundation (BMGF) has split into two entities, but it existed as BMGF when we received funding. Evidently Melinda French Gates was interested in test-optional, which led to the funding of two projects. To learn more, go to www.cafcolab.org.
30. I find the "tOSU" branding to be pretty funny.
31. It was a race-conscious merit scholarship. Yes, I know that I spend a lot of time critiquing merit aid while being a beneficiary. Back then, Vanderbilt really was desperate for racial/ethnic diversity, so there was more benefit to the campus itself than the typical "enrollment incentive" type of merit aid.
32. HEOC/Moore 3019!
33. I am constantly recapping this factoid to my children. "Thirty minutes! Tiny one room grocery store! [Like a one-room school house.] No H-Mart!"
34. Julie J. Park and Amanda E. Assalone, "Over 40%: Asian Americans and the Road (s) to Community Colleges," *Community College Review* 47, no. 3 (2019): 274–94.
35. Julie J. Park, *When Diversity Drops: Race, Religion, and Affirmative Action in Higher Education* (Rutgers University Press, 2013).
36. Julie J. Park, *Race on Campus: Debunking Myths with Data* (Harvard Education Press, 2018).

Chapter 1

1. Daniel Golden, ProPublica, and Kunal Purohit, "The Newest College Admissions Ploy: Paying to Make Your Teen a 'Peer-Reviewed' Author," *ProPublica*, May 18, 2023, https://www.propublica.org/article/college-high-school-research-peer-review-publications. The investigation was also supported by the Chronicle of Higher Education.
2. In 2023 dollars. Depending on when you're reading this, rates may be even higher depending on inflation. Of course, graduate students, adjuncts, and postdocs are notoriously underpaid, so this supplemental income is much-needed for many. It's an example of the weird interconnectedness of higher education: Underpay your staff, and they have to take on side hustles that inadvertently contribute to greater inequality in the system. Inequality breeds inequality.
3. "Supplementary Materials," Columbia University Undergraduate Admissions, accessed August 17, 2024, https://undergrad.admissions.columbia.edu/supplementary-materials; "Supplementary Materials," Yale University Office of Undergraduate Admissions, accessed August 17, 2024, https://admissions.yale.edu/supplementary.
4. Golden et al., "Newest College Admissions Ploy."
5. Caitlin Zaloom, *Indebted: How Families Make College Work at Any Cost* (Princeton University Press, 2019).
6. Jay Caspian Kang, "Summer Camp and Parenting Panics," *The New Yorker*, May 24, 2024, https://www.newyorker.com/news/fault-lines/summer-camp-and-parenting-panics.
7. Sadly, typing in "write me a book about navigating the college admissions landscape following the *Students for Fair Admission v. Harvard* ruling" into ChatGPT did not yield quality results, so you're stuck with this book.

8. Ozan Jaquette, "State University No More: Out-of-State Enrollment and the Growing Exclusion of High-Achieving, Low-Income Students at Public Flagship Universities," Jack Kent Cooke Foundation, 2017, https://www.jkcf.org/research/state-university-no-more-out-of-state-enrollment-and-the-growing-exclusion-of-high-achieving-low-income-students-at-public-flagship-universities/.
9. All of this to get yourself a ticket to the Yale holiday dinner, which really is dystopian! It's an appropriate feast for the winners of the college admissions Hunger Games. We'll circle back to that one soon. An actual dystopian portrayal of the college admissions process would be the Korean drama *Sky Castle*.
10. I insert the word "sometimes" purposefully. Admissions has been described as "zero-sum," and this was the language used in the SCOTUS majority ruling. At the same time, I don't see race-conscious admissions as resulting in the pushing out of other groups.
11. See Joy Ann Williamson, *Black Power on Campus: The University of Illinois, 1965–75* (University of Illinois Press, 2003); Juan Carlos Garibay, Christian West, and Christopher Mathis, "'It Affects Me in Ways That I Don't Even Realize': A Preliminary Study on Black Student Responses to a University's Enslavement History," *Journal of College Student Development* 61, no. 6 (2020): 697–716; Juan C. Garibay and Christopher Mathi, "Does a University's Enslavement History Play a Role in Black Student–White Faculty Interactions? A Structural Equation Model," *Education Sciences* 11, no. 12 (2021): 809.
12. See Craig Steven Wilder, *Ebony and Ivy: Race, Slavery, and the Troubled History of America's Universities* (Bloomsbury Publishing USA, 2013); Julia W. Bernier, "Georgetown and Slavery, from Plantation to Campus," *Journal of the Early Republic* 44, no. 1 (2024): 87–114.
13. Christopher M. Span and James D. Anderson, "The Quest for 'Book Learning': African American Education in Slavery and Freedom," in *A Companion to African American History*, ed. Alton Hornsby (Blackwell Publishing, 2005), 295–311; Robert L. Reece and Heather A. O'Connell, "How the Legacy of Slavery and Racial Composition Shape Public School Enrollment in the American South," *Sociology of Race and Ethnicity* 2, no. 1 (2016): 42–57.
14. Mae M. Ngai, *The Lucky Ones: One Family and the Extraordinary Invention of Chinese America* (Princeton University Press, 2012).
15. Charles Wollenberg, "Mendez v. Westminster: Race, Nationality and Segregation in California Schools," *California Historical Quarterly* 53, no. 4 (1974): 317–32.
16. Ann Piccard, "Death by Boarding School: The Last Acceptable Racism and the United States' Genocide of Native Americans," *Gonzaga Law Review* 49 (2013): 137; Andrea Smith, *Conquest: Sexual Violence and American Indian Genocide* (Duke University Press, 2015).
17. Christina Ciocca Eller and Thomas A. DiPrete, "The Paradox of Persistence: Explaining the Black-White Gap in Bachelor's Degree Completion," *American Sociological Review* 83, no. 6 (2018): 1171–214. Troublingly, the disproportionate negative impact of the student debt crisis on Black students is also reflective of the considerable investment that Black communities have made in education: Black students and families see education as the key to success, but this belief has been exploited by the for-profit, predatory sector of institutions. Sadly, this same group of institutions has benefited from the end of race-conscious admissions in states with affirmative action bans; see

David Mickey-Pabello, "The Anti-Affirmative Action Avalanche: The Rise of Underrepresented Minority Enrollment at For-Profit Institutions," *Sociology of Education* 97, no. 1 (2024): 37–57.

18. Paul David Nelson, "Experiment in Interracial Education at Berea College, 1858–1908," *The Journal of Negro History* 59, no. 1 (1974): 13–27; James Oliver Horton, "Black Education at Oberlin College: A Controversial Commitment," *The Journal of Negro Education* 54, no. 4 (1985): 477–99; Adam Harris, *The State Must Provide: Why America's Colleges Have Always Been Unequal—and How to Set Them Right* (Ecco, 2021).
19. Margaret A. Nash, "Entangled Pasts: Land-Grant Colleges and American Indian Dispossession," *History of Education Quarterly* 59, no. 4 (2019): 437–67. See Tristan Ahtone, Robert Lee, Amanda Tachine, An Garagiola, Audrianna Goodwin, Maria Parazo Rose, and Clayton Aldern, "Misplaced Trust," *Grist*, February 7, 2024, https://grist.org/project/indigenous/land-grant-universities-indigenous-lands-fossil-fuels/, for how to this day, public universities actively profit off of trust lands, which are "expropriated Indigenous territories . . . held and managed by the state for the school's continued benefit" (Ahtone et al.).
20. Amy E. Slaton, "Engineering Segregation: The University of Maryland in the Twilight of Jim Crow," *Organization of American Historians Magazine of History* 24, no. 3 (2010): 15–23.
21. Harris, *The State Must Provide.*
22. Hilary Herbold, "Never a Level Playing Field: Blacks and the GI Bill," *The Journal of Blacks in Higher Education* 6 (1994): 104–8.
23. Dafina-Lazarus Stewart, "Whiteness as Collective Memory in Student Publications at Midwestern Liberal Arts Colleges, 1945–1965," *American Educational Research Journal* 56, no. 1 (2019): 3–38; Jesse Wang and Diamond Steward-Hutton, "History of Black Student Housing at UI," *The Daily Illini*, September 10, 2023, https://dailyillini.com/news-stories/around-campus/campus-life/2023/09/10/a-history-of-black-student-housing-at-ui/.
24. Alfred McClung Lee, *Fraternities Without Brotherhood: A Study Of Prejudice on the American Campus* (The Beacon Press, 1955), 93. For more on how other contexts remain informally segregated, see Julie J. Park, *Race on Campus: Debunking Myths with Data* (Harvard Education Press, 2018); Zachary Bleemer and Aashish Mehta, "College Major Restrictions and Student Stratification," Research & Occasional Paper Series: CSHE. 14.2021 (Center for Studies in Higher Education, 2021); Ebony Omotola McGee, *Black, Brown, Bruised: How Racialized STEM Education Stifles Innovation* (Harvard Education Press, 2021); Jason T. Hilton and Jessica Jordan, "The Recruitment and Retention of Diverse Students in Honors: What the Last Twenty Years of Scholarship Say," *Journal of the National Collegiate Honors Council* 22, no. 1 (2021): 115–33, https://digitalcommons.unl.edu/nchcjournal/673/.
25. "The Numbers Don't Lie: HBCUs Are Changing the College Landscape," UNCF (United Negro College Fund), accessed August 17, 2024, https://uncf.org/the-latest/the-numbers-dont-lie-hbcus-are-changing-the-college-landscape.
26. "Fast Facts: Historically Black Colleges and Universities (HBCUs)," National Center for Education Statistics, accessed August 17, 2024, https://nces.ed.gov/fastfacts/display.asp?id=667.

27. Alexis Marshall, "HBCUs Have Been Underfunded by $12 Billion, Federal Officials Reveal," *NPR*, October 9, 2023, https://www.npr.org/2023/10/09/1204614576/hbcus-have-been-underfunded-by-12-billion-federal-officials-reveal.
28. Marshall, "HBCUs Have Been Underfunded."
29. That form of inequality has literally compounded over the years, as university endowments are practically untaxed, which for better or worse has benefited historically White institutions, especially private ones.
30. Travis Knoll, "Supreme Court Is Poised to Dismantle an Integral Part of LBJ's Great Society: Affirmative Action," *The Conversation*, June 29, 2023, https://theconversation.com/supreme-court-is-poised-to-dismantle-an-integral-part-of-lbjs-great-society-affirmative-action-201247.
31. "Constitutional Requirements for Affirmative Action in Higher Education Admissions and Financial Aid," UCLA Civil Rights Project, 2002, https://civilrightsproject.ucla.edu/legal-developments/legal-memos/constitutional-requirements-for-affirmative-action-in-higher-education-admissions-and-financial-aid/constitutional-affirmative-action-financial-aid.pdf.
32. April J. Anderson, "Race-Conscious Admissions and Equal Protection in Higher Education," Congressional Research Service, April 19, 2024, https://crsreports.congress.gov/product/pdf/R/R48043.
33. American Psychological Association, "Amicus Brief of the American Psychological Association in Support of Respondents," website of Harvard University, August 2022, https://www.harvard.edu/admissionscase/wp-content/uploads/sites/6/2022/08/Amicus-Brief-APA5.pdf.
34. US Government Accountability Office, "K-12 Education: Student Population Has Significantly Diversified, but Many Schools Remain Divided Along Racial, Ethnic, and Economic Lines," GAO-22-104737, September 2022, https://www.gao.gov/products/gao-22-104737.
35. Richard Rothstein, *The Color of Law: A Forgotten History of How Our Government Segregated America* (Liveright Publishing, 2017).
36. Nicholas Lemann, *The Big Test: The Secret History of the American Meritocracy* (Macmillan, 2000); Awilda Rodriguez and Keon M. McGuire, "More Classes, More Access? Understanding the Effects of Course Offerings on Black-White Gaps in Advanced Placement Course-Taking," *The Review of Higher Education* 42, no. 2 (2019): 641–79; Camille Z. Charles, Vincent J. Roscigno, and Kimberly C. Torres, "Racial Inequality and College Attendance," *Social Science Research* 36, no. 1 (2007): 329–52; Julia Bryan, Jungnam Kim, and Chang Liu, "How the Culture in School Counseling Programs Shapes College-Going Outcomes: Do the Effects Vary by Race?," *Professional School Counseling* 27, no. 1a (2023): 2156759X231153392.
37. Consider the case of *Dayo Adetu, et al. v. Sidwell Friends School*. See Caroline Kelly, "She Was Rejected from 13 Schools and Blames Her Elite School," *CNN*, June 13, 2019, https://www.cnn.com/2019/06/13/politics/sidwell-friends-supreme-court/index.html.
38. Eller and DiPrete, "Paradox of Persistence," 1195.
39. Of course, beyond direct benefits to students of color, all students on a campus benefit from being able to engage with racial diversity during college, and the corresponding benefits to society at large.

40. Wang and Steward-Hutton, "History of Black Student Housing"; Williamson, *Black Power on Campus*; Division of Management Information, "New Beginning Freshmen, Fall 1968: 'Unofficial' Demographic Profile," University of Illinois, https://www.dmi.illinois.edu/stuenr/frosh/frosh68.html.
41. Division of Management Information, "New Beginning Freshmen"; Division of Management Information, "UIUC Student Enrollment: Six-Year Graduation Rates for New Beginning Freshman," University of Illinois, https://www.dmi.illinois.edu/stuenr/index.htm#gradrates.
42. In 1965, 27% of Black students graduated from high school, but in 2019 in the state of Illinois, 77% of Black students graduated from high school. Not all of these graduates would necessarily gain admission to UIUC or want to go if admitted. Still, certainly the pool of Black high school graduates eligible to attend is considerably larger than it was in 1968. See "Public High School Graduation Rates," National Center for Education Statistics, https://nces.ed.gov/programs/coe/indicator/coi; US Census Bureau, "Education," in *Statistical Abstract of the United States*, https://www.census.gov/prod/99pubs/99statab/sec04.pdf; The Annie E. Casey Foundation, "High School Graduation Rates by Race-Ethnicity—Illinois and Chicago," Kids Count Data Center, https://datacenter.kidscount.org/data/tables/9735-high-school-graduation-rates-by-race-ethnicity--illinois-and-chicago#detailed/2/any/false/1696,1648,1603,1539,1381,1246,1124/2160,4739,2159,2161,2757,3307/18997.
43. Andrew Nichols, "Segregation Forever: The Continued Underrepresentation of Black and Latino Undergraduates at the Nation's 101 Most Selective Public Colleges and Universities," *The Education Trust*, July 21, 2020, https://edtrust.org/wp-content/uploads/2014/09/Segregation-Forever-The-Continued-Underrepresentation-of-Black-and-Latino-Undergraduates-at-the-Nations-101-Most-Selective-Public-Colleges-and-Universities-July-21-2020.pdf. Rest in power, Dr. Nichols.
44. Meredith Kolodner, "Many Flagship Universities Don't Reflect Their States' Black or Latino High School Graduates," *The Hechinger Report*, July 30, 2021, https://hechingerreport.org/many-flagship-universities-dont-reflect-their-states-black-or-latino-high-school-graduates/.
45. Kolodner, "Many Flagship Universities Don't Reflect Their States."
46. Office of Institutional Research, Planning, and Assessment, "UMD Undergraduate Student Profile," October 2024, https://irpa.umd.edu/CampusCounts/Enrollments/stuprofile_allug.pdf.
47. U.S. Census Bureau, "Quick Facts: Maryland," https://www.census.gov/quickfacts/fact/table/MD/BZA115222.
48. prabhdeep singh kehal, Daniel Hirschman, and Ellen Berrey, "When Affirmative Action Disappears: Unexpected Patterns in Student Enrollments at Selective U.S. Institutions, 1990–2016," *Sociology of Race and Ethnicity* 7, no. 4 (2021): 543–60.
49. Middle status included those classified as very competitive, competitive, and less competitive but not maximally competitive. kehal et al., "When Affirmative Action Disappears," 544.
50. Our CAF Co-LAB team found that test-optional policy adoption during the pandemic was linked with increased Black enrollment at mid-selective institutions. It's possible that this group of schools relied more on test scores to weed out students, and going test-optional facilitated access for Black students. Returning to the kehal team study,

pre-pandemic test score requirements may have inhibited some of the potential of race-conscious admissions to support the enrollment of Black students within this group of schools.

51. Some have become more highly rejective since the 2020s.
52. Victor Ray, "A Theory of Racialized Organizations," *American Sociological Review* 84, no. 1 (2019): 26–53. Ray of course builds off of the important work of Eduardo Bonilla-Silva and others. Hopefully the theory of racialized organizations, a.k.a. TRO, doesn't become subject to the same treatment as some of its other easy-to-abbreviate predecessors, since that seems to be part of the playbook—find something with an acronym, use the acronym without explaining the concept, and demonize the heck out of it.
53. OiYan Poon, Douglas H. Lee, Eileen Galvez, Joanne Song Engler, Bri Sérráno, Ali Raza, Jessica M. Hurtado, and Nikki Kahealani Chun, "A Möbius Model of Racialized Organizations: Durability of Racial Inequalities in Admissions," *The Journal of Higher Education* 95, no. 3 (2024): 7.
54. Shawn Hubler and Soumya Karlamangla, "California Bans Legacy Admissions at Private Universities," *New York Times*, September 30, 2024, https://www.nytimes.com/2024/09/30/us/california-bans-legacy-admissions-private-universities.html.
55. Basically, the legacy of legacy admissions.
56. Sarah Reber and Gabriela Goodman, "How Widespread Is the Practice of Giving Special Consideration to Relatives of Alumni in Admissions?," The Brookings Institution, December 5, 2019, https://www.brookings.edu/articles/how-widespread-is-the-practice-of-giving-special-consideration-to-relatives-of-alumni-in-admissions/.
57. I used the word "weird" to describe legacy admissions before Tim Walz used the word to describe Trump/Vance, and I still find it fitting for all of them. Weird!
58. Kudos to James Murphy at Education Reform Now, and others, for beating the drum on legacy.
59. Of course there are those who say that now is a bad time to get rid of legacy admissions because the alumni pool is finally more diverse than it has been in previous generations. White students and the rich are still disproportionately more likely to benefit from the bump, and as I said—on what planet is getting a "bump" for your bloodline defensible?
60. Richard Kahlenberg, "Trump Claims He Supports Meritocracy? Why Is He Silent on Legacy Admissions," *MSNBC.com*, March 28, 2025, https://www.msnbc.com/opinion/msnbc-opinion/trump-silence-college-legacy-admissions-merit-race-rcna198635.
61. Jaquette, *State University No More*; Ozan Jaquette and Bradley R. Curs, "Creating the Out-of-State University: Do Public Universities Increase Nonresident Freshman Enrollment in Response to Declining State Appropriations?," *Research in Higher Education* 56 (2015): 535–65; Aaron Klein, "The Great Student Swap," The Brookings Institution, https://digitalscholarship.unlv.edu/brookings_policybriefs_reports/7.
62. Karina G. Salazar, Ozan Jaquette, and Crystal Han, "Coming Soon to a Neighborhood Near You? Off-Campus Recruiting by Public Research Universities," *American Educational Research Journal* 58, no. 6 (2021): 1270–314; Jaquette, *State University No More*; Ozan Jaquette, Bradley R. Curs, and Julie R. Posselt, "Tuition Rich, Mission Poor: Nonresident Enrollment Growth and the Socioeconomic and Racial Composition of Public Research Universities," *The Journal of Higher Education* 87, no. 5 (2016): 635–73.

63. Stephen Burd, "High Merit Aid Public Flagships See Substantial Shifts to Wealthier Students," *New America*, https://na-production.s3.amazonaws.com/documents/Moving-on-Up.pdf, 33.
64. Salazar et al., "Coming Soon," 1270.
65. Karina G. Salazar, "Recruitment Redlining by Public Research Universities in the Los Angeles and Dallas Metropolitan Areas," *The Journal of Higher Education* 93, no. 4 (2022): 585.
66. Office of Institutional Research and Assessment, "Fall 2023 Enrollment at a Glance," University of Alabama, https://oira.ua.edu/new/reports/6504792f75c4420b3e594dc5; OSU Analysis and Reporting, "15th Day Student Enrollment Overview, Fall 2024," The Ohio State University, https://dataviz.rae.osu.edu/t/public/views/15thDayStudentEnrollment/EnrollmentSummaryByTerm?%3Aembed=y&%3AisGuestRedirectFromVizportal=y; Elaine S. Povich, "State Universities Admit More Out-of-State Students for the Tuition Bump," *West Virginia Watch*, February 19, 2024, https://westvirginiawatch.com/2024/02/19/state-universities-admit-more-out-of-state-students-for-the-tuition-bump/.
67. J. D. Vance, "Senator Vance Raises Concerns to Incoming OSU President over Discriminatory DEI Initiatives," US Senate Press Releases of J. D. Vance, December 7, 2023, https://www.vance.senate.gov/press-releases/senator-vance-raises-concerns-to-incoming-osu-president-over-discriminatory-dei-initiatives/.
68. Office of Student Academic Success, *Accelerating Excellence, Access and Service: Strategic Enrollment Plan for The Ohio State University, 2022–2024*, the Ohio State University, May 2021, accessed June 4, 2025, https://web.archive.org/web/20220327074832/https://osas.osu.edu/pdf/enrollment-plan.pdf, 6-7. The previous link for the plan was https://osas.osu.edu/pdf/enrollment-plan.pdf but it is no longer posted online. Thanks to the Wayback Machine for archiving it.
69. Krista Mattern and Jeff N. Wyatt, "Student Choice of College: How Far Do Students Go for an Education," *Journal of College Admission* 203 (2009): 18–29; Ruth N. López Turley, "When Parents Want Children to Stay Home for College," *Research in Higher Education* 47 (2006): 823–46.
70. Christopher Avery, Andrew Fairbanks, and Richard Zeckhauser, *The Early Admissions Game: Joining the Elite* (Harvard University Press, 2009).
71. Or whatever it's called—Genie Plus? Genie Fast Pass Plus?
72. I know a few, and due to my networks, most are either the children of pastors, former pastors, or current/former missionaries. In Asian American Christian circles, this group includes kids from highly educated families who don't have a ton of money, which makes their progeny attractive to competitive schools: high test scores, modest financial backgrounds.
73. Scott Jaschik, "Tulane Admitted Two-Thirds of Students Through Early Decision," *Inside Higher Ed*, https://www.insidehighered.com/admissions/article/2022/06/27/tulane-admitted-two-thirds-its-class-early-year#.YtQj6wtC5NA.link.
74. Julie J. Park, Pearl Lo, Elizabeth Wadsen Oudin, Victoria Alexander, Rachel DiDonna, and Nancy Wong, "Contradictory Aims: How Institutions Undermine Racial and Economic Equity in Undergraduate Admissions," *Journal of Diversity in Higher Education* (in press).
75. Hilton and Jordan, "Recruitment and Retention," McGee, *Black, Brown, Bruised*; Varsha Singh and Sujoy Chakravarty, "Are Quantitative Skills Critical for Business

Education Program or an Entry-Barrier for Diversity?," *Psychological Studies* 63, no. 3 (2018): 325–34; Bleemer and Mehta, "College Major Restrictions."

76. Stephen J. Burd, ed., *Lifting the Veil on Enrollment Management: How a Powerful Industry is Limiting Social Mobility in American Higher Education* (Harvard Education Press, 2024).
77. Ozan Jaquette and Karina G. Salazar, "A Sociological Analysis of Structural Racism in 'Student List' Lead Generation Products," *Educational Evaluation and Policy Analysis* 46, no. 2 (2024): 301; Karina Salazar, Ozan Jaquette, and Crystal Han, "Geodemographics of Student List Purchases by Public Universities: A First Look," The Institute for College Access & Success, https://ticas.org/wpcontent/uploads/2022/09/Geodemographics-ofStudent-List-Purchases_A-First-Look.pdf.
78. Rick Seltzer, "A Look in the Mirror," *Inside Higher Ed*, September 15, 2017, https://www.insidehighered.com/news/2017/09/15/speaker-implores-nacac-attendees-change-practices-he-believes-are-racist; National Association for College Admission Counseling (NACAC), "DEI Challenges in the College Admission Counseling Profession," Salesforce.org, https://www.salesforce.org/wp-content/uploads/2022/05/sfdo-nacac-dei-report-032222.pdf.
79. NACAC, "DEI Challenges."
80. Nicholas A. Bowman and Michael N. Bastedo, "What Role May Admissions Office Diversity and Practices Play in Equitable Decisions?," *Research in Higher Education* 59 (2018): 430–47.
81. Bowman and Bastedo, "Equitable Decisions?," 441.
82. Bowman and Bastedo, "Equitable Decisions?," 442.
83. Bowman and Bastedo, "Equitable Decisions?," 441–42.
84. Bowman and Bastedo, "Equitable Decisions?," 443.
85. Recent graduates are a natural hiring pool for entry-level positions: someone who worked in the admissions office as an undergraduate, loves their alma mater, and isn't quite sure what to do after graduation. ("I just couldn't leave!") However, alumni hiring may backfire against efforts to expand access and equity unless institutions are proactive about counteracting some of trends identified by the authors.
86. Scott Jaschik, "The Growth of Part-Time Readers," *Inside Higher Ed*, August 7, 2022, https://www.insidehighered.com/admissions/article/2022/08/08/part-time-readers-grow-applications.
87. Park et al., "Contradictory Aims."
88. Michael N. Bastedo, Kristen M. Glasener, K. C. Deane, and Nicholas A. Bowman, "Contextualizing the SAT: Experimental Evidence on College Admission Recommendations for Low-SES Applicants," *Educational Policy* 36, no. 2 (2022): 282–311.
89. "Digest of Education Statistics 2013, Table 219.10, High School Graduates," National Center for Education Statistics, https://nces.ed.gov/programs/digest/d17/tables/dt17_219.10.asp.
90. Julie J. Park and Amy Liu, "Interest Convergence or Divergence?," *The Journal of Higher Education* 85, no. 1 (2014): 36–64.
91. There was some nice momentum around Coalition sign-ups, as it had one of the "all the cool kids are doing it" vibes that help drive equity-related initiatives in the admissions world.
92. Common App does a lot of great things, and I myself was an early beneficiary. I photocopied my Common Application last minute to what would become my alma

mater, and I probably wouldn't have applied if I had to complete a separate application. (Yes, there was no online Common App back then, I used a typewriter.) That said, the "apply to multiple schools through just one application" function has gone to another level in this era of admissions-in-the-era-of-late-stage-capitalism, and it's hard to get the genie back in the bottle. For more on in-state students feeling frustrated that they're being rejected from their flagship state institution, see Kevin Thompson, "Many Students Ask 'Why Can't I Get into UF,'" *The Palm Beach Post*, December 22, 2015, https://www.palmbeachpost.com/story/special/2015/12/22/many-students-ask-why-can/7026094007/; Elli Jacobs, "Breaking Down UMD's Increasing Rejection Rates," *The Tide*, April 11, 2023, https://thermtide.com/18540/popular/breaking-down-umds-increasing-rejection-rates/. There are also numerous posts on forums like Reddit, College Confidential, and the like.

93. I'm not a fan of much of Jonathan Haidt's other work, but am very much on board with the idea of delaying and limiting smartphone use, as someone who used a flip phone until around 2021.
94. Derek Thompson, "We're Missing a Key Driver of Teen Anxiety," *The Atlantic*, March 8, 2023, https://www.theatlantic.com/newsletters/archive/2023/03/teen-anxiety-elite-schools-sat-act-paradox-wealthy-nations/673307/.
95. William Fitzsimmons, "Time Out or Burn Out for the Next Generation," *New York Times*, December 6, 2000, https://www.nytimes.com/2000/12/06/national/time-out-or-burn-out-for-the-next-generation.html.
96. Cornell University Institutional Research and Planning, "Fall 2003 Profile," Cornell University, https://irp.dpb.cornell.edu/wp-content/uploads/2021/02/Fall-2003-Profile.pdf; "College Report: College Admissions on Course, Says Behnke," *University of Chicago Magazine*, October 1999, https://magazine.uchicago.edu/9910/html/collegereport1.htm#:~:text=At%20the%20same%20time%2C%20Chicago's,ever%20been%20below%2050%20percent.
97. Anastasia Thumser, "College Is Nothing Like the Movies, and That's Okay," *The Vanderbilt Hustler*, October 16, 2023, https://vanderbilthustler.com/2023/10/16/thumser-college-is-nothing-like-the-movies-and-thats-okay/.
98. Thumser, "College Is Nothing Like the Movies."
99. Frank Bruni, *Where You Go Is Not Who You'll Be: An Antidote to the College Admissions Mania* (Hachette UK, 2015).
100. William Stixrud and Ned Johnson, *The Self-Driven Child: The Science and Sense of Giving Your Kids More Control Over Their Lives* (Penguin, 2019).
101. Nancy Wong, OiYan Poon, Julie J. Park, Jia Zheng, and Pearl Lo, "Test-Optional Policies in the Era of COVID-19: Responses from the College Admissions Community," College Admissions Futures Co-Laborative, https://cafcolab.org/s/NACAC_UMD-College-Admissions-Futures_Report-v5.pdf, 7.

Chapter 2

1. *Students for Fair Admissions v. Harvard*, 600 U.S. 181 (2023), https://www.supremecourt.gov/opinions/22pdf/20-1199_hgdj.pdf.
2. The entire quote is: "'Race-based admissions' is a made-up nonsense term, and people should stop saying/writing/using it, even if that gets them in trouble w their neocon

editors." Eric Hoover (@erichoov), "Race-based admissions," September 25, 2024, X (website), https://x.com/erichoov/status/1839035018603110582.

3. Alisa Nelson, "Following U.S. Supreme Court Decisions, Bailey Informs Missouri Universities and Cities to End Affirmative Action Policies," *Missouri.net*, June 29, 2023, https://www.missourinet.com/2023/06/29/following-u-s-supreme-court-decisions-bailey-informs-missouri-universities-and-cities-to-end-affirmative-action-policies/.
4. David Hinojosa, "Re: Critical Points on Affirmative Action Decision and Response to Blum Letter," Lawyers' Committee for Civil Rights Under Law, July 14, 2023, https://www.lawyerscommittee.org/wp-content/uploads/2023/07/FINAL-Open-Letter-re-SFFA-July-12-Letter.pdf.
5. "The Death of Affirmative Action," *NPR*, June 29, 2023, https://www.npr.org/2023/06/29/1185176218/the-death-of-affirmative-action.
6. Elie Mystal, "The Supreme Court Has Killed Affirmative Action," *The Nation*, June 30, 2023, https://www.thenation.com/article/society/supreme-court-killed-affirmative-action/.
7. I myself was asked to speak on a webinar titled "The End of Race-Based Admissions," and immediately pointed out that the programs at Harvard and UNC weren't "race-based" to begin with.
8. Craig Trainor, "Dear Colleague," US Department of Education, February 14, 2025, https://www.ed.gov/media/document/dear-colleague-letter-sffa-v-harvard-109506.pdf.
9. In this prior version of race-conscious admissions, students could get points for an array of characteristics, from race/ethnicity to coming from rural Michigan, special talents, and other factors. SCOTUS saw the practice as being an improper way to consider race/ethnicity.
10. For a perspective arguing that *Grutter* was effectively gutted, see Bill Watson, "Did the Court in *SFFA* Overrule *Grutter*?," *Notre Dame Law Review Reflection* 99 (2023): 113.
11. Benjamin Eidelson and Deborah Hellman, "Unreflective Disequilibrium: Race-Conscious Admissions After *SFFA*," *American Journal of Law and Equality* 4 (2024): 316.
12. *Students for Fair Admissions*, 6.
13. Liliana M. Garces and Uma M. Jayakumar, "Dynamic Diversity: Toward a Contextual Understanding of Critical Mass," *Educational Researcher* 43, no. 3 (2014): 115–24.
14. *Students for Fair Admissions*, 8.
15. *Students for Fair Admissions*, 39. If you're scratching your head on why SCOTUS would still allow for discussion of race at the individual level, I suggest Sonja Starr's great paper on the issue and how Roberts's framing of race as relevant to individual traits still falls within a traditional conservative approach. See Sonja B. Starr, "Admissions Essays After SFFA," *Indiana Law Journal* (forthcoming), https://papers.ssrn.com/sol3/papers.cfm?abstract_id=4806726.
16. This would be a good place to insert one of those "side-by-side" memes: "What SCOTUS says is okay"; "What the admissions community is already doing." For one example on how race was considered in the holistic admissions process at Harvard, see "Harvard's Proposed Findings of Fact and Conclusions of Law: Document 619," Harvard University, December 19, 2018, https://www.harvard.edu/admissionscase/wp-content/uploads/sites/6/2021/06/harvard_fof_col_with_appendix-as_filed.pdf, 19.

17. *Students for Fair Admissions*, 40.
18. The backwards colorblindness approach reminds me of the cringeworthy backhanded "compliment" often given to people of color, some variant of "well, I don't see you as having a race, but as a person" or "I see you as a human being, or a member of the human race." Once again, Starr's paper does a nice job of unpacking how this discussion of race is in sync with traditional conservative norms.
19. Eidelson and Hellman, "Unreflective Disequilibrium," 324.
20. As noted earlier, disagreement exists over whether race-conscious admissions and affirmative action in higher education are even the same thing, despite the terms often being used interchangeably. Once again, I'll echo Art Coleman of EducationCounsel's statement that within the admissions sphere, the issue taken up by SCOTUS was race-conscious admissions and not affirmative action. Conventional race-conscious admissions could open the door for an institution to act affirmatively, but did not guarantee any particular outcome for an applicant.
21. Eidelson and Hellman, "Unreflective Disequilibrium," 296.
22. Eidelson and Hellman, "Unreflective Disequilibrium," 306. I found a few references to "race-sensitive admissions" from the late 1990s; the term was used to refer to conventional race-conscious admissions. I wouldn't mind resurrecting the term to refer to what we have after *SFFA*.
23. Donald J. Trump, "Ending Illegal Discrimination and Restoring Merit-Based Opportunity," White House website, January 21, 2025, https://www.whitehouse.gov/presidential-actions/2025/01/ending-illegal-discrimination-and-restoring-merit-based-opportunity/.
24. Trump, "Ending Illegal Discrimination."
25. Trainor, "Dear Colleague," 2.
26. Art Coleman, "Overreaching and Misleading: An Analysis of the U.S. Department of Education's February 14, 2025 'Dear Colleague' Letter on Diversity, Equity and Inclusion Policies and Programs," EducationCounsel, February 19, 2025, https://www.nelsonmullins.com/storage/AyMazdRpsfYnAbDpCNQE6kE7LsCIke5ATu3C7g09.pdf, 3.
27. Liliana Garces, "Hitting Pause on the 'Dear Colleague Letter,'" *Chronicle of Higher Education*, February 18, 2025, https://www.chronicle.com/article/hitting-pause-on-the-dear-colleague-letter.
28. Kathryn Abrams et al., "DEI Programs Are Lawful Under Federal Civil Rights Laws and Supreme Court Precedent," February 20, 2025, https://www.nacua.org/docs/default-source/new-cases-and-developments/2025/ogc-memo-re-trump-dei-and-sffa-2025-02-20.pdf.
29. Liam Knox, "Ed Blum Takes a Victory Lap," *Inside Higher Ed*, February 19, 2025, https://www.insidehighered.com/news/government/politics-elections/2025/02/19/sffa-president-affirmative-action-bans-growing-impact. As noted in the article: "Blum doesn't actually believe the decision itself extends to those programs. He does think they're illegal—there just hasn't been a successful case challenging them yet. 'I haven't really made myself clear on this, which is my fault, but the SFFA opinion didn't change the law for those policies' in internships and scholarships,' he said. 'But those policies have always been, in my opinion, outside of the scope of our civil rights law and actionable in court.'"
30. Coleman, "Overreaching," 3.

31. Julie J. Park, "Some DEI Programs Are Vulnerable, Not Illegal," *Inside Higher Ed*, April 14, 2025, https://www.insidehighered.com/opinion/views/2025/04/14/some-dei-programs-are-vulnerable-not-illegal-opinion.
32. Cue nostalgia for the phone-free era.
33. All of this is moot speculation since I'm also from a group that is well-represented at many institutions, but that wasn't necessarily the case when I applied to college in the 1990s.
34. *Students for Fair Admissions*, 39, 8.
35. See Eidelson and Hellman, "Unreflective Disequilibrium," for insight into this issue.
36. Jazper Lu, "Duke No Longer Giving Numerical Rating to Standardized Testing, Essays in Undergraduate Admissions," *Duke Chronicle*, February 7, 2024, https://www.dukechronicle.com/article/2024/02/duke-university-undergraduate-admissions-changes-numerical-rating-standardized-testing-essays-covid-test-optional-ai-generated-college-consultants.
37. MEChA is the Movimiento Estudiantil Chicano de Aztlán (Chicano Student Movement of Aztlán), Aztlán being the ancestral home of the Aztec/Mexica people. Thank you to my copyeditor for suggesting that phrasing.
38. "Q&A: Undergraduate Admissions in the Wake of Supreme Court Ruling," *MIT News*, August 21, 2024, https://news.mit.edu/2024/qa-undergraduate-admissions-in-wake-of-supreme-court-ruling-0821.
39. Hinojosa, "Critical Points," 2.
40. See, for example, "University of California Freshman Applications by Campus and Race/Ethnicity," University of California Office of the President, 2022, https://www.ucop.edu/institutional-research-academic-planning/_files/factsheets/2022/table-2.1-california-freshman-applications-by-campus-and-race-ethnicity.pdf.
41. Hinojosa, "Critical Points," 2.
42. "Statutory Requirement for Reporting IPEDS Data," National Center for Education Statistics (NCES), https://surveys.nces.ed.gov/ipeds/public/statutory-requirement.
43. *Students for Fair Admissions*, 22.
44. See Phil Stewart and Idrees Ali, "Exclusive: U.S. Military Academies Should Not Use Race-Conscious Admissions, Trump's Pentagon Pick Says," Reuters, January 24, 2025, https://www.reuters.com/world/us/us-military-academies-should-not-use-race-admissions-trumps-pentagon-pick-says-2025-01-24/.
45. Bianca Quilantan, "Federal Judge Allows Naval Academy to Continue Using Race in Admissions—for Now," *Politico*, December 14, 2023, https://www.politico.com/news/2023/12/14/naval-academy-affirmative-action-00131876; Liam Knox, "Supreme Court Passes On West Point Affirmative Action Case," *Inside Higher Ed*, February 5, 2024, https://www.insidehighered.com/news/quick-takes/2024/02/05/supreme-court-declines-west-point-affirmative-action-case; Melissa Quinn, "Judge Upholds U.S. Naval Academy's Race-Conscious Admissions Program," *CBS News*, https://www.cbsnews.com/news/judge-upholds-u-s-naval-academys-race-conscious-admissions-program/.
46. "Brief for the United States as Amicus Curiae," Supreme Court of the United States, December 2021, https://www.supremecourt.gov/DocketPDF/20/20-1199/204668/20211209161118061_20-1199%20-%20SFFA%20v%20Harvard%20CVSG%20-%20Corrected.pdf.

47. "Brief of Adm. Charles S. Abbot, Adm. Dennis C. Blair, Gen. Charles F. Bolden, Jr., Gen. Thomas P. Bostick, Gen. Vincent K. Brooks, Adm. Walter E. Carter, Jr., et al., as Amici Curiae in Support of Respondents," Harvard University, August 2022, https://www.harvard.edu/admissionscase/wp-content/uploads/sites/6/2022/08/Amicus-Brief-Military-Brief72.pdf.
48. Olivia Sanchez, "The Supreme Court Affirmative Action Decision Left a Head-Scratching Exemption for Military Academies: Here's Why It Matters," *Hechinger Report*, July 1, 2023, https://hechingerreport.org/the-supreme-court-affirmative-action-decision-left-a-head-scratching-exemption-for-military-academies-heres-why-it-matters/.
49. For studies documenting benefits linked with engaging with racial/ethnic diversity, see American Psychological Association, "Amicus Brief of the American Psychological Association in Support of Respondents," Harvard University, August 2022, https://www.harvard.edu/admissionscase/wp-content/uploads/sites/6/2022/08/Amicus-Brief-APA5.pdf. Shout out to my friends from college who had no idea they would end up as FBI agents. I can't say enough about how lucky the FBI is to have them—bicultural, multilingual women of color who understand complex cross-cultural dynamics and, even better, can blend into settings in ways that others cannot.
50. *Students for Fair Admissions*, 40.
51. Usha Lee McFarling, "In Counties with More Black Doctors, Black People Live Longer," *STAT News*, April 14, 2023, https://www.statnews.com/2023/04/14/black-doctors-primary-care-life-expectancy-mortality/. The article referenced is John E. Snyder, Rachel D. Upton, Thomas C. Hassett, Hyunjung Lee, Zakia Nouri, and Michael Dill, "Black Representation in the Primary Care Physician Workforce and Its Association with Population Life Expectancy and Mortality Rates in the US," *JAMA Network Open* 6, no. 4 (2023): e236687–e236687. Can Black individuals still be well-served by doctors of other races? Oftentimes, and usually they have no choice. Still, given the numerous reasons for African American individuals to distrust the medical profession (Tuskegee, anyone?), sometimes having someone who looks like you can affect whether you're willing to listen to directions for care. It can also influence whether a doctor is going to take the time to listen carefully to your concerns (which doctors are disincentivized to do thanks to our healthcare system) and take them seriously.
52. See McFarling, "In Counties," for commentary on data preparation.
53. Greenwood et al., "Physician-Patient Racial Concordance," 22194. In Justice Jackson's dissent, this same statistic was presented but with slightly different wording. It was challenged in the *Wall Street Journal* on the grounds that it was statistically impossible to double a survival rate. The error was likely a misread of the original article by a clerk. Basically, the Greenwood team article states that the risk of dying, when compared to White infants, is cut in half. The clerk probably read that to mean a doubling of the survival rate, versus the mortality rate being reduced. Either way, the bottom line remains that, on average, Black babies do better under the Black doctors.
54. Brad N. Greenwood, Rachel R. Hardeman, Laura Huang, and Aaron Sojourner, "Physician–Patient Racial Concordance and Disparities in Birthing Mortality for Newborns," *Proceedings of the National Academy of Sciences* 117, no. 35 (2020): 21194. See also the crisis related to Black women, mortality, and other issues when giving birth, which can even affect celebrities like Serena Williams. Serena Williams, "What My

Life-Threatening Experience Taught Me About Giving Birth," *CNN*, February 20, 2018, https://www.cnn.com/2018/02/20/opinions/protect-mother-pregnancy-williams-opinion/index.html.

55. Olivia Sanchez, "As Supreme Court Considers Affirmative Action, a Former Critic of the Policy Voices Regret," *USA Today*, May 31, 2023, https://www.usatoday.com/story/news/education/2023/05/31/affirmative-action-critic-has-regrets/70263878007/.
56. Sanchez, "Supreme Court Considers Affirmative Action."
57. "Complaint in *Students for Fair Admissions v. Harvard*," Students for Fair Admissions, November 2014, https://studentsforfairadmissions.org/wp-content/uploads/2014/11/SFFA-v.-Harvard-Complaint.pdf, 5.
58. "U.S. District Court District of Massachusetts Findings of Fact and Conclusions of Law Document 672," Harvard University, October 30, 2019, https://www.harvard.edu/admissionscase/wp-content/uploads/sites/6/2021/06/2019-10-30_dkt_672_findings_of_fact_and_conclusions_of_law.pdf, 53–54.
59. "U.S. District Court of Massachusetts," SFFA, 41–43.
60. "U.S. District Court of Massachusetts," SFFA, 43.
61. "Complaint," SFFA, 101.
62. "Petition for Writ of Certorari," Students for Fair Admissions, February 25, 2021, https://www.supremecourt.gov/DocketPDF/20/20-1199/169941/20210225095525027_Harvard%20Cert%20Petn%20Feb%2025.pdf, ii.
63. Cam E. Kettles and Claire Yuan, "Did Harvard Intentionally Discriminate? In Admissions Discrimination Suit, the Supreme Court Doesn't Say," *Harvard Crimson*, July 20, 2023, https://www.thecrimson.com/article/2023/7/20/sffa-decision-asian-american-discrimination/.
64. Kettles and Yuan, "Did Harvard Intentionally Discriminate?"
65. Kettles and Yuan, "Did Harvard Intentionally Discriminate?"
66. *Students for Fair Admissions*, 91.
67. *Students for Fair Admissions*, 114.
68. *Students for Fair Admissions*, 27.
69. "*Students for Fair Admissions v. Harvard* Appeal from the United States District Court," United States Court of Appeals for the First Circuit, November 12, 2020, http://media.ca1.uscourts.gov/pdf.opinions/19-2005P-01A.pdf, 73.
70. "*Students for Fair Admissions v. Harvard* Appeal," 73.
71. "*Students for Fair Admissions v. Harvard* Appeal," 73.
72. *Students for Fair Admissions*, 27.
73. April J. Anderson, "Race-Conscious Admissions and Equal Protection in Higher Education," Congressional Research Service, April 19, 2024, https://crsreports.congress.gov/product/pdf/R/R48043.
74. Jill Radsken, "Harvard Files Motion Backing Student Testimony at Trial," *Harvard Gazette*, September 21, 2018, https://news.harvard.edu/gazette/story/2018/09/harvard-motion-supports-student-testimony-at-trial/.
75. Kettles and Yuan, "Did Harvard Intentionally Discriminate?"
76. Kettles and Yuan, "Did Harvard Intentionally Discriminate?"
77. For examples of this dynamic, see OiYan Poon, *Asian American Is Not a Color: Conversations on Race, Affirmative Action, and Family* (Beacon Press, 2024).

78. Joan Biscupik, "Lawsuit: Harvard Ranks Asian American Students Lower on Personality Traits," *CNN*, July 3, 2018, https://www.cnn.com/2018/06/15/politics/harvard-admissions-asian-american/index.html.
79. "Oral Arguments, *Students for Fair Admissions v. Harvard*," Supreme Court of the United States (SCOTUS), 2022, https://www.supremecourt.gov/oral_arguments/argument_transcripts/2022/20-1199_bi7a.pdf, 3.
80. See, for example, Prasad Krishnamurthy, "Harvard's Cult of Personality," *The Hill*, October 26, 2022, https://thehill.com/opinion/education/3704542-harvards-cult-of-personality/.
81. Krishnamurthy, "Harvard's Cult of Personality."
82. "Oral Arguments," SCOTUS, 3–4.
83. "Harvard's Proposed Findings," Harvard, 14.
84. "Harvard's Proposed Findings," Harvard, 14.
85. Peter Arcidiacono, "Expert Report of Peter S. Arcidiacono: *Students for Fair Admissions, Inc. v. Harvard*," on the website of Brown University, June 15, 2018, https://www.brown.edu/Departments/Economics/Faculty/Glenn_Loury/louryhomepage/teaching/Affirmative_Action/Meeting_V/supporting_documents/Doc%20415-8%20-%20(Arcidiacono%20Expert%20Report).pdf, 52. White students ranked in the top 10% academically were between 4.4 and 6.3 percentage points more likely than Asian Americans to get a top rating on the two teacher letters, and about 7.6 percentage points more likely to snag a top rating for the counselor letter. See Arcidiacono, "Expert Report," 48. The same group of White students also received slightly higher ratings from alumni. It's easy to imagine alumni being the most enthusiastic when rating students: "These darn youngsters, they're amazing!" Common refrains from all of my friends who do alumni interviewing are (1) they would not be able to get admitted to their alma maters today, and today's students are way more accomplished than we were; and (2) despite being more accomplished than said alumni, almost none of the interviewees end up getting admitted, with some exceptions for recruited athletes.
86. Julie J. Park and Sooji Kim, "Harvard's Personal Rating: The Impact of Private High School Attendance," *Asian American Policy Review* 30 (2020): 79–80.
87. Jonathan D. Schwarz, "Lost in Translation: Elite College Admission and High School Differences in Letters of Recommendation," PhD dissertation, University of Notre Dame, 2016.
88. Tara Nicola and Sebastian Munoz-Najar Galvez, "Writing the Same Thing? Exploring Text Similarity in Counselor Recommendation Letters," paper presented at the ASHE (Association for the Study of Higher Education) Annual Conference, Las Vegas, NV, November 18, 2022.
89. I wrote for the *Chronicle of Higher Education* on the issue: "During the trial, Justice Samuel Alito asked Harvard's counsel how the personal rating for Asian Americans could be lower when alumni interviewers rated them just as well as other groups. Actually, Whites still outscored Asian Americans on alumni ratings when you break students out by academic ranking, and they outscored Asian Americans overall on the alumni personal rating. Alumni tended to give everyone better scores than teachers, counselors, and admissions officers. It makes sense because they evaluate fewer students so they are easier to impress than a teacher or a counselor: It's not hard to envision a middle aged alum gushing about how accomplished the youngsters are these days." See

Julie J. Park, "Does Harvard Really Discriminate Against Asian American Students?," *Chronicle of Higher Education*, March 7, 2023, https://www.chronicle.com/article/does-harvard-really-discriminate-against-asian-american-students.

90. "Document 672," Harvard, 110–11.
91. "Document 672," Harvard, 124.
92. "Document 672," Harvard, 112.
93. "Digest of Education Statistics 2013, Table 219.10, High School Graduates," NCES, https://nces.ed.gov/programs/digest/d17/tables/dt17_219.10.asp.
94. Anderson, "Race-Conscious Admissions," 11.
95. Kimberly West-Faulcon, "Affirmative Action After *SFFA v. Harvard*: The Other Defenses," *Syracuse Law Review* 74 (2024): 1101–78.
96. West-Faulcon, "Affirmative Action," 1146.
97. Thank you, Wikipedia: See "City of Richmond v. J.A. Croson Co.," Wikipedia, accessed November 10, 2025, https://en.wikipedia.org/wiki/City_of_Richmond_v._J.A._Croson_Co. In Richmond, prior to the case, only 0.67% of major construction contracts went to businesses under minority ownership, thanks in large part to discrimination. The city set a target for 30% of municipal contracts to be awarded to minority-owned businesses.
98. West-Faulcon, "Affirmative Action," 1150.
99. *Students for Fair Admissions*, 8.
100. *Students for Fair Admissions*, 20.
101. West-Faulcon, "Affirmative Action," 1160.
102. West-Faulcon, "Affirmative Action," 1162.
103. West-Faulcon, "Affirmative Action," 1165.
104. Anderson, "Race-Conscious Admissions," 14.

Chapter 3

1. Joe Biden, "Remarks by President Biden on the Supreme Court's Decision on Affirmative Action," White House website, June 29, 2023, https://www.whitehouse.gov/briefing-room/speeches-remarks/2023/06/29/remarks-by-president-biden-on-the-supreme-courts-decision-on-affirmative-action/.
2. Thomas Espenshade and Alexandra Walton Radford, *No Longer Separate: Race and Class in Elite College Admission and Campus Life* (Princeton University Press, 2009), 85–86. This group includes low-income Asian American students. Prior to the Harvard trial, a sentiment I commonly heard was the need to strike down race-conscious admissions so that low-income Asian Americans could benefit. People failed to realize that low-income Asian Americans were already benefiting from institutional policies that considered both race and social class in admissions.
3. Richard D. Kahlenberg, *The Remedy: Class, Race, and Affirmative Action* (HarperCollins, 1996).
4. Kahlenberg, *The Remedy*. He makes similar arguments in his book released in 2025, *Class Matters: The Fight to Get Beyond Race Preferences, Reduce Inequality, and Build Real Diversity at America's Colleges*.
5. Aatish Bhatia and Emily Badger, "Can You Create a Diverse College Class without Affirmative Action?," *New York Times*, March 9, 2024, https://www.nytimes.com/interactive/2024/03/09/upshot/affirmative-action-alternatives.html.

6. For more on undermatch, see Michael N. Bastedo and Allyson Flaster, "Conceptual and Methodological Problems in Research on College Undermatch," *Educational Researcher* 43, no. 2 (2014): 93–99. Richer institutions = the kind that likes to roll out chocolate fondue fountains for special occasions. Of course, chocolate fondue fountains are a crucial part of a high-quality educational experience. If you based college rankings on expenditures for fancy receptions, you'd probably just end up with the same list of schools, with the exception of the UCs (University of California institutions). No money for free chocolate fondue at the UCs! As a graduate student at UCLA, I remember sometimes missing the "free" food receptions that were common at my private undergraduate institution, but those dollars were put to better use for things like, you know, advancing social mobility. Of course, nothing is really free, and also, who needs a fondue fountain when you have $1 Taco Tuesdays at Rubio's?
7. Julie J. Park, "Will the Supreme Court Admissions Decision Boost Economic Diversity? Think Twice," *Dallas Morning News*, July 3, 2023, https://www.dallasnews.com/opinion/commentary/2023/07/03/will-the-supreme-court-admissions-decision-boost-economic-diversity-think-twice/.
8. "LDF Criticizes Recent Legal Claims About Thomas Jefferson High School Admissions Policy That Were Rejected by Federal Appeals Court," Legal Defense Fund, May 22, 2025, https://www.naacpldf.org/press-release/ldf-criticizes-recent-legal-claims-about-thomas-jefferson-high-school-admissions-policy-that-were-rejected-by-federal-appeals-court/.
9. People go bonkers about TJ, as in some people move to the area from overseas just to try for TJ. Think I'm kidding? Fairfax County is referenced in the ultimate Korean dystopian drama on college admissions, *Sky Castle*. Arguably as twisted as *Squid Games*! Like many magnet programs, TJ has experienced tremendous challenges in enrolling Black, Latinx, and lower-income students. In TJ's admissions system, the majority of seats are allocated through a race-neutral percent plan. Each middle school in the county can send up to 1.5% of its graduating class to TJ. In the new plan, not every student who is TJ eligible by being in the "top 1.5%" necessarily goes, but there is more representation from different middle schools in the county (and thus more diversity, both racial and economic) than there was before. The remaining seats go to students who score well on the TJ entrance exam, as well as students from neighboring counties, private schools, and the like. For more on the case, see Liebert, Cassidy, and Whitmore, "High School Admissions Process Deemed Non-Discriminatory," LCW Legal, June 22, 2023, https://www.lcwlegal.com/news/high-schools-admissions-process-deemed-non-discriminatory/.
10. Jonathan Feingold, "Trump's War Against DEI Isn't Going So Well in Virginia," *The Hill*, June 8, 2025, https://thehill.com/opinion/education/5337479-trump-dei-policy-fairfax-schools/.
11. Richard D. Kahlenberg, "Alito's Furious Dissent in a New Admissions Case Is a Good Sign for Student Body Diversity," *Slate*, February 22, 2024, https://slate.com/news-and-politics/2024/02/alito-thomas-jefferson-dissent-admissions-scotus.html. I kind of feel like I'm talking about a playground squabble or drama between high school cliques. "I thought we were friends!!! Why are you sitting with them?!"
12. Park, "Will the Supreme Court."
13. HAIL was phased out in 2023, leaving Go Blue for students with family incomes of $75,000 or less—I'll discuss some of the nuances of these programs in detail later.

14. See this helpful tweet from Professor Sarah Turner at the University of Virginia about how changes in Pell numbers are mostly due to shifts in how the eligibility formula is calculated versus institutional change. Sarah E. Turner (@turnersarahe), "PSA for people who write university press releases," X (website), August 29, 2024, https://x.com/turnersarahe/status/1829160074344071204.
15. "2022 Progress Report," American Talent Initiative, August 2022, https://americantalentinitiative.org/wp-content/uploads/2022/08/0819_ATI_2022-Progress-Report_v2-003.pdf.
16. "Progress," American Talent Initiative, accessed June 16, 2025, https://americantalentinitiative.org/progress/.
17. "Progress," American Talent Initiative.
18. "Progress," American Talent Initiative. Still waiting for the 2024 report in 2025.
19. "Five Strategies to Advance Progress," American Talent Initiative, April 2024, https://americantalentinitiative.org/wp-content/uploads/2024/04/ATI-FiveStrategiesToAdvanceProgress.pdf. Note this is the 2023 report.
20. "Five Strategies," American Talent Initiative.
21. $67,100 was the current threshold to qualify in April 2024. Household assets exclude home ownership and retirement funds, but includes assets like savings/checking, investments, and business net worth. For more information, see "Illinois Commitment Frequently Asked Questions," UIUC Office of Student Financial Aid, https://osfa.illinois.edu/types-of-aid/other-aid/illinois-commitment/illinois-commitment-frequently-asked-questions/.
22. Students work ten to twelve hours a week and also receive special support and mentoring through the program. For more, see "Illinois Promise," UIUC Office of Student Financial Aid, https://osfa.illinois.edu/types-of-aid/other-aid/illinois-promise/.
23. "Progress," American Talent Initiative. For example, Washington University in St. Louis nearly doubled the number of Pell Grant recipients, enrolling an additional 551 students from 2015 to 2022. Representation grew at Claremont McKenna from 13% in 2015 to 20% in 2022, representing a 69% growth rate.
24. Sean F. Reardon, Rachel Baker, Matt Kasman, Daniel Klasik, and Joseph B. Townsend, "Can Socioeconomic Status Substitute for Race in Affirmative Action College Admissions Policies? Evidence from a Simulation Model," white paper, Educational Testing Service, 2015, https://www.ets.org/Media/Research/pdf/reardon_white_paper.pdf.; Sean F. Reardon, Rachel Baker, Matt Kasman, Daniel Klasik, and Joseph B. Townsend, "What Levels of Racial Diversity Can Be Achieved with Socioeconomic-Based Affirmative Action? Evidence from a Simulation Model," *Journal of Policy Analysis and Management* 37, no. 3 (2018): 630–57.
25. To note, in the simulation, "strong" consideration to race was not very different from the consideration given to race/ethnicity in selective college admissions prior to the SCOTUS ruling, but "strong" consideration to class would be considerably more than what most campuses were doing at the time.
26. Bhatia and Badger, "Can You Create a Diverse Class."
27. The scenario where students only received preferences for income yielded an admitted pool that was 10% low-income (as measured by being in the bottom quarter of household income), with 13% of students being Black or Latinx. When Reardon gave a considerable extra boost to students who attended a high school with a high

concentration of poverty, low-income representation among admits inched up to 11%, and Black and Latinx representation grew to 18%.

28. Bhatia and Badger, "Can You Create a Diverse Class."
29. In this scenario, students of any race with an SAT of 1000 or more in high schools where at least 75% of students were from racially minoritized backgrounds would be in the selective college applicant pool thanks to serious investments in high school recruitment and outreach. Of note, there are a good number of students who fit this profile, but don't apply to elite colleges for a variety of reasons. Hmm, could a $90,000–$100,000 plus per year sticker price be a possible deterrent for anyone? Gulp.
30. Catherine Rickman, "TikTok Controversy at Yale's Holiday Dinner," *Food Republic*, January 3, 2024, https://www.foodrepublic.com/1483581/tiktok-controversy-yale-holiday-dinner/.
31. Caitlyn (@c.a.i.t.l.y.n), "yale holiday dinner accidentally radicalized me," TikTok, August 1, 2024, https://www.tiktok.com/@c.a.i.t.l.y.n/video/7318489949639249198?lang=en.
32. See for example Kamaron McNair, "Carolina Williams Chose Auburn over Yale, Has No Regrets," *CNBC*, June 14, 2024, https://www.cnbc.com/2024/06/14/carolina-williams-chose-auburn-over-yale-has-no-regrets.html.
33. Increases in applications did happen under test-optional admissions at many elite institutions, including some of those that have chosen to abandon the policy. Only time will tell how things will turn out for them in a new policy landscape where they no longer have access to a student's racial/ethnic demographic data. See Kelly Rosinger, Dominique J. Baker, Joseph Sturm, Wan Yu, Julie J. Park, OiYan Poon, Brian Heseung Kim, and Stephanie Breen, "Exploring the Relationship between Test-Optional Admissions and Selectivity and Enrollment Outcomes During the Pandemic," EdWorkingPaper 24-982 (Annenberg Institute for School Reform at Brown University, 2024).
34. Mark C. Henderson, Charlene Green, and Candice Chen, "What Does It Mean for Medical School Admissions to Be Socially Accountable?" *AMA Journal of Ethics* (December 2021), https://journalofethics.ama-assn.org/article/what-does-it-mean-medical-school-admissions-be-socially-accountable/2021-12.
35. Henderson et al., "What Does It Mean."
36. Usha Lee McFarling, "How One Medical School Became Remarkably Diverse Without Considering Race," *STAT News*, March 7, 2023, https://www.statnews.com/2023/03/07/how-one-medical-school-became-remarkably-diverse-without-considering-race/.
37. Nicholas A. Bowman and Michael N. Bastedo, "What Role May Admissions Office Diversity and Practices Play in Equitable Decisions?," *Research in Higher Education* 59 (2018): 430–47.
38. For more detail on the UC Davis admissions scale, see Joshua J. Fenton, Kevin Fiscella, Anthony F. Jerant, Francis Sousa, Mark Henderson, Tonya Fancher, and Peter Franks, "Reducing Medical School Admissions Disparities in an Era of Legal Restrictions: Adjusting for Applicant Socioeconomic Disadvantage," *Journal of Health Care for the Poor and Underserved* 27, no. 1 (2016): 22–34. Among efforts to consider socioeconomic challenge at the graduate school level, Kahlenberg lauds an approach used by UCLA School of Law, where students are asked to report their family's net worth, among other factors, and data are cross-checked against the FAFSA. (Disclosure, my brother is a professor there, and currently serving as Vice Dean for Community,

Equality, and Justice. He doesn't have any input into admissions.) Generally, low-income students are even more underrepresented in law schools than at the undergraduate level. In 2023 at UCLA School of Law, about 18% of the first-year class was first-generation college students. This is an improvement over when UCLA School of Law did not consider wealth at all, but there's still much room for growth, so I'm not sure it's really an exemplar. Consider that in 2022 for the first year class, UCDSOM had a first-generation enrollment of 42%, with 84% from economically disadvantaged backgrounds—showing that when there's a will, there's a way. In 2014, over a decade after UCLA Law started considering wealth, only 33 out of 1100 law students identified as Black/African American, sparking student protests. In more recent years, that number has gone up slightly, to 5.3% of the student body in 2023, which works out to roughly fifty-four Black students. Seeing that students reported a pretty negative climate in 2014 with only thirty-three Black students, I doubt that the enrollment of an extra 20 students has made a huge difference, although it's better than nothing. Latinx enrollment has fared better, at 17.3% of the class. While the country's racial wealth gap is persistent, there are a number of reasons why just adding wealth won't level the playing field. In an article for *The Atlantic*, Richard Rothstein, author of *The Color of Law*, who has argued for race-conscious solutions to race-related problems, noted how wealth-conscious affirmative action still "exclude[s] middle-class Black youths whose families' multigenerational experience of discrimination and exclusion still leaves them at a disadvantage compared with their white peers." Altogether, adding wealth to the socioeconomic measures that institutions receive from students seems to fit into the category of "it can't hurt, but isn't going to do that much," especially without additional institutional change. To note, while holistic in nature, the admissions program at UCLA School of Law is more formulaic than the process of holistic review utilized at most selective undergraduate institutions, in that decisions are driven largely by a series of indices related to undergraduate GPA and LSAT score, and students receive extra "boosts" related to SES. The field needs more research on how decision-making might differ in the undergraduate context when admission reviewers have access to this information.

39. Related to high school, information includes the name of the high school, some information on the locale (e.g., "city: small" or "town: remote"), size of the senior class, percent of students eligible for free and reduced-price lunch, average SAT scores at colleges attended (so of colleges that graduates attended, the average of median first-year SAT scores), percentage of seniors who took at least one AP course, average number of AP courses, average AP score, and overall number of AP courses taken. (Scores are generally three-year averages.) When a reviewer sees a student's SAT or ACT score (if provided), the 25th, 50th, and 75th percentile of SAT scores from the student's high school from the last three years is also provided, along with a metric showing the percentage of the senior class that took the SAT. Neighborhood and community information include a metric predicting the likelihood that a student from the high school or neighborhood attends a four-year institution, a measure reflecting information on the number of families that are married or coupled and single parent, and children living under the poverty line, median family income within the neighborhood/ high school district, a measure of housing stability (related to information on "vacancy rates, rental vs. home ownership, and mobility/housing turnover"), a measure of

educational attainment reached by adults in the community, and statistics on the likelihood of being a victim of a crime in the neighborhood or high school area. Besides information for the individual metrics, the reader gets a number 1–100 that represents an average for the six metrics (one average for the neighborhood, and another one for the high school, with a higher number reflecting "a higher level of challenge related to educational opportunities." See "Landscape Comprehensive Data and Methodology Overview," College Board, accessed November 1, 2024, https://secure-media.collegeboard.org/landscape/comprehensive-data-methodology-overview.pdf.

40. "The Landscape of Higher Education Research," University of Michigan Marsal School of Education, fall 2019, https://sites.marsal.umich.edu/mac/wp-content/uploads/sites/29/2022/11/Bastedo-landscape.pdf; Zachary Mabel, Michael D. Hurwitz, Jessica Howell, and Greg Perfetto, "Can Standardizing Applicant High School and Neighborhood Information Help to Diversify Selective Colleges?," *Educational Evaluation and Policy Analysis* 44, no. 3 (2022): 505–31; Michael N. Bastedo, D'Wayne Bell, Jessica S. Howell, Julian Hsu, Michael Hurwitz, Greg Perfetto, and Meredith Welch, "Admitting Students in Context: Field Experiments on Information Dashboards in College Admissions," *Journal of Higher Education* 93, no. 3 (2022): 327–74.
41. Once again, I'd love to be proven wrong, so we'll see—but I'm not betting the farm.
42. Mabel et al., "Can Standardizing Applicant High School."
43. Mabel et al., "Can Standardizing Applicant High School," 523.
44. Michael N. Bastedo and Nicholas A. Bowman, "Improving Admission of Low-SES Students at Selective Colleges: Results from an Experimental Simulation," *Educational Researcher* 46, no. 2 (2017): 67–77.
45. Additional information on the high school included the percentage enrolling at two and four-year colleges, average SAT/ACT scores, percentage on free or reduced lunch, and percentage of those who took an AP and received at least a 3 on the test.
46. Bastedo and Bowman, "Improving Admission," 67.
47. University of Michigan Marsal School of Education, 19.
48. Hailey Talbert, "In First Yale Class Since the End of Affirmative Action, Black and Latine Enrollment Share Remains Stable While Asian American Decreases," *Yale Daily News*, September 4, 2024, https://yaledailynews.com/blog/2024/09/04/in-first-yale-class-since-the-end-of-affirmative-action-black-and-latine-enrollment-share-remains-stable-while-asian-american-decreases/.
49. "Yale in MOHtion," Yale University, December 15, 2025, https://admissions.yale.edu/Yale-in-MOHtion.
50. Michael N. Bastedo, Mark Umbricht, Emma Bausch, Bo-Kyung Byun, and Yiping Bai, "Contextualized High School Performance: Evidence to Inform Equitable Holistic, Test-Optional, and Test-Free Admissions Policies," *AERA Open* 9 (2023): 23328584231197413.
51. To be more specific: "This [measure] is equal to the raw score minus the median score at a student's high school, divided by the standard deviation of the score at the school. Thus, the contextualized high school GPA measures how far a student is from the median student in their high school." See Bastedo et al., "Contextualized High School Performance," 6.
52. Bastedo et al., "Contextualized High School Performance,"14.
53. Bastedo et al., "Contextualized High School Performance," 12.

54. Michael N. Bastedo, Mark Umbricht, Emma Bausch, Bo-Kyung Byun, and Yiping Bai, "How Well Do Contextualized Admissions Measures Predict Success for Low-Income Students, Women, and Underrepresented Students of Color?," *Journal of Diversity in Higher Education* (2023): 1–16.
55. Bastedo et al., "How Well Do Contextualized Admissions Measures," 10–11.
56. Rosinger et al., "Exploring the Relationship."
57. Some institutions that have brought back testing may see some growth in low and moderate-income enrollment, but it will be difficult to attribute it to being test-required, since some are boosting financial aid at the same time. For example, after announcing a move back to test-required, Dartmouth announced that it will now foot the full bill of tuition, room, board, and fees for students from families making under $125,000 in March 2024. Previously, it covered these expenses for students from families making $65,000 or less. See "Dartmouth Receives Its Largest Scholarship Bequest," Dartmouth University Office of Communications, March 2024, https://student-affairs.dartmouth .edu/news/2024/03/dartmouth-receives-its-largest-ever-scholarship-bequest.
58. David Leonhardt, "The Misguided War on the SAT," *New York Times*, January 7, 2024, https://www.nytimes.com/2024/01/07/briefing/the-misguided-war-on-the-sat.html.
59. Indeed, I only applied to my ultimate destination because they visited my school and I wanted an excuse to skip physics that day.
60. Ozan Jaquette and Karina G. Salazar, "A Sociological Analysis of Structural Racism in 'Student List' Lead Generation Products," *Educational Evaluation and Policy Analysis* 46, no. 2 (2024): 301; Karina Salazar, Ozan Jaquette, and Crystal Han, "Geodemographics of Student List Purchases by Public Universities: A First Look," Institute for College Access & Success, September 2022, https://ticas.org/wpcontent/uploads/2022/09 /Geodemographics-ofStudent-List-Purchases_A-First-Look.pdf.
61. Taylor Odle and Jennifer Delaney, "Experimental Evidence on 'Direct Admissions' from Four States: Impacts on College Application and Enrollment," EdWorkingPaper 23-834 (Annenberg Institute at Brown University, 2023), https://doi.org/10.26300/6xtn -2j84.
62. Elizabeth Burland, Susan Dynarski, Katherine Michelmore, Stephanie Owen, and Shwetha Raghuraman, "The Power of Certainty: Experimental Evidence on the Effective Design of Free Tuition Programs," *American Economic Review: Insights* 5, no. 3 (2023): 293–310; Susan Dynarski, C. J. Libassi, Katherine Michelmore, and Stephanie Owen, "Closing the Gap: The Effect of Reducing Complexity and Uncertainty in College Pricing on the Choices of Low-Income Students," *American Economic Review* 111, no. 6 (2021): 1721–56.
63. Burdland et al., "Power of Certainty."
64. Burdland et al., "Power of Certainty."
65. The rollout was plagued with multiple issues, from delayed availability to website glitches to families having trouble opening accounts.
66. Laura W. Perna, Jeremy Wright-Kim, and Nathan Jiang, "Money Matters: Understanding How Colleges and Universities Use Their Websites to Communicate Information About How to Pay College Costs," *Educational Policy* 35, no. 7 (2021): 1333.
67. Phillip Levine, "A Problem of Fit: How the Complexity of College Pricing Hurts Students—And Universities," MyinTuition, accessed December 1, 2024, https:// myintuition.org/a-problem-of-fit/.

68. "Ohio State University—Columbus Campus," College Board, 2025, https://bigfuture.collegeboard.org/colleges/ohio-state-university-columbus-campus/tuition-and-costs.
69. Christopher Bennett, Brent Evans, and Christopher Marsicano, "Taken for Granted? Effects of Loan-Reduction Initiatives on Student Borrowing, Admission Metrics, and Campus Diversity," *Research in Higher Education* 62 (2021): 569–99.
70. Thanks to AP credit, I triple majored, studied abroad, and graduated in four years. I excelled at finding courses that would fulfill multiple major requirements. Military Culture—really a fascinating class—knocked out requirements for English, sociology, and women's studies. Others with lots of AP credit just graduate early, saving tuition money.
71. "Retention and Graduation Rates for New First-Year Students: The Ohio State University - Columbus Campus: Entering Autumn Terms 2013-2022," Ohio State University, 2023, https://oesar.osu.edu/pdf/grad_rates/RETENTION_SUMMARY.pdf.
72. Eli Dvorkin and Brody Viney, "New York's Free Tuition Program Falling Short," Center for an Urban Future, https://files.eric.ed.gov/fulltext/ED606560.pdf.
73. Lisa Philip, "Western Illinois University Revokes, Then Reinstates Scholarships for Students of Color," *WBEZ*, July 31, 2023, https://www.wbez.org/education/2023/07/31/western-illinois-university-revokes-then-reinstates-scholarships-for-students-of-color.
74. Liam Knox, "Ed Blum Takes a Victory Lap," *Inside Higher Ed*, February 19, 2025, https://www.insidehighered.com/news/government/politics-elections/2025/02/19/sffa-president-affirmative-action-bans-growing-impact. As noted in the article: "Blum doesn't actually believe the decision itself extends to those programs. He does think they're illegal—there just hasn't been a successful case challenging them yet. 'I haven't really made myself clear on this, which is my fault, but the SFFA opinion didn't change the law for those policies' in internships and scholarships, he said. 'But those policies have always been, in my opinion, outside of the scope of our civil rights law and actionable in court.'"
75. Some audiences are more receptive than others to discussions on reparations. Still, it's often hard to get a conversation going, in my experience.
76. Dominique Baker, this one's for you.
77. Liam Knox, "Could Reparations Replace Race-Conscious Admissions?," *Inside Higher Ed*, November 27, 2023, https://www.insidehighered.com/news/admissions/traditional-age/2023/11/27/could-reparations-replace-race-conscious-admissions.
78. This comment isn't to say that continuing legacy admissions is a good idea, just pointing out the ridiculousness of it all.
79. Knox, "Could Reparations Replace."
80. Students for Fair Admissions v. Harvard, 600 U.S. 181 (2023) (statement of Thomas, J. concurring), https://www.supremecourt.gov/opinions/22pdf/20-1199_hgdj.pdf, 20.
81. For an overview, see "Toward an Understanding of Percentage Plans in Higher Education: Are They Effective Substitutes for Affirmative Action?," US Commission on Civil Rights, April 1, 2001, https://www.usccr.gov/files/pubs/percent/stmnt.htm.
82. The late Ruth Bader Ginsburg pointed out that only an "ostrich" would see percent plans as truly race neutral. (In other words, only an ostrich with its head stuck in the sand would be oblivious to how percent plans only work due to pervasive racial segregation in K–12 education.) No offense to the actual ostriches out there. Richard

Primus, "Affirmative Action in College Admissions: Here to Stay," *New York Times*, June 23, 2016, https://www.nytimes.com/2016/06/23/opinion/affirmative-action-in-college-admissions-here-to-stay.html.

83. Scott Jaschik, "Report Questions Benefits of 10 Percent Admissions Plans," *Inside Higher Ed*, January 19, 2021, https://www.insidehighered.com/admissions/article/2021/01/19/report-questions-benefits-10-percent-admissions-plans.
84. Zachary Bleemer, "Affirmative Action and Its Race-Neutral Alternatives," *Journal of Public Economics* 220 (2023): 104839.
85. "Toward an Understanding," US Commission on Civil Rights; see also Jaschik, "Report Questions Benefits."
86. Bleemer, "Affirmative Action"; see Appendix A, 8.
87. Park, "Will the Supreme Court."
88. Jaschik, "Report Questions Benefits."
89. Matt S. Giani, Richard Murphy, Stella M. Flores, Jori Barash, Brian Dixon, and Julio Mena Bernal, "From Passive Promises to Proactive Guarantees: The Efficacy of Financial Certainty Interventions Among Automatically (In-) Admissible Students," EdWorkingPaper No. 25-1158 (Annenberg Institute for School Reform at Brown University, March 2025), 1, https://doi.org/10.26300/bk34-s137.
90. Giani et al., "From Passive Promises," 5.
91. Bryan Walsh, "Why the Ivy League Should Use a Lottery System for Admissions," *Vox*, April 19, 2023, https://www.vox.com/future-perfect/2023/4/19/23689402/college-admissions-lottery-ivy-league; Frederick M. Hess, "A Modest Proposal Regarding College Admissions," *Forbes*, March 15, 2019, https://www.forbes.com/sites/frederickhess/2019/03/15/a-modest-proposal-regarding-college-admissions/?sh=4db084c11fe5; Elizabeth Grace Matthew, "College Admission by Lottery Isn't a Bad Idea—Here's How to Make It Work," *The Hill*, July 10, 2023, https://thehill.com/opinion/education/3969019-college-admission-by-lottery-isnt-a-bad-idea-heres-how-to-make-it-work/.
92. Alia Wong, "The Case for a College Admissions Lottery," *The Atlantic*, August 2, 2018, https://www.theatlantic.com/education/archive/2018/08/lottery-college-admissions/566492/.
93. Of course when you actually think through the scenario of a lottery, it's a little more offensive than the implied neutrality and randomness of "lottery" suggests. Do you have your big Powerball cage of Ping-Pong balls for low-income students, and then pick the first one hundred or so? Lottery advocates would say no, you'd have the computer do it! But basically it's the same scenario, just done by computer sampling. For decades, people argued that race-conscious admissions stigmatized racially minoritized students, making them think they were being picked just for their race/ethnicity. (Of course, I would beg to disagree, and you can read David Card's expert report in the *SFFA* case for a deep dive on the independent effect linked with race/ethnicity in admissions at Harvard.) Strangely, no one brings up this same argument when talking about lotteries, even though it seems like it would be pretty reductionist.
94. Anthony Carnevale and Stephen Rose, "Socioeconomic Status, Race/Ethnicity, and Selective College Admissions," in *America's Untapped Resource: Low-Income Students in Higher Education*, ed. Richard D. Kahlenberg (Century Foundation, 2003), 101–56, https://www.immagic.com/eLibrary/ARCHIVES/GENERAL/TCF_US/C030320C.pdf.

95. Rebecca Zwick, "College Admissions in Twenty-First-Century America: The Role of Grades, Tests, and Games of Chance," *Harvard Educational Review* 77, no. 4 (2007): 419–29.
96. Dominique J. Baker and Michael N. Bastedo, "What If We Leave It Up to Chance? Admissions Lotteries and Equitable Access at Selective Colleges," *Educational Researcher* 51, no. 2 (2022): 134–45.
97. Baker and Bastedo, "What If We Leave It Up," 138.
98. Baker and Bastedo, "What If We Leave It Up," 139.
99. Due to data issues, they were unable to conduct stratified sampling by race.
100. Interestingly, the share of male students would drop notably (by up to 40%) if GPA were used as the sole criteria.
101. Stephen J. Burd, ed., *Lifting the Veil on Enrollment Management: How a Powerful Industry is Limiting Social Mobility in American Higher Education* (Harvard Education Press, 2024); Stephen Burd, "Crisis Point: How Enrollment Management and the Merit-Aid Arms Race Are Derailing Public Higher Education," New America, February 13, 2020, https://www.newamerica.org/education-policy/reports/crisis-point-how-enrollment-management-and-merit-aid-arms-race-are-destroying-public-higher-education/.
102. Stephen Burd, "Too Much Merit Aid for Those Not in Need," New America, August 17, 2023, https://www.newamerica.org/weekly/too-much-merit-aid-for-those-not-in-need/.
103. Vige Barrie, "Hamilton to Eliminate Merit Scholarships," Hamilton College, March 14, 2024, https://www.hamilton.edu/news/story/hamilton-to-eliminate-merit-scholarships.
104. Eric Hoover, "There's No Secret Sauce: An Enrollment Leader Looks Back at 35 Years," *Chronicle of Higher Education*, July 25, 2024, https://www.chronicle.com/article/theres-no-secret-sauce-an-enrollment-leader-looks-back-at-35-years.
105. I have great memories of doing a panel on race-conscious admissions at Hamilton on a snowy night before the world shut down in early 2020. Hamilton brought in both pro and con perspectives and we had a robust, collegial debate. Despite the cold temperatures, the building was packed, and I remember being impressed at the curiosity and engagement shown by the students.
106. Donald E. Heller, "Financial Aid and Admission: Tuition Discounting, Merit Aid and Need-Aware Admission," paper presented at the National Association for College Admission Counseling, Seattle, WA, 2008.
107. Rick Seltzer, "What Happens When Colleges Drop Need-Blind Admissions," *Inside Higher Ed*, July 21, 2016, https://www.insidehighered.com/news/2016/07/21/what-happens-when-colleges-drop-need-blind-admissions.
108. Hoover, "There's No Secret Sauce."
109. Hoover, "There's No Secret Sauce."
110. Ian Morse, "Expansion Creates Means for Future Need-Blind Status," *The Lafayette*, April 10, 2023, https://lafayettestudentnews.com/25078/news/expansion-creates-means-for-future-need-blind-status/.
111. Jeffrey Selingo, *Who Gets In and Why: A Year Inside College Admissions* (Scribner, 2020).
112. Anthony Carnevale, Zachary Mabel, Kathryn Peltier Campbell, *Race-Conscious Affirmative Action in College Admissions: A Review of Evidence and Policy Options* (Georgetown Center for Education and the Workforce, 2020), https://cew.georgetown.edu/wp-content/uploads/cew-race_conscious_affirmative_action-fr.pdf, 11.

113. Scott Jaschik, “Without Preference, Amherst Legacy Admits Fell 11 Percent,” *Inside Higher Ed*, June 12, 2023, https://www.insidehighered.com/news/admissions/traditional-age/2023/06/12/without-preference-amherst-legacy-admits-fell-11-percent.
114. Raj Chetty, David J. Deming, and John N. Friedman, “Diversifying Society’s Leaders? The Causal Effects of Admission to Highly Selective Private Colleges,” no. w31492 (National Bureau of Economic Research, 2023). Those from the top 1% of household incomes are about 58% more likely to enroll at an “Ivy-Plus” school than students who have the same SAT/ACT scores coming from the 70th to 80th percentile ($93,000–$114,000) of household incomes.

Chapter 4

1. I still remember calling the College Board to find out my scores early from a payphone, and then having to wait in suspense until the actual scores came because I thought I misheard the robot reporter.
2. “Test Optional-Growth Chronology 2005–2022,” FairTest, September 4, 2024, https://www.fairtest.org/sites/default/files/Optional-Growth-Chronology.pdf.
3. “Test-Optional List,” FairTest, accessed September 4, 2024, https://fairtest.org/test-optional-list/.
4. Some people will readily acknowledge their worldview while others will say, “Huh? What’s a worldview? I don’t have a worldview!” And that, folks, is a worldview.
5. Nicholas Lemann, *The Big Test: The Secret History of the American Meritocracy* (Macmillan, 2000).
6. Christopher Bennett, “Untested Admissions: Examining Changes in Application Behaviors and Student Demographics Under Test-Optional Policies,” *American Educational Research Journal* 59, no. 1 (2022): 180–216.
7. Bennett, “Untested Admissions,” 200.
8. Jill Barshay, “Test-Optional Policies Didn’t Do Much to Diversify College Student Populations,” *Hechinger Report*, May 10, 2021, https://hechingerreport.org/proof-points-test-optional-policies-didnt-do-much-to-diversify-college-student-populations/.
9. That would be a 1.5 percentage point difference. Don’t forget the half point! Why do I say 10 to 15%? Well, it looks like an increase of 15% when you just calculate the gain, but Zach describes the gain as “perhaps 10 percent” in his paper, so maybe he wanted to hedge his bets a little. See Zachary Bleemer, “Affirmative Action and Its Race-Neutral Alternatives,” *Journal of Public Economics* 220 (2023): 2. Also see Bennett, “Untested Admissions,” 200.
10. Zachary Bleemer, email to the author, November 22, 2024.
11. Bleemer, “Affirmative Action and Its Race-Neutral Alternatives,” 1.
12. Andrew S. Belasco, Kelly O. Rosinger, and James C. Hearn, “The Test-Optional Movement at America’s Selective Liberal Arts Colleges: A Boon for Equity or Something Else?,” *Educational Evaluation and Policy Analysis* 37, no. 2 (2015): 206–23. For an overview of other studies on test-optional since 2015, not including our most recent CAF Co-LAB study, see Reginald M. Gooch, Vinetha K. Belur, Sara B. Haviland, and Ou Lydia Liu, “Test-Optional Policies: Impacts to Date and Recommendations for Equity in Admissions,” *Journal of Postsecondary Student Success* 3, no. 4 (2024): 1–19.
13. Kelly Rosinger, Dominique J. Baker, Joseph Sturm, Wan Yu, Julie J. Park, OiYan Poon, Brian Heseung Kim, and Stephanie Breen, “Exploring the Relationship Between

Test-Optional Admissions and Selectivity and Enrollment Outcomes During the Pandemic," EdWorkingPaper 24-982 (Annenberg Institute for School Reform at Brown University, 2024).

14. See Belasco et al., "Test-Optional Movement."
15. Trust me: On multiple occasions, I've wanted to blast results out via social media or op-eds, and they have pulled me back time and time again. During the pandemic, test-optional was linked with higher Pell Grant student enrollment at highly selective institutions in some, but not all, of the models. Kelly urged me to include the qualifier that the result was not significant in all of the models that the team ran. This issue brings up the interpretive aspect of statistics—when to pay attention to a finding or not. Given that we very well could have seen enrollment trends go in the opposite direction (i.e., a notable drop in low-income enrollment at highly selective universities due to the crushing effect of the pandemic on families), I still think the finding around low-income enrollment at highly selective schools is worth paying attention to, although it's less of a "slam-dunk" finding.
16. Shout out to Joseph Strum, Stephanie Breen, and Wan Yu for doing the heavy lifting on the verification of the dataset.
17. Thinking back to discussion from chapter 1 on how use of race-conscious admissions wasn't linked with higher Black enrollment at mid-selective institutions, it's possible that these institutions were using test scores in a more rote, cut-off fashion. Thus, test-optional may have been especially beneficial for students who would have been shut out under test-required. prabhdeep singh kehal, Daniel Hirschman, and Ellen Berrey, "When Affirmative Action Disappears: Unexpected Patterns in Student Enrollments at Selective US Institutions, 1990–2016," *Sociology of Race and Ethnicity* 7, no. 4 (2021): 543–60.
18. "University of Michigan—Ann Arbor Enrollment Headcounts by Academic Level & Citizenship Status," University of Michigan Office of Budget and Planning, October 6, 2023, https://obp.umich.edu/wp-content/uploads/pubdata/factsfigures/enrollment_umaa.pdf.
19. Julie J. Park, Nancy Wong, Pearl Lo, Jia Zheng, OiYan Poon, and Kelly Rosinger, "Test-Free Admissions at Selective Institutions: Perspectives From Admissions Professionals," *Journal of College Student Development* 65, no. 4 (2024): 438–42.
20. See for example "Common Dataset Info on Test Scores," DC Urban Moms & Dads, accessed September 4, 2024, https://www.dcurbanmom.com/jforum/posts/list/1221659.page.
21. For more on the very unequal roots of standardized testing, see Lemann, *Big Test*. It's interesting to wonder whether we would have the same swing back to test-required if the country had continued the momentum that seemed so promising in 2020.
22. Stuart Schmill, "MIT's Stuart Schmill on Why the SAT and ACT Are No Longer Required," *MIT News*, March 28, 2022, https://news.mit.edu/2022/stuart-schmill-sat-act-requirement-0328.
23. See Paul Tough, *The Inequality Machine: How Universities Are Creating a More Unequal World-and What to Do About It* (Random House, 2021). The College Board responded to Tough's criticism; see "Fact Checking Paul Tough's The Years that Matter Most," College Board, accessed December 1, 2024, https://newsroom.collegeboard.org/pages/paul-tough. Their critique seemed to miss Tough's point that the number of

lower-income students who actually used the Khan Academy program for the number of hours needed to improve one's score was pretty small.

A report by the ACT points to how a challenge with online test prep effectiveness is actually getting students to use the program; see Edgar I. Sanchez and Ty M. Cruce, "No Pain, No Gain: Lessons from a Test Prep Experiment," Research Report 2019-3 (ACT, 2019), accessed December 1, 2024, https://files.eric.ed.gov/fulltext/ED602026.pdf. The authors note: "Overall, most students did not use the course as intended. Despite all the students in our sample expressing interest in using the product for free prior to their test date, many of the students who were assigned to the treatment group did not actually use the product during the month prior to their test date. These results indicate that simply granting a population of students access to a self-directed test preparation product such as [ACT Online Program] would not be sufficient for improving the college readiness of this population, as many of these students would not make adequate use of the product. Students may not be self-directed enough to engage with an unstructured test preparation program despite motivation to perform well on a standardized test."

24. Derek C. Briggs, "Preparation for College Admission Exams," 2009 NACAC Discussion Paper (National Association for College Admission Counseling, 2009).
25. Soo-yong Byun and Hyunjoon Park, "The Academic Success of East Asian American Youth: The Role of Shadow Education," *Sociology of Education* 85, no. 1 (2012): 40–60.
26. Tamar Lewin, "Abuse Feared as SAT Test Changes Disability Policy," *New York Times*, July 15, 2002, https://www.nytimes.com/2002/07/15/us/abuse-feared-as-sat-test-changes-disability-policy.html. When all else fails, some parents have resorted to outright buying higher scores for their kids (cough, Felicity Huffman). Yes, the Varsity Blues scandal included "only" about fifty kids (whose parents paid a cumulative $25 million. Twenty. Five. Million!) but it still spoke volumes about both the lengths that wealthy parents are willing to go to get their children into a prestigious university, as well as the loopholes in the system vulnerable to exploitation.
27. Or that anyone can gauge whether they should submit test scores or not because the Common Dataset is publicly available.
28. Sanchez and Cruce, "No Pain, No Gain," 2.
29. "Which Tests Does Each State Require?," *Education Week*, February 2017, https://www.edweek.org/teaching-learning/what-tests-does-each-state-require/2017/02.
30. Joshua Hyman, "ACT for All: The Effect of Mandatory College Entrance Exams on Postsecondary Attainment and Choice," *Education Finance and Policy* 12, no. 3 (2017): 281–311.
31. To note, at the time of Hyman's work, the national average on the ACT was a 21.
32. Susan Dynarski, "How Universal College Admission Tests Help Low-Income Students," *New York Times*, July 14, 2017, https://www.nytimes.com/2017/07/14/upshot/how-universal-college-admission-tests-help-low-income-students.html.
33. Forget high school, my first grader took the iReady math test three times this year, as well as a literacy screener, which was also taken three times. I'm not saying that kids should be targeted for college based on their first-grade scores—definitely not—but the point is that there is no shortage of testing out there. If anything, there's too much.
34. Wai is the brother-in-law of my friend Miles Chen, esteemed cofounder of the series "Lecture and a Film," a.k.a. LAAF.

35. For critiques, see M. W. Feldman and Jessica Riskin, "Why Biology Is Not Destiny," *New York Review*, April 21, 2022, https://www.nybooks.com/articles/2022/04/21/why-biology-is-not-destiny-genetic-lottery-kathryn-harden/; Anne O'Connor, Brenna M. Henn, Emily Klancher Merchant, and Tina Rulli, "Why DNA Is No Key to Social Equality: On Kathryn Paige Harden's 'The Genetic Lottery,'" *Los Angeles Review of Books*, September 21, 2021, https://lareviewofbooks.org/article/why-dna-is-no-key-to-social-equality-on-kathryn-paige-hardens-the-genetic-lottery/.
36. "SAT Program Results Show Increased Participation for the Class of 2022," College Board, September 22, 2022, https://newsroom.collegeboard.org/sat-program-results-show-increased-participation-class-2022.
37. "Morning Consult Survey Commissioned by College Board Reveals Attitudes Toward College and Admissions," College Board, March 21, 2023, https://allaccess.collegeboard.org/morning-consult-survey-commissioned-college-board-reveals-attitudes-toward-college-and-admissions. For the full report, see Morning Consult, "Student and Parent Attitudes on College Admissions," College Board, 2021, https://research.collegeboard.org/media/pdf/student-parent-attitudes-college-admissions.pdf, 27. Don't take away students' choices; it's un-American!
38. Another choice tidbit from the College Board survey: "Parents and students are in consensus that college entrance exams, along with GPA, provide students the most equal opportunity to showcase their strengths over other admissions criteria" (16). Basically, students and parents received ten options to pick from in response to the question "Which of the following admissions criteria do you think provides students the most equal opportunity to showcase their strengths, regardless of their background? Select your top three" (16). First, students and parents technically aren't in consensus: Students put teacher or counselor letters of recommendation ahead of test scores, while parents put test scores as their second top pick. Second, the ten options are chock-full of items rife with inequities, such as internships, extracurricular activities, application interviews, and legacy status, so it's not that surprising that students and families would view test scores as a more equitable opportunity than, say, legacy status. One interesting tidbit is that both students and parents viewed class rank as being much less likely to provide equal opportunity to showcase strengths, maybe because only so many students can rank in the top 10% of a class. It's quite possible that respondents interpreted "most equal opportunity" as being equated to "what everyone technically has the ability to do," versus being really reflective of equity, which might explain why admissions criteria like GPA, test scores, and letters are viewed as having more equal opportunity for respondents—because technically everyone can have a GPA, test score (if fees are waived), or letter.
39. Rankin & Associates, "Dartmouth College Climate Assessment," Dartmouth College, May 2016, https://www.dartmouth.edu/oir/rankinandassociates_final_revised_report.pdf.
40. Liam Knox, "Harvard and Caltech Restore Test Requirements," *Inside Higher Ed*, April 12, 2024, https://www.insidehighered.com/news/admissions/traditional-age/2024/04/12/sudden-move-harvard-caltech-return-test-requirements.
41. The Upshot, "The Best and Worst Places to Grow Up: How Your Area Compares," *New York Times*, May 3, 2015, https://www.nytimes.com/interactive/2015/05/03/upshot/the-best-and-worst-places-to-grow-up-how-your-area-compares.html; Aatish Bhatia and

Claire Cain Miller, "Explore How Income Influences Attendance at 139 Top Colleges," *New York Times*, September 11, 2023, https://www.nytimes.com/interactive/2023/09/11/upshot/college-income-lookup.html.

42. John Friedman, Bruce Sacerdote, and Michele Tine, "Standardized Test Scores and Academic Performance at Ivy-Plus Colleges," Opportunity Insights, January 2024, https://opportunityinsights.org/wp-content/uploads/2024/01/SAT_ACT_on_Grades.pdf.
43. Elizabeth Cascio, Bruce Sacerdote, Doug Staiger, and Michele Tine, "Report from Working Group on the Role of Standardized Test Scores in Undergraduate Admissions," Dartmouth College, January 2024, https://home.dartmouth.edu/sites/home/files/2024-02/sat-undergrad-admissions.pdf. These were simpler days for President Beilock; a few months later she was censured by her faculty for having the police arrest students just two hours after they had set up a nonviolent encampment. Now of course the Trump administration loves her, or at least they did as of mid-2025.
44. David Leonhardt, "The Misguided War on the SAT," *New York Times*, January 7, 2024, https://www.nytimes.com/2024/01/07/briefing/the-misguided-war-on-the-sat.html.
45. As noted in David Leonhardt, "Affordable Housing and the NIMBY Problem," *New York Times*, August 8, 2019, https://www.nytimes.com/2019/08/08/opinion/affordable-housing-nimby-seattle.html.
46. Nell Gluckman and Francie Diep, "Does Raj Chetty Practice What He Preaches?," *Chronicle of Higher Education*, September 23, 2023, https://www-chronicle-com/article/does-raj-chetty-practice-what-he-preaches.
47. Gluckman and Diep, "Does Raj Chetty." Also, trivia: Chetty is the William A. Ackman Professor of Public Economics at Harvard, with William A. Ackman being the Trump-supporting billionaire who has been on the warpath against "DEI" while espousing support for "diversity with a lower case *d*." See: Elizabeth Dwoskin, "How a Liberal Billionaire Became America's Leading Anti-DEI Crusader," *Washington Post*, February 11, 2024. Would people be happy if we just said we were supporting "little d-diversity?" Bonus trivia: Ackman wrote his senior thesis at Harvard on college admissions. Yes, we're coming full circle here.
48. Indeed, I repeatedly tried to get my then toddler to eat okra because of an article in *The Atlantic* where Chetty said his mom fed him a lot of okra because she thought it was good for brain development. Sadly, said toddler wasn't into okra, but that's okay.
49. A quick detour to share my own worldview on testing: I'm somewhat of an agnostic. I definitely have benefited from the system, as I tested well growing up and attended college on a full-tuition scholarship thanks to my test scores. While it's too early to know how my kids will do with tests, the older one has already had tons of standardized testing in first grade (thanks iReady!) and so far is doing fine with it. Their dad tests well, and even if they don't, we have the resources and know how to get them better scores. Of course, through nonshady means. We definitely can't afford the Varsity Blues path. Over the years, I've known many brilliant people who didn't test well. I also know many "book-smart" people who test well and are certainly intelligent, but I don't think society is best served when elite institutions are dominated by this population.
50. Friedman et al., "Standardized Test Scores," 1.
51. Cascio et al., "Report from Working Group," 9.
52. Leonhardt, "Misguided War."

53. The undercurrent seemed to be something like, "Well, you definitely want to keep this subpar, '3.25 material' out of the Ivies."
54. Cascio et al., "Report from Working Group," 9.
55. "Yale Announces New Test-Flexible Admissions Policy," *Yale News*, February 22, 2024, https://news.yale.edu/2024/02/22/yale-announces-new-test-flexible-admissions-policy.
56. I was aware that I needed something in the 3.5 or higher ballpark to look better for graduate school applications. Junior year helped a lot when I studied abroad, padding my GPA with courses with generous grading.
57. Teresa Watanabe, "UC Applications Rise for Fall 2024 with Gains in Diversity and Transfer Applicants," *Los Angeles Times*, March 6, 2024, https://www.latimes.com/california/story/2024-03-06/uc-applications-rise-for-fall-2024-with-gains-in-diversity-and-transfer-applicants.
58. Cascio et al., "Report from Working Group," 16.
59. Brian Heseung Kim, Mark Freeman, Trent Kajikawa, Honeiah Karimi, and Preston Magouirk, "Unpacking Applicant Race and Ethnicity, Part 2," Common App, October 2022, https://s3.us-west-2.amazonaws.com/ca.research.publish/Research_Briefs_2022/2022_2023_Report_RaceEthnicity_2_2022.10.10.pdf, 21–22.
60. Michael N. Bastedo, Mark Umbricht, Emma Bausch, Bo-Kyung Byun, and Yiping Bai, "Contextualized High School Performance: Evidence to Inform Equitable Holistic, Test-Optional, and Test-Free Admissions Policies," *AERA Open* 9 (2023): 23328584231197413.
61. Michael N. Bastedo, Kristen M. Glasener, K. C. Deane, and Nicholas A. Bowman, "Contextualizing the SAT: Experimental Evidence on College Admission Recommendations for Low-SES Applicants," *Educational Policy* 36, no. 2 (2022): 282–311.
62. Leonhardt, "Misguided War."
63. I say that as someone who graduated with a decent college GPA, but guess what—I didn't have to work! Embarrassingly, thanks to coming from an upper middle-class household and attending university on a full-tuition scholarship, money was a highly abstract concept to me during my undergraduate years. I remember swiping my student ID—the "Vandy card"—loaded with cash supplied by my parents to buy a $3 Naked Juice without a second thought. In the meantime, I patted myself on the back for being highly involved in extracurricular activities, oblivious to how my involvement was enabled by financial privilege. For more on how working can affect students' lives, see Rebecca Summer, Megan McCoy, Isabelle Trujillo, and Esperanza Rodriguez, "Support for Working Students: Understanding the Impacts of Employment on Students' Lives," *Journal of College Student Retention: Research, Theory & Practice* 26, no. 4 (2025): 1123–46.
64. Friedman et al., "Standardized Test Scores," 1.
65. Jake Vigdor (@JakeVigdor), "Here's a sentence you won't read in @ProfDavidDeming's pro-testing @theAtlantic essay," Twitter (now X), March 15, 2023, https://x.com/JakeVigdor/status/1765843449969008776.
66. Jesse Rothstein (@jrothst.bsky.social), "My Letter to the NYT Editor," Bluesky, August 15, 2024, https://bsky.app/profile/jrothst.bsky.social/post/3kiktnuob272s.
67. Saul Geiser, *SAT/ACT Scores and College Admissions: An Analysis of the Role of Standardized Test Scores in College Admissions* (Center for Studies in Higher Education, University of California, Berkeley, March 18, 2020), https://cshe.berkeley

.edu/sites/default/files/publications/2.rops.cshe.1.2020.geisersatactommitted_variables.3.18.2020.pdf.

68. Bastedo, et al., "Contextualized High School Performance."
69. "Caltech Announces Updates to Admissions Practices," California Institute of Technology, September 18, 2023, https://www.caltech.edu/about/news/caltech-announces-updates-to-admissions-practices.
70. Emily Yu, "Decision Making for Standardized Tests," *The California Tech*, June 4, 2024, https://tech.caltech.edu/2024/06/04/decision-making-for-standardized-tests/. Also see Michael Gutierrez, Eneko Arrizabalaga, and Mahak Mathur, "President, Provost, and VP of Student Affairs Convene Faculty," *The California Tech*, February 6, 2024, https://tech.caltech.edu/2024/02/06/president-provost-vpsa-convene-faculty/.
71. For more on how high-income students are more likely to be rewarded when SAT scores are evaluated in context, see Bastedo et al., "Contextualizing the SAT."
72. Am I the only one who thinks of "binders full of women" when I hear "hundreds of low-income students with 1400s"? Okay, just me? For discussion of the issue in the Dartmouth report, see Cascio et al., "Report from Working Group," 6.
73. Vigdor, "Here's a Sentence."
74. Controlling for additional variables, our CAF Co-LAB research team found that low-income enrollment was higher at highly selective schools under test-optional in some of the models that we ran analyzing IPEDS data. Rosinger et al., "Exploring the Relationship."
75. See Bruce Sacerdote, Douglas O. Staiger, and Michele Tine, "How Test Optional Policies in College Admissions Disproportionately Harm High Achieving Applicants from Disadvantaged Backgrounds," No. w33389 (National Bureau of Economic Research, 2025), https://www.nber.org/system/files/working_papers/w33389/w33389.pdf, 16 for a more in-depth analysis of some of the arguments they advanced in the original Dartmouth report. My thoughts on the paper: It makes it sound like Dartmouth didn't admit any high-achieving low-income students under test-optional admissions when Dartmouth certainly did, they just weren't the group that the team seems to prefer (those with higher test scores). Their main takeaway is that score inclusion is linked with a higher likelihood of admission for low SES students when compared to non-submitting low SES peers. Still, that doesn't mean that simply requiring score submission will result in huge gains in low SES student admission, because score inclusion for lower SES, relatively high-scoring students might overlap with other characteristics in the application that aren't accounted for in the analysis. Now, if required score inclusion is paired with new massive investments in financial aid (which Dartmouth is trying to do), we might see increased economic diversity, but the independent causality is hard to prove given the concurrent investment in financial aid.
76. Christopher Bennett, Brent Evans, and Christopher Marsicano, "Taken for Granted? Effects of Loan-Reduction Initiatives on Student Borrowing, Admission Metrics, and Campus Diversity," *Research in Higher Education* 62 (2021): 569–99; Zachary Mabel, Michael D. Hurwitz, Jessica Howell, and Greg Perfetto, "Can Standardizing Applicant High School and Neighborhood Information Help to Diversify Selective Colleges?," *Educational Evaluation and Policy Analysis* 44, no. 3 (2022): 505–31.
77. Sean F. Reardon, Rachel Baker, Matt Kasman, Daniel Klasik, and Joseph B. Townsend, "Can Socioeconomic Status Substitute for Race in Affirmative Action College

Admissions Policies? Evidence from a Simulation Model," white paper, Educational Testing Service, 2015, https://www.ets.org/Media/Research/pdf/reardon_white_paper.pdf.; Sean F. Reardon, Rachel Baker, Matt Kasman, Daniel Klasik, and Joseph B. Townsend, "What Levels of Racial Diversity Can Be Achieved with Socioeconomic-Based Affirmative Action? Evidence from a Simulation Model," *Journal of Policy Analysis and Management* 37, no. 3 (2018): 630–57.

78. "Q&A: Undergraduate Admissions in the Wake of Supreme Court Ruling," *MIT News*, August 21, 2024, https://news.mit.edu/2024/qa-undergraduate-admissions-in-wake-of-supreme-court-ruling-0821. In his *New York Times* article, Leonhardt lauded MIT as an exemplar for other institutions in bringing back standardized testing. While I have mixed feelings about MIT's return to required testing, I appreciate that it has already rejected legacy admissions and early decision policies, as well as its decision to limit the number of extracurricular activities that students report. While MIT sees tests as value-added, the idea that everyone should bring back required tests because MIT likes them doesn't feel like a compelling rationale. I can see how MIT feels that having a test score is useful to assess whether a student can "cut it" in their heavy math and science curriculum, although other STEM schools have gone in the other direction to experiment with test-free admissions. Nonetheless, MIT finds the SAT to be useful; okay, I can see that. At the same time, the vast majority of selective higher education institutions don't have the same overridingly dominant STEM focus as MIT. Yes, yes, I know you can be an English major at MIT.
79. There are some parallels with the example from the UC system that I discuss later in this chapter. The UC system allegedly had "thousands" of low-income and URM students who became UC-eligible through the statewide index that includes test scores. Does that mean that tests are great for equity? As Sarah Reber showed, in the end, "thousands" of students being eligible translated into a few dozen low-income and/or URM students enrolling at UC Merced. Keep on reading this chapter for more explanation. In the case of Ivies, you may have had a few hundred low-income students with 1400s who didn't submit their scores under test-optional, but I'm not sure that's going to translate into a big boom in low-income student enrollment at the Ivies. There's a long road from "eligibility" (which is much hazier at the Ivies than in the UC system) to actual "enrollment."
80. Ran Abramitzky, Jennifer K. Kowalski, Santiago Pérez, and Joseph Price, "The GI Bill, Standardized Testing, and Socioeconomic Origins of the US Educational Elite over a Century," No. w33164 (National Bureau of Economic Research, 2024). The key relevant finding is that "two major policy changes in the history of American higher education, namely the G.I. Bill after World War II and the introduction of standardized tests for admissions, had little success in increasing the representation of lower- and middle-income students at elite colleges."
81. Bastedo et al., "Contextualizing the SAT."
82. Bastedo et al., "Contextualizing the SAT," 302.
83. Bastedo et al., "Contextualizing the SAT," 302.
84. Bastedo et al., "Contextualizing the SAT," 304.
85. Raj Chetty, David J. Deming, and John N. Friedman, "Diversifying Society's Leaders? The Causal Effects of Admission to Highly Selective Private Colleges," No. w31492 (National Bureau of Economic Research, 2023).

86. More or less, they're all connected.
87. Walt Bogdanich and Michael Forsythe, *When McKinsey Comes to Town: The Hidden Influence of the World's Most Powerful Consulting Firm* (Anchor, 2022).
88. Rebecca Steinitz, "To the Editor," *New York Times*, January 27, 2024, https://www.nytimes.com/2024/01/27/opinion/sat-tests.html.
89. Another thought is that schools being test-optional or test-free won't result in a dearth of people working at top firms or going to top graduate schools. Those places will always fill their ranks, and most likely they'll still be filled with people from the most elite of the name-brand institutions.
90. Kudos to Bruce Sacerdote, who mentioned on a webinar we did for ETS that the Dartmouth report's findings were most relevant to Dartmouth and not necessarily other contexts.
91. "Smith v. Regents of University of California," Public Counsel, https://publiccounsel.org/our-cases/smith-v-regents-of-university-of-california/.
92. UC Academic Council Standardized Testing Task Force, "Report of the UC Academic Council Standardized Testing Task Force (STTF)," January 27, 2020, University of California, https://senate.universityofcalifornia.edu/_files/committees/sttf/sttf-report.pdf.
93. UC Academic Council, "Report of the STTF," 4, 35.
94. UC Academic Council, "Report of the STTF," 33. Overall, 4,931 of students who qualified through the statewide index were from low-income backgrounds; 5,609 were Black, Latinx, or Indigenous; and 5,704 were first-generation college students. This doesn't mean that 16,244 of the 22,613 were from marginalized backgrounds due to overlap between the groups. Still, the numbers are notable, before we realize that very few students actually attended a UC school through this route.
95. Caitlin Flanagan, "The University of California Is Lying to Us," *The Atlantic*, July 27, 2021, https://www.theatlantic.com/ideas/archive/2021/07/why-university-california-dropping-sat/619522/.
96. Michal Kurlaender, Sarah Reber, and Jesse Rothstein, "UC Regents Should Consider All Evidence and Options in Decision on Admissions Policy," Policy Analysis for California Education (PACE), April 22, 2020, https://edpolicyinca.org/newsroom/uc-regents-should-consider-all-evidence-and-options-decision-admissionspolicy, 13. Also, remember that only some of the 22,613 students who qualified through the statewide index were from low-income or URM backgrounds, meaning the number of low-income and/or URM students who enrolled at UC Merced due to the statewide index was even smaller than 168. Maybe about fifty, for a ballpark estimate?
97. Kurlaender et al., "UC Regents," 14. Reber also noted that technically a student "cannot be made eligible for admission (in the ETR sense) based on his or her SAT score. Students who meet the a–g requirements and take the SAT (or ACT) are 'eligible for admission to UC' regardless of their score" (14).
98. UC Academic Council, "Report of the STTF," 19.
99. Saul Geiser, "SAT/ACT Scores, High-School GPA, and the Problem of Omitted Variable Bias: Why the UC Taskforce's Findings Are Spurious," Center for Studies in Higher Education, University of California, Berkeley, March 18, 2020, https://cshe.berkeley.edu/sites/default/files/publications/2.rops.cshe.1.2020.geisersatactommitted_variables.3.18.2020.pdf, 1–4.

100. University of California, "UC Announces Record-Breaking Admissions for Fall 2024," *University of California News*, August 21, 2024, https://www.universityofcalifornia.edu/news/uc-announces-record-breaking-admissions-fall-2024.
101. Campaign for College Opportunity, "Expert Spotlight: Olufemi 'Femi' Ogundele," August 21, 2024, https://collegecampaign.org/publication/expert-spotlight-olufemi-femi-ogundele.
102. Rosinger et al., "Exploring the Relationship," 5–6.
103. Gary Clark, "A Year Like No Other: Test Free at the UC," *Admitted* (blog), at National Association of College Admissions Counselors (NACAC), August 23, 2021, https://admitted.nacacnet.org/wordpress/index.php/2021/08/23/a-year-like-no-other-test-free-at-the-uc/#more-4900.
104. Board of Admissions and Relations with Schools Systemwide Academic Senate University of California, "Annual Report on Undergraduate Admissions Requirements and Comprehensive Review June 2023," University of California, https://senate.universityofcalifornia.edu/_files/committees/boars/boars-cr-report-june-2023.pdf, 63.
105. Julie J. Park, Nancy Wong, Pearl Lo, Jia Zheng, OiYan Poon, and Kelly Rosinger, "Test-Free Admissions at Selective Institutions: Perspectives From Admissions Professionals," *Journal of College Student Development* 65, no. 4 (2024): 440.
106. Park et al., "Test-Free Admissions."
107. Park et al., "Test-Free Admissions."
108. Paul Tough, "What College Admissions Offices Really Want," *New York Times Magazine*, September 10, 2019, https://www.nytimes.com/interactive/2019/09/10/magazine/college-admissions-paul-tough.html.
109. Clark, "Year Like No Other."
110. For more on how the College Board is playing up polling data showing more favorable attitudes towards test-optional versus test-free admissions, see College Board and Morning Consult, "Student and Parent Attitudes," 19. A ninth grader told me that the College Board must be worried that they're losing money since they rolled out a new AP for Pre-Calculus, which is not seen as a college-level course at his affluent high school. You know it's bad when fourteen-year-olds are noticing these things.
111. "SAT Program Results Show Increased Participation for the Class of 2022," College Board, September 28, 2022, https://newsroom.collegeboard.org/sat-program-results-show-increased-participation-class-2022.
112. To go back to the College Board survey of students and families, interestingly enough, students ($n = 1{,}006$) and parents ($n = 605$) did view test-optional more favorably than test-free admissions. However, it may have something to do with how the College Board phrased the questions. Of respondents, only 19% of students and 17% of parents supported the option of "All students are not permitted to submit ACT or SAT scores to colleges for consideration when applying"; see College Board and Morning Consult, "Student and Parent Attitudes," 19. However, as any good pollster knows, responses to questions vary considerably depending on how the question is phrased. Test-free admissions comes off as restrictive and repressive—students are "not permitted" to submit scores. In the survey, test-free admissions is portrayed as downright draconian, while test-optional comes off as cool and open-minded: "We're just keeping things light and casual over here, just like a good dating app!" It fits the ethos of our current era of

noncommitment, where everyone wants the ability to hold off as long as possible before making a choice.

That said, I can see why the majority of students and parents in the survey voiced support for test-optional over test-free or test-required, and I don't know if you'd get radically different survey results if the question about test-free admissions was rephrased. By and large, people want to hope that they could have that extra special day where they get an awesome test score, while keeping the backup plan of not submitting scores if they are too low. Every parent wants to believe in the potential of their child. The College Board has milked this phenomenon in their messaging as well. It's a very American sensibility—don't take away my choices!

113. Bastedo et al., "Contextualizing the SAT."
114. "Yale Announces."
115. Cascio et al., "Report from Working Group," 9.
116. Bleemer, email to the author, November 22, 2024; Bleemer, "Affirmative Action and Its Race-Neutral Alternatives," 1.

Chapter 5

1. Jerome Karabel, *The Chosen: The Hidden History of Admission and Exclusion at Harvard, Yale, and Princeton* (Houghton Mifflin Harcourt, 2005); Nicholas Lemann, *The Big Test: The Secret History of the American Meritocracy* (Macmillan, 2000); Wayne Au, "Testing for Whiteness? How High-Stakes, Standardized Tests Promote Racism, Undercut Diversity, and Undermine Multicultural Education," in *Visioning Multicultural Education* (Routledge, 2020).
2. *Students for Fair Admissions v. Harvard* forced Harvard to peel back the curtain on their admissions system, and we learned a lot about how components beyond test scores influence the process. Still, both sides' experts only had access to ratings attached to certain documents (e.g., rating for a counselor or teacher letter), versus the actual letters themselves; no one had the time or resources to analyze actual letters anyway. At Harvard, the essay didn't even get a specific rating or score; it was included as part of the personal rating assigned to applicants.
3. See, for example, Jesse Rothstein, "Qualitative Information in Undergraduate Admissions: A Pilot Study of Letters of Recommendation," *Economics of Education Review* 89 (2022): 1–14.
4. In my area, getting an afterschool nanny is the holy grail of childcare—a reliable person who can pick up kids, shuttle them to activities, and help with homework. Big bonus if they can do meal prep.
5. I've had people tell me that if a kid hasn't secured a spot on a good club swim team by age eight, they may have difficulty ever getting on a team, in which case they can forget swimming competitively down the line.
6. A sad irony is that in some wealthy areas, half of the kids who do all of these things won't get to play for their high school team because there's a surplus of kids who follow the said formula for soccer, baseball, and the like.
7. Fred P. Graham, "Court Says Cities May Close Pools to Bar Racial Mix: 5–4 Ruling Backs," *New York Times*, June 15, 1971, https://www.nytimes.com/1971/06/15/archives/court-says-cities-may-close-pools-to-bar-racial-mix-54-ruling-backs.html.

8. Rachel Martin and Jeff Wiltse, "Racial History of American Swimming Pools," *NPR*, May 6, 2008, https://www.npr.org/2008/05/06/90213675/racial-history-of-american-swimming-pools.
9. "Black Youth at Highest Risk of Drowning," YMCA (originally Young Men's Christian Association), https://www.ymca.org/ystories/healthy-living/black-youth-at-highest-risk-of-drowning. In the suburbs of the greater Washington, DC, area where I live, private neighborhood swim clubs that were either officially or in essence "Whites only" proliferated as part of efforts to resist integration, with many being founded in the mid-1950s and early 1960s. Decades later, many private swim clubs continue to be predominantly White, or predominantly White and Asian American. As noted, an estimated almost 60% of African American children cannot swim. In my area, you can spend five or more years on a waitlist for your neighborhood pool. After a year or two (or five), you'll be blessed (ha) to pay $850–$1,000 or more a season to "rent" a membership. For our family, it took five years before we got to pay a depressingly high amount to get a real membership, and now in the mid-2020s, we "only" have to pay $650 or so a year to swim for three months per year. The rec center fees are not cheap here, which probably discourages swimming if you're plunking down $50 for your family every time you go to the pool. Swimming almost every day during multiple summers definitely helped my kids be comfortable in the water and learn how to swim, and it's a shame that this opportunity is so restricted in many areas.
10. Some schools offer a period built into the school day for students to participate in clubs, which naturally supports participation.
11. Example of how parental capital matters: My brother stepped up to coach his kids' debate team. Now their school gets to have a debate team run by a law school professor/former top debater on the national high school circuit, attracting more affluent families and parental capital.
12. Thank you, wonderful people of southwestern Ohio: all of my OM coaches and, for extemporaneous speaking, the late, great Ralph Bender. My immigrant parents were glad to reap the benefits of their move to the suburbs. I grumbled about having to sell raffle tickets and coupon books, but I was totally oblivious to how much parent volunteers worked to make all of our programs run. I don't know whether to be proud or a little sad that the offerings seem to have been more robust than what my kids have today, which means that I have to pitch in more.
13. Even with that support (he also drove my extemporaneous speaking team to Chicago so we could compete), I'd still categorize my parents as uninvolved by today's standards, as they rarely if ever attended any of our numerous competitions. They weren't alone, it just wasn't really a thing to have your parents at every event back then. Back then, many upper middle-class parents just dropped their kids off and wrote the checks, which sounds great to me.
14. Resource-intensive programs like speech and debate don't exist in many high schools, although initiatives like the Urban Debate League have worked to expand access.
15. Part of this might be a quirk of how elementary schools are K–6 in some school districts, so only sixth grade (I believe?) competes. Still, the fact that this activity is even available at some elementary schools when it's missing from many a lower-income high school says a lot. Kudos to some school districts that have dedicated resources so Science Olympiad can exist at Title I middle schools, a great idea.

16. Jennifer Lee and Min Zhou, *The Asian American Achievement Paradox* (Russell Sage Foundation, 2015); Julie J. Park, "It Takes a Village (or an Ethnic Economy): The Varying Roles of Socioeconomic Status, Religion, and Social Capital in SAT Preparation for Chinese and Korean American Students," *American Educational Research Journal* 49, no. 4 (2012): 624–50.
17. The popularity of spelling bees among South Asian Americans has spread to the point where the finalist pool of the Scripps spelling bee is reliably packed with South Asian American youth. Do South Asians have some magical talent for spelling? It's nothing genetic. Over time, as more South Asian American kids took up spelling, word spread within tight-knit ethnic communities. As is the case for pretty much any ethnic community, do not underestimate the power of the auntie gossip network. In the *New York Times*, a reporter noted that "over the past two decades, spelling bees tailored to South Asian children have proliferated. So have spelling bee coaching companies founded by South Asian Americans. Flyers for local bees are handed out at Indian supermarkets, and the activity is spread through word of mouth at temple events." Anna P. Kambhampaty, "How Indian Americans Came to Love the Spelling Bee," *New York Times*, July 3, 2021, https://www.nytimes.com/2021/07/03/style/spelling-bee-south-asian-americans.html. It's a prime example of how young people get socialized into an activity, which in turn is reinforced by high availability/opportunity and community actors (fliers, ethnic media, coaching companies). When a South Asian kid goes to Scripps, they likely won't feel isolated or marginalized because they are part of the dominant group. Kudos to these young people!
18. See David Card, "Report of David Card, Ph.D.," December 15, 2017, Harvard University, https://projects.iq.harvard.edu/files/diverse-education/files/expert_report_-_2017-12-15_dr._david_card_expert_report_updated_confid_desigs_redacted.pdf.
19. Thomas J. Espenshade and Alexandria Walton Radford, *No Longer Separate, Not Yet Equal: Race and Class in Elite College Admission and Campus Life* (Princeton University Press, 2009). To note, the researchers were unable to control for other factors that institutions consider, such as essays and leadership roles. Still, after controlling for variables like demographics, GPA, and test scores, having more extracurriculars was linked with admissions.
20. Card, "Report," 28. During the 2014–2019 period, 1,340 students who received a top athletic rating but no other top ratings applied to Harvard. If they were accepted on average at a rate of 88%, that translates into about 235 per year being admitted. Granted, not all of them accepted the offer of admission, but Harvard's yield is exceptionally high. Also, the 235 per year does not include students who received a top athletic rating, but top ratings in other categories, which means the number of recruited athletes/class may be higher.
21. Card, "Report," 31.
22. Students for Fair Admissions v. Harvard, "U.S. District Court District of Massachusetts Findings of Fact and Conclusions of Law Document 672," Harvard University, October 30, 2019, https://www.harvard.edu/admissionscase/wp-content/uploads/sites/6/2021/06/2019-10-30_dkt_672_findings_of_fact_and_conclusions_of_law.pdf, 56.
23. Kirsten Hextrum, *Special Admission: How College Sports Recruitment Favors White Suburban Athletes* (Rutgers University Press, 2021).
24. Hextrum was a two-time NCAA Division 1 national champion.

25. I got into a debate with a journal editor over this issue. They insisted that due to the diversity within more "omnivorous," somewhat more accessible sports (e.g., basketball, football), collegiate athletes are a fairly racially diverse group. However, I spent some time looking at rosters for two schools, Amherst (Division III) and the University of Michigan (Division I). Athletic rosters were actually less diverse than I thought they'd be. With the exception of football, most rosters were not just predominantly White, but overwhelmingly or almost all White, although there was some Asian American involvement in certain sports. Some sports, like basketball, are more diverse, although not always; it depends on the school. Still, the roster size for a sport like basketball is relatively small so the overall percentage of athletes of color at an institution is smaller than some would predict, even if some sports like basketball are more diverse. This dynamic is even more prevalent in women's sports because institutions don't sponsor football (oftentimes the most racially diverse sport) for women at the intercollegiate level. To make up the imbalance in roster spots per Title IX requirements, women's sports feature additional teams that tend to be almost or completely White.
26. For another key study highlighting inequality in athletics and activities, see: Uma Mazyck Jayakumar and Scott E. Page, "Cultural Capital and Opportunities for Exceptionalism: Bias in University Admissions," *Journal of Higher Education* 92, no. 7 (2021): 1109–39.
27. Julie J. Park, Brian Heseung Kim, Nancy Wong, Jia Zheng, Stephanie Breen, Pearl Lo, Dominique J. Baker, Kelly Rosinger, Mike Hoa Nguyen, and OiYan A. Poon, "Inequality Beyond Standardized Tests: Trends in Extracurricular Activity Reporting in College Applications Across Race and Class," *American Educational Research Journal* 62, no. 2 (2025): 336–77. In case you are wondering, the 860,003 students represent 41% of the overall number of students who submitted an application through Common App during the two cycles. Applications were almost all submitted prior to the pandemic lockdown which hit in March 2020, meaning that we have test scores for the sample, and students' academic and extracurricular records reflect "the before times" of the era that existed before we all ended up spending way too much time on Zoom.
28. A bit on the process: The first step was building a dictionary, basically a list of key terms that fit the construct of interest. Through a process called "topic modeling," the computer first generated a list of the first hundred or so clusters of how students were writing about their accomplishments. Our team parsed through these and identified terms that reflected each construct. We also parsed through rubrics and training materials obtained from admissions offices, and mined our collective knowledge to add to the list of terms, which involved some fun reminiscing about high school activities here. We also ran additional lists for different racial/ethnic and socioeconomic groups to be able to spot terms that popped up more frequently within subpopulations but that were not as common within the overall sample. From there we engaged in a process using the ever-so-technical term of *hashing it out* to reconcile disagreements about whether certain terms really reflected top-level leadership or honors/awards. We also had to think of numerous rules or qualifiers to help direct the computer—for example, when the computer might spot a term within a phrase, but the term or phrase didn't really reflect top-level leadership or honors/awards. We also brainstormed ways that students might commonly misspell terms (chiarman, anyone?). The end result was a dictionary that you can access on Brian Kim's GitHub website, at https://github.com

/brhkim/extracurricular_trends_common_app. There are some additional steps that you can read about in the paper posted on the CAF Co-Lab website, www.cafcolab.org/research, or you can read the paper as now published in the *American Educational Research Journal* 62, no. 2 (see earlier endnote for full citation). We then fed the dictionary to the computer, which went through almost six million applications and let us know how many times the terms were spotted in the overall database.

29. Now there are AI tools that students can use to jazz up their activity descriptions, but all of our data come from the pre-AI period.
30. William G. Bowen and Sarah A. Levin, *Reclaiming the Game: College Sports and Educational Values* (Princeton University Press, 2011); Card, "Report," 28–31.
31. I guess it's a good thing his board wasn't opposed to reparations, but still.
32. Yes, I recognize that this would create its own mess, but one can dream.
33. Annette Lareau, *Unequal Childhoods: Class, Race, and Family Life* (University of California Press, 2003).
34. Scott Morse, "Lafayette to Reduce Common App Activities Submissions," *Lafayette News*, August 2, 2023, https://news.lafayette.edu/2023/08/02/lafayette-to-reduce-common-app-activities-submissions/. Lafayette's president is Nicole Hurd, who founded the College Advising Corp and was already sensitive to the opportunity gap in extracurricular participation/reporting.
35. MIT does not use Common App.
36. Pearl Lo, "Reconsidering Extracurriculars in Admissions," *Inside Higher Ed*, June 5, 2023, https://www.insidehighered.com/opinion/views/2023/06/05/reconsidering-extracurriculars-admissions-opinion.
37. Yes, extracurricular activities are great, but I'm glad that I got to balance them with an abundance of mall, TV, and sleepover time when growing up about an hour away from Vivek Ramaswamy, who evidently had no time for such frivolities. See David Brooks, "Vivek Ramaswamy Is Uninvited from My Sleepover," *The Atlantic*, December 30, 2024, https://www.theatlantic.com/ideas/archive/2024/12/david-brooks-ramaswamy/681188/.
38. Hey, that's after working a full-time job and taking care of two high-energy children who will pay your Social Security one day. Needless to say, I'm amazed at all of the things I used to do with my spare time before having kids. This is part of why student-parents are incredibly impressive. "Activity: Parent. Hours: Nonstop, endless, even in my sleep."
39. Anne Helen Petersen, *Can't Even: How Millennials Became the Burnout Generation* (Mariner Books, 2021).
40. Another selective public university, the University of Illinois, Champaign-Urbana, does not require them.
41. To note, the current national student-to-counselor ratio was 385:1 in 2022–2023; see "School Counselor Roles and Ratios," American School Counselor Association, https://www.schoolcounselor.org/About-School-Counseling/School-Counselor-Roles-Ratios. That number is still an improvement over the average 482:1 ratio a decade earlier in 2012–2013. Still, there are some issues with overrelying on the national ratio as a proxy of quality in school counseling; see Tara P. Nicola, "Understanding the Recommended Student-to-Counselor Ratio's Persistence," *Journal of Education* 204, no. 3 (2024): 634–48. That said, there are obviously differences between workload and student-to-counselor ratios within and between private and public school contexts.

42. Jonathan D. Schwarz, "Lost in Translation: Elite College Admission and High School Differences in Letters of Recommendation," PhD dissertation, University of Notre Dame, 2016, 61.
43. People can only do the travel work of admissions for so long, so becoming a full-time college counselor at a private school is a typical next step for many in the field.
44. Schwarz, "Lost in Translation," 34. NACAC is a wonderful organization, playing a vital role in representing admissions professionals and working to improve the field. At the same time, public school counselors, especially those at historically underresourced schools, are less likely to be involved in the organization, and often don't have the funds (or time off) to attend the organization's annual conference, which is held smack in the middle of fall semester. I spoke with a public school counselor from a Title I school who lamented that she was one of very few counselors from schools like hers, and that counselors in similar positions could not afford to leave their schools for a professional development opportunity: Too much was going on. As a result, the heavy presence of the private school counseling crowd at such conferences further solidifies the relationships that already exist between college admissions professionals and high school counselors from more affluent communities.
45. Julie R Posselt, "Trust Networks: A New Perspective on Pedigree and the Ambiguities of Admissions," *Review of Higher Education* 41, no. 4 (2018): 497–521; Jessica M. Nicklin and Sylvia G. Roch, "Letters of Recommendation: Controversy and Consensus from Expert Perspectives," *International Journal of Selection and Assessment* 17, no. 1 (2009): 76–91.
46. Tara Nicola and Sebastian Munoz-Najar, "Writing the Same Thing? Exploring Text Similarity in Counselor Recommendation Letters," paper presented at the ASHE (Association for the Study of Higher Education) Annual Conference, Las Vegas, NV, November 18, 2022.
47. At my well-resourced but large high school, I remember feeling lucky that my counselor even knew my name; I had to go out of my way to get to know her.
48. Peter Arcidiacono, "Expert Report of Peter S. Arcidiacono," Brown University, June 15, 2018, https://www.brown.edu/Departments/Economics/Faculty/Glenn_Loury/louryhomepage/teaching/Affirmative_Action/Meeting_V/supporting_documents/Doc%20415-8%20-%20(Arcidiacono%20Expert%20Report).pdf, 48.
49. Dania V. Francis, Angela CM De Oliveira, and Carey Dimmitt, "Do School Counselors Exhibit Bias in Recommending Students for Advanced Coursework?," *BE Journal of Economic Analysis & Policy* 19, no. 4 (2019): 20180189; Frank Linnehan, Christy H. Weer, and Paul Stonely, "High School Guidance Counselor Recommendations: The Role of Student Race, Socioeconomic Status, and Academic Performance," *Journal of Applied Social Psychology* 41, no. 3 (2011): 536–58.
50. See for example Rita Kohli and Daniel G. Solórzano, "Teachers, Please Learn Our Names! Racial Microagressions and the K–12 Classroom," *Race Ethnicity and Education* 15, no. 4 (2012): 441–62; Brea M. Banks, Kara S. Cicciarelli, and Julie Pavon, "It Offends Us Too! An Exploratory Analysis of High School-Based Microaggressions," *Contemporary School Psychology* 26, no. 2 (2022): 182–94; Rita Kohli, Marcos Pizarro, and Arturo Nevárez, "The 'New Racism' of K–12 Schools: Centering Critical Research on Racism," *Review of Research in Education* 41, no. 1 (2017): 182–202.

51. Seth Gershenson, Stephen B. Holt, and Nicholas W. Papageorge, "Who Believes in Me? The Effect of Student–Teacher Demographic Match on Teacher Expectations," *Economics of Education Review* 52 (2016): 209–24.
52. Research on letters written for college applications is relatively scant, but more studies exist on letters of recommendation written for other opportunities, such as medical school residency and internships. Here we find some fairly consistent patterns, where historically underrepresented groups are written about less positively than their White and in some cases, Asian American peers. For example, one study found that "grindstone" words were used more commonly for students of color, while standout words like *outstanding*, *superb*, and *remarkable* were used more frequently for White students; see Alexa Powers, Katherine M. Gerull, Rachel Rothman, Sandra A. Klein, Rick W. Wright, and Christopher J. Dy, "Race-and Gender-Based Differences in Descriptions of Applicants in the Letters of Recommendation for Orthopaedic Surgery Residency," *JBJS Open Access* 5, no. 3 (2020): e20.
53. Brian Heseung Kim, Julie J. Park, Pearl Lo, Dominique J. Baker, Nancy Wong, Stephanie Breen, Huong Truong, Jia Zheng, Kelly Ochs Rosinger, and OiYan Poon, "Inequity and College Applications: Assessing Differences and Disparities in Letters of Recommendation from School Counselors with Natural Language Processing," EdWorkingPaper 24-953 (Annenberg Institute at Brown University, 2024), https://doi.org/10.26300/pmv2-r349. We thank the Bill & Melinda Gates Foundation and Common App for their support of the work. This paper was accepted by *Research in Higher Education* shortly before the book went to press, so you can see a final version there.
54. Brian Kim, "What's in a Letter? Using Natural Language Processing to Investigate Systematic Differences in Teacher Letters of Recommendation," paper presented at the 47th Annual Conference of the Association of Education Finance and Policy, Denver, CO, March 2022. On the whole, Black students' letters had fewer positive sentences and slightly more negative sentences. Teachers were more likely to talk about community engagement and leadership than academics for Black students, particularly in letters to highly selective institutions. Asian American students' letters were slightly more positive than letters submitted for White students. Teachers highlighted topics such as community engagement, extracurriculars, STEM subjects, and future potential in letters for Asian American more often than for White students. Asian American students' letters contained less emphasis on intellectual promise. Kim did not find any difference in discussion of personal/character-based topics (e.g., character excellence, diligence) between Asian Americans and Whites in teacher letters sent to highly selective institutions.
55. Raj Chetty, David J. Deming, and John N. Friedman, "Diversifying Society's Leaders? The Causal Effects of Admission to Highly Selective Private Colleges," No. w31492 (National Bureau of Economic Research, 2023).
56. Leslie Killgore, "Merit and Competition in Selective College Admissions," *Review of Higher Education* 32, no. 4 (2009): 469–88; Card, "Report," 28–31.
57. Nicola and Munoz-Najar Galvez, "Writing the Same Thing?"
58. Rothstein, "Qualitative Information," 13.
59. Rothstein, "Qualitative Information," 1.
60. Jesse Rothstein, *The Impact of Letters of Recommendation on UC Berkeley Admissions in the 2016–17 Cycle* (California Policy Lab, 2017), 28.

61. Eli Ben-Michael, Avi Feller, and Jesse Rothstein, "Varying Impacts of Letters of Recommendation on College Admissions," No. w30940 (National Bureau of Economic Research, 2023), 2.
62. For a great breakdown on how institutions shifted essay prompts after the ruling, see Sonja B. Starr, "Admissions Essays After SFFA," *Indiana Law Journal* (forthcoming), https://papers.ssrn.com/sol3/papers.cfm?abstract_id=4806726. Shout-out AM2017!
63. Michael N. Bastedo, Kristen M. Glasener, K. C. Deane, and Nicholas A. Bowman, "Contextualizing the SAT: Experimental Evidence on College Admission Recommendations for Low-SES Applicants," *Educational Policy* 36, no. 2 (2022): 282–311.
64. Jazper Lu, "Duke No Longer Giving Numerical Rating to Standardized Testing, Essays in Undergraduate Admissions," *Duke Chronicle*, February 7, 2024, https://www.dukechronicle.com/article/2024/02/duke-university-undergraduate-admissions-changes-numerical-rating-standardized-testing-essays-covid-test-optional-ai-generated-college-consultants.
65. I really did try to get it to write this book and the results weren't pretty. That said, thanks, ChatGPT, for assisting with the endnotes.
66. A. J. Alvero, Sonia Giebel, Ben Gebre-Medhin, Anthony Lising Antonio, Mitchell L. Stevens, and Benjamin W. Domingue, "Essay Content and Style Are Strongly Related to Household Income and SAT Scores: Evidence from 60,000 Undergraduate Applications," *Science Advances* 7, no. 42 (2021): eabi9031.
67. Alvero et al., "Essay Content," 7. See Mitchell L. Stevens, *Creating a Class* (Harvard University Press, 2009).
68. "Harvard Announces Return to Required Testing," *Harvard Gazette*, April 4, 2024, https://news.harvard.edu/gazette/story/2024/04/harvard-announces-return-to-required-testing/.
69. Ran Abramitzky, Jennifer K. Kowalski, Santiago Pérez, and Joseph Price, "The GI Bill, Standardized Testing, and Socioeconomic Origins of the US Educational Elite Over a Century," No. w33164 (National Bureau of Economic Research, 2024).
70. Abramitzky et al., "GI Bill."
71. What's behind the SAT/ACT's makeover from gatekeeper to beacon of equity? Besides the College Board PR machine, some institutions, such as Harvard and MIT, cite free tools like Khan Academy test prep as game changers that are leveling the playing field. Even though Khan Academy is free, the benefits appear to be pretty uneven. The practical existence of an online tool doesn't lead to equity; inequality will affect who uses these tools and how they use them.
72. See Liz Mineo, "New Study Finds Wide Gap in SAT/ACT Scores Between Wealthy, Lower-Income Kids," *Harvard Gazette*, November 22, 2023, https://news.harvard.edu/gazette/story/2023/11/new-study-finds-wide-gap-in-sat-act-test-scores-between-wealthy-lower-income-kids/.
73. See Alvero et al., "Essay Content," 1–10.
74. Alvero et al., "Essay Content," 7.
75. Rothstein, "Qualitative Information."
76. Bastedo et al., "Contextualizing the SAT." Deming's work with the Opportunity Insights team also points to how higher scoring low-income students are far outnumbered by higher scoring affluent peers; see Mineo, "New Study Finds Wide Gap."
77. See Kim et al., "Inequity and College Applications."

78. A key shortcoming (and to some, a virtue) of standardized tests is that test scores stand on their own—you just see a number; there's no qualitative component or automatic contextualization. Even if the evaluator has a sense of context for the student's circumstances through a tool like Landscape, the score still comes devoid of critical information that can explain how the score came to be: the type of test prep a student may or may not have received, the impact of the peer environment and socialization around testing, and the like. Some schools have concluded that they have enough information to contextualize and thereby assess the value of scores, but others have decided differently.

Chapter 6

1. James Murphy, "Tracking the Impact of the SFFA Decision on College Admissions," *Ed Reform Now*, September 9, 2024, https://edreformnow.org/2024/09/09/tracking-the-impact-of-the-sffa-decision-on-college-admissions/.
2. Murphy, "Tracking the Impact."
3. Anemona Hartcollis and Stephanie Saul, "Black Enrollment: How Schools Are Adapting After Affirmative Action," *New York Times*, August 30, 2024, https://www.nytimes.com/2024/08/30/us/black-enrollment-affirmative-action-amherst-tufts-uva.html.
4. Liliana M. Garces, Brianna Davis Johnson, Evelyn Ambriz, and Dwuana Bradley, "Repressive Legalism: How Postsecondary Administrators' Responses to On-Campus Hate Speech Undermine a Focus on Inclusion," *American Educational Research Journal* 58, no. 5 (2021): 1032–69.
5. Antar A. Tichavakunda, "Black Joy on White Campuses: Exploring Black Students' Recreation and Celebration at a Historically White Institution," *Review of Higher Education* 44, no. 3 (2021): 297–324; Antar A. Tichavakunda, "Taking Black Joy Seriously in Higher Education," *Change: The Magazine of Higher Learning* 54, no. 5 (2022): 52–56.
6. Confederate Memorial Hall was alive and well at my alma mater Vanderbilt until 2016.
7. Those efforts included initiatives like Posse, which brings students from urban regions to campuses they probably would not have otherwise considered. My alma mater Vanderbilt was the founding partner campus. While I know that cohorts of New Yorkers have been bewildered by being suddenly plunked into Nashville, I benefited tremendously from their presence and campus leadership. For more on critical mass and the concept of dynamic diversity, see Liliana M. Garces and Uma M. Jayakumar, "Dynamic Diversity: Toward a Contextual Understanding of Critical Mass," *Educational Researcher* 43, no. 3 (2014): 115–24.
8. I say "some" because due to the lack of diversity on campus, I don't think we maximized the learning and engagement that could have happened on a more racially diverse campus.
9. A.k.a. the Big 18, and probably still growing.
10. America Counts Staff, "Maryland's Population Grew 7% to 6,177,224 Last Decade," US Census Bureau, August 25, 2021, https://www.census.gov/library/stories/state-by-state/maryland-population-change-between-census-decade.html.
11. Julie J. Park and Young K. Kim, "Interracial Friendship and Structural Diversity: Trends for Greek, Religious, and Ethnic Student Organizations," *Review of Higher Education* 37, no. 1 (2013): 1–24; Uma Jayakumar, "Can Higher Education Meet the Needs of an

Increasingly Diverse and Global Society? Campus Diversity and Cross-Cultural Workforce Competencies," *Harvard Educational Review* 78, no. 4 (2008): 615–51; Nicholas A. Bowman and Julie J. Park, "Interracial Contact on College Campuses: Comparing and Contrasting Predictors of Cross-Racial Interaction and Interracial Friendship," *Journal of Higher Education* 85, no. 5 (2014): 660–90; Nida Denson and Mitchell J. Chang, "Racial Diversity Matters: The Impact of Diversity-Related Student Engagement and Institutional Context," *American Educational Research Journal* 46, no. 2 (2009): 322–53.

12. Peter Blau and Joseph E. Schwartz, *Crosscutting Social Circles: Testing a Macrosocial Theory of Intergroup Relations* (Academic Press, 1984), 13.
13. Julie J. Park, *When Diversity Drops: Race, Religion, and Affirmative Action in Higher Education* (Rutgers University Press, 2013).
14. Literally, there was a dialogue program called "Race Matters."
15. I don't want to minimize interracial friendships between Whites and Asian Americans because they don't happen as often as you'd think, even in communities dominated by the two groups. That said, opportunities to form interracial friendships with Black and/or Latinx students were severely limited due to the mentioned conditions.
16. Bowman and Park, "Interracial Contact."
17. Liliana M. Garces and Courtney D. Cogburn, "Beyond Declines in Student Body Diversity: How Campus-Level Administrators Understand a Prohibition on Race-Conscious Postsecondary Admissions Policies," *American Educational Research Journal* 52, no. 5 (2015): 828–60.
18. Julie J. Park, *Race on Campus: Debunking Myths with Data* (Harvard Education Press, 2018). I critiqued this myth in chapter 3 of *Race on Campus*, which I like to refer to as the "Malia Obama effect," meaning that we see students like Ms. Obama attending places like Harvard and then overgeneralize to the overall population thanks to a combination of cognitive bias and our own ignorance.
19. Park, *Race on Campus*. Yes, on average, Black students enrolled at selective colleges and universities are from higher socioeconomic backgrounds than Black students enrolled in community colleges. However, White students are much more likely to come from affluent backgrounds than Black students at selective institutions. As Derek Bok and Howard Bowen noted in their classic examination of selective college admissions, *The Shape of the River*, Black students were seven times more likely to come from the lowest socioeconomic category than White students (14% versus 2%) on such campuses. (Inclusion in the category meant that students came from both a low-income background *and* they were a first-generation college student.) Overall, 71% of Black students came from families categorized as middle-class, and 15% from families that fit the criteria for being from an upper-class socioeconomic background. That may sound like Black students enrolled at selective institutions are overwhelmingly affluent, but to compare with other populations, 44% of White students came from the highest socioeconomic bracket, and only 54% of White students came from families categorized as middle-class. As I discuss in *Race on Campus*, some of the public confusion around SES and Black students comes from some strategic cherry-picking and collapsing of SES-related categories.
20. "In 2022, the median White household held $284,310 in wealth, more than six times that of the median Black household at $44,100 and 4 times that of Hispanic households

at $62,120. Black households have a wealth gap of 85% compared to White households, and Hispanic households have a wealth gap of 78%." Joseph Dean, "The Racial Wealth Gap 1992 to 2022," National Community Reinvestment Coalition, October 2024, https://ncrc.org/the-racial-wealth-gap-1992-to-2022/. Dean comments on how the wealth of Black households is often concentrated in assets related to homeownership, which is highly precarious given the instability of the housing market.

21. Regarding Black students being admitted but choosing to attend another institution, see Eddie Comeaux, Thandeka K. Chapman, and Frances Contreras, "The College Access and Choice Processes of High-Achieving African American Students," *American Educational Research Journal* 57, no. 1 (2020): 411–39. Tracking enrollment trends across both race and SES will be difficult, and we're even having trouble tracking trends by race/ethnicity following the ruling.
22. Gordon W. Allport, "The Nature of Prejudice," *Addison-Wesley* (1954): 59–82.
23. For a powerful example of how these dynamics affected students during COVID-19, see Anthony Abraham Jack, *Class Dismissed: When Colleges Ignore Inequality and Students Pay the Price* (Princeton University Press, 2024).
24. Julie J. Park, Nida Denson, and Nicholas A. Bowman, "Does Socioeconomic Diversity Make a Difference? Examining the Effects of Racial and Socioeconomic Diversity on the Campus Climate for Diversity," *American Educational Research Journal* 50, no. 3 (2013): 466–96.
25. Julie J. Park, Nicholas Bowman, Nida Denson, and Kevin Eagan, "Race and Class beyond Enrollment: The Link between Socioeconomic Diversity and Cross-Racial Interaction," *The Journal of Higher Education* 90, no. 5 (2019): 665–89.
26. Park et al., "Does Socioeconomic Diversity Make a Difference?"; Jeffrey F. Milem, Paul D. Umbach, and Christopher T. H. Liang, "Exploring the Perpetuation Hypothesis: The Role of Colleges and Universities in Desegregating Society," *Journal of College Student Development* 45, no. 6 (2004): 688–700.
27. Donut talk makes me wonder what the ideal donut metaphor is for a college. Apple fritter? Strawberry donut from the famed Donut Man in Glendora, CA?
28. Elizabeth Aries, *Race and Class Matters at an Elite College* (Temple University Press, 2008).
29. Milem et al., "Exploring the Perpetuation Hypothesis."
30. Park et al., "Does Socioeconomic Diversity Make a Difference?"
31. Nathan Ferguson, "In Media Res: Tracing #ConcernedStudent1950's Story," *Society Pages*, November 15, 2015, https://thesocietypages.org/cyborgology/2015/11/17/in-medias-res-tracing-concernedstudent1950s-story/.
32. For an overview of the research, see "Amicus Brief of the American Psychological Association in Support of Respondents," Harvard University, August 2022, https://www.harvard.edu/admissionscase/wp-content/uploads/sites/6/2022/08/Amicus-Brief-APA5.pdf.
33. See Park, *When Diversity Drops*, for how this dynamic played out at "California University" as Black enrollment dwindled.
34. See, for example, Jessica Blake, "U of Alabama Requires Black and LGBTQ Groups to Relocate," *Inside Higher Ed*, August 26, 2024, https://www.insidehighered.com/news/quick-takes/2024/08/26/u-alabama-requires-black-and-lgbtq-groups-relocate.
35. "Title VI of the Civil Rights Act of 1964," US Department of Labor, https://www.dol.gov/agencies/oasam/regulatory/statutes/title-vi-civil-rights-act-of-1964.

36. "Racial Incidents and Harassment Against Students," US Department of Education, March 10, 1994, https://www2.ed.gov/about/offices/list/ocr/docs/race394.html.
37. Julie J. Park and Jonathan Feingold, "How Universities Can Build and Sustain Welcoming and Equitable Campus Environments," Campaign for College Opportunity, October 2024, https://collegecampaign.org/wp-content/uploads/2024/10/2024_WelcomingCampuses_FINAL_web.pdf, 8.
38. Office of the Governor of Virginia, "Executive Order 1: Ending the Use of Inherently Divisive Concepts, Including Critical Race Theory, and Restoring Excellence in K-12 Public Education in the Commonwealth," January 15, 2022, https://www.governor.virginia.gov/media/governorvirginiagov/governor-of-virginia/pdf/eo/EO-1-Ending-the-Use-of-Inherently-Divisive-Concepts.pdf, 3.
39. Jared Cole, "Race Discrimination at School: Title VI and the Department of Education's Office for Civil Rights," Congressional Research Service, July 21, 2023, https://crsreports.congress.gov/product/pdf/IF/IF12455.
40. Park and Feingold, "How Universities Can Build," 8–9.
41. See for example Bill Chappell, "Alabama Governor Signs Ban on DEI Funds,'" NPR, March 20, 2024, https://www.npr.org/2024/03/20/1239635678/alabama-dei-funding-ban-divisive-concepts.
42. Art Coleman, "Overreaching and Misleading: An Analysis of the U.S. Department of Education's February 14, 2025 'Dear Colleague' Letter on Diversity, Equity and Inclusion Policies and Programs," EducationCounsel, February 19, 2025, https://www.nelsonmullins.com/storage/AyMazdRpsfYnAbDpCNQE6kE7LsCIke5ATu3C7g09.pdf.
43. Anthony Lising Antonio, "Faculty of Color Reconsidered: Reassessing Contributions to Scholarship," *Journal of Higher Education* 73, no. 5 (2002): 582–602.
44. Nicholas A. Bowman and Nida Denson, "Institutional Racial Representation and Equity Gaps in College Graduation," *Journal of Higher Education* 93, no. 3 (2022): 399–423.
45. "UCI Black Thriving Initiative Cluster Hiring Program," University of California, Irvine (UCI), https://inclusion.uci.edu/core-programs/uci-black-thriving-initiative/uci-black-thriving-initiative-cluster-hiring-program/.
46. "UCI Black Thriving," UCI.
47. The dead link for the program is "Anti-Racism Initiatives," University of Michigan Office of the Provost, https://provost.umich.edu/initiatives/anti-racism/. You can use the Wayback Machine to see what used to exist: https://web.archive.org/web/20250421181428/https://provost.umich.edu/initiatives/anti-racism/#expand.
48. "University of California Presidential Postdoctoral Fellowship," University of California President's Postdoctoral Fellowship Program, https://ppfp.ucop.edu/info/. Yes, let's not forget how much women, including White women, have benefited from affirmative action.
49. We heard about this in departments when conducting interviews with faculty: The programs and funds were there, but senior faculty refused to use them. C'mon people, free money! Don't turn it down! Also, am I the only one who thinks of Statler and Waldorf from the Muppets when I hear "old boys' club"?
50. See for example KerryAnn O'Meara, "Leveraging, Checking, and Structuring Faculty Discretion to Advance Full Participation," *Review of Higher Education* 44, no. 4 (2021): 555–85; KerryAnn O'Meara, Lindsey L. Templeton, Damani K. White-Lewis, Dawn Culpepper, and Julia Anderson, "The Safest Bet: Identifying and Assessing Risk in

Faculty Selection," *American Educational Research Journal* 60, no. 2 (2023): 330–66. Personally I am not a rubric lover for things like evaluating assignments and so on, but it is interesting to use them for faculty searches. Committing to thoroughly reading each application and rating them systematically is cumbersome, but really forces a committee to go through every application. In the end, some of the finalists were (very talented) people who maybe would not have risen to the top if we hadn't used the rubric, and I thought the process was productive.

51. Kathryn Abrams et al., "DEI Programs Are Lawful Under Federal Civil Rights Laws and Supreme Court Precedent," memorandum, February 20, 2025, https://www.nacua.org/docs/default-source/new-cases-and-developments/2025/ogc-memo-re-trump-dei-and-sffa-2025-02-20.pdf.
52. See Nolan L. Cabrera, Jeffrey F. Milem, Ozan Jaquette, and Ronald W. Marx, "Missing the (Student Achievement) Forest for All the (Political) Trees: Empiricism and the Mexican American Studies Controversy in Tucson," *American Educational Research Journal* 51, no. 6 (2014): 1084–118; Thomas S. Dee and Emily K. Penner, "The Causal Effects of Cultural Relevance: Evidence from an Ethnic Studies Curriculum," *American Educational Research Journal* 54, no. 1 (2017): 127–66 (2017).
53. Marcia B. Baxter Magolda and Patricia M. King, eds., *Learning Partnerships: Theory and Models of Practice to Educate for Self-Authorship* (Taylor & Francis, 2023). There are also interesting developments in the "science of learning" world emphasizing the importance of background knowledge to reading comprehension and literacy. While one policy initiative is to expose early readers to curriculum that helps them build their depository of background knowledge, another is to use Ethnic Studies as a springboard to harness the already-existing background knowledge that students of color often have from their own communities. Both approaches can and should be used in combination with each other.
54. Nida Denson, "Do Curricular and Cocurricular Diversity Activities Influence Racial Bias? A Meta-Analysis," *Review of Educational Research* 79, no. 2 (2009): 805–38; Nicholas A. Bowman, "College Diversity Courses and Cognitive Development among Students from Privileged and Marginalized Groups," *Journal of Diversity in Higher Education* 2, no. 3 (2009): 182; Nicholas A. Bowman, Nida Denson, and Julie J. Park, "Racial/Cultural Awareness Workshops and Post-College Civic Engagement: A Propensity Score Matching Approach," *American Educational Research Journal* 53, no. 6 (2016): 1556–87.
55. Think STEM is immune? There's plenty of controversy in Biology, with evolution, bioethics, cloning, and the like. Should we just stop teaching Biology? A slim minority will say yes, but the majority fortunately recognizes the value of retaining the subject while working to build more inclusive environments.
56. Nicholas Bowman, Christine Logel, Jennifer Lacosse, Elizabeth A. Canning, Katherine T. U. Emerson, and Mary C. Murphy, "The Role of Minoritized Student Representation in Promoting Achievement and Equity within College STEM Courses," *AERA Open* 9 (2023): 23328584231209957.
57. Zachary Bleemer and Aashish Mehta, "College Major Restrictions and Student Stratification," Research & Occasional Paper Series, CSHE 14.2021 (Center for Studies in Higher Education, 2021).
58. Bleemer and Mehta, "College Major Restrictions," 4–5.

59. Zoey Thomas, "Florida Shut Down State Funding for Diversity, Equity and Inclusion," *Independent Florida Alligator*, January 29, 2024, https://www.alligator.org/article/2024/01/dei.
60. Thomas, "Florida Shut Down."
61. Alissa Gary, "UF Eliminates Diversity, Equity, and Inclusion Offices," *Independent Florida Alligator*, March 1, 2024, https://www.alligator.org/article/2024/03/uf-eliminates-diversity-equity-and-inclusion-offices.
62. Lori D. Patton, ed., *Culture Centers in Higher Education: Perspectives on Identity, Theory, and Practice* (Taylor & Francis, 2010).
63. Patrick McDonald, "UF Rebrands Its 'Inclusion and Multicultural Engagement' Center to Comply with State Anti-DEI Law," Campus Reform, August 6, 2024, https://www.campusreform.org/article/uf-rebrands-inclusion-multicultural-engagement-center-comply-state-anti-dei-law/26072.
64. See "West Point Shuts Down Clubs for Women and Students of Color in Response to Trump's DEI Policies," Associated Press, February 5, 2025, https://apnews.com/article/west-point-student-clubs-diversity-trump-dei-a8e992f1bbceda4bf217db6dfebd6b92. Michigan State University (MSU) put itself in an awkward position by cancelling a Lunar New Year celebration shortly after the executive order. MSU apologized later and saying that they had overreacted to the order. See "MSU Apologizes for Cancelling Chinese Student Event after Trump Order," Bridge Michigan, February 5, 2025, https://www.bridgemi.com/talent-education/msu-apologizes-canceling-chinese-student-event-after-trump-order.
65. Bowman and Park, "Interracial Contact."
66. Jennifer A. Richeson and J. Nicole Shelton, "Negotiating Interracial Interactions: Costs, Consequences, and Possibilities," *Current Directions in Psychological Science* 16, no. 6 (2007): 316–20.
67. Rodolfo Mendoza-Denton, Geraldine Downey, Valerie Purdie, Angelina Davis, and Janina Pietrzak, "Sensitivity to Status-Based Rejection: Implications for African-American Students' College Experience," *Journal of Personality and Social Psychology* 83, no.4 (2002): 896–918. For more discussion of how students benefit from both intraracial and interracial engagement, see Elizabeth Page-Gould, Elizabeth, Rodolfo Mendoza-Denton and Wendy Berry Mendes, "Stress and Coping in Interracial Contexts: The Influence of Race-Based Rejection Sensitivity and Cross-Group Friendship in Daily Experiences of Health," *Journal of Social Issues* 70, no. 2 (2014): 256–78, https://doi.org/10.1111/josi.12059; Elizabeth Page-Gould, Rodolfo Mendoza-Denton, J. M. Alegre, and J. O. Siy, "Understanding the Impact of Cross-Group Friendship on Interactions with Novel Outgroup Members," *Journal of Personality and Social Psychology* 98, no. 5 (2010): 775–93, https://doi.org/10.1037/a0017880; Rodolfo Mendoza-Denton and Elizabeth Page-Gould, "Can Cross-Group Friendships Influence Minority Students' Well-Being at Historically White Universities?," *Psychological Science* 19, no. 9 (2008): 933–39, https://doi.org/10.1111/j.1467-9280.2008.02179.x.
68. Sherry L. Deckman, *Black Space: Negotiating Race, Diversity, and Belonging in the Ivory Tower* (Rutgers University Press, 2022).
69. I thought people didn't like cancel culture? Jessica Blake, "Mizzou Renames Long-Standing Black Student Group Event," *Inside Higher Ed*, August 19, 2024,

https://www.insidehighered.com/news/quick-takes/2024/08/19/mizzou-renames-long-standing-black-student-group-event.

70. Blake, "U of Alabama Requires." Actions speak louder than words: UA recently poured millions of dollars into building a new admissions welcome center to lure new students (especially affluent nonresidents), while pushing out Black students who actually made it to UA despite its legacy of exclusion. See "New Randall Welcome Center Showcases Alabama Experience," *UA News Center*, January 19, 2024, https://news.ua.edu/2024/01/new-randall-welcome-center-showcases-alabama-experience/. For costs associated with the welcome center project, see Marc Hughes Cobb, "University of Alabama Leaders, Randall Family Break Ground on New Campus Welcome Center," *Tuscaloosa News*, April 1, 2022, https://www.tuscaloosanews.com/story/news/2022/04/01/ua-leaders-randall-family-break-ground-new-campus-welcome-center/7232069001/.
71. "Theme Programs," University of California, Berkeley Residence Life, https://reslife.berkeley.edu/academics/theme-programs/; "Living Learning Communities," UCLA Residence Life, https://reslife.ucla.edu/living-learning-communities.
72. Karen Kurotsuchi Inkelas and Matthew Soldner, "Undergraduate Living–Learning Programs and Student Outcomes," in *Higher Education: Handbook of Theory and Research*, vol. 26 (Springer, 2011).
73. Erica L. Green and Zach Montague, "Trump Cracks Down on Diversity Initiatives Celebrated in His First Term," *New York Times*, February 14, 2025, https://www.nytimes.com/2025/02/14/us/politics/trump-diversity-education-department.html.
74. Chappell, "Alabama Governor Signs Ban."
75. Chappell, "Alabama Governor Signs Ban."
76. You know what's chock full of divisive concepts? Christianity! I say that as a Christian. Sure we love unity and peace (in theory) but there are plenty of things that upset people about our faith. Check Matthew 10:35—super divisive!
77. Chris Cooper, "A Call for Moderate Voices on DEI," *Inside Higher Ed*, June 12, 2025, https://www.insidehighered.com/opinion/views/2025/06/12/call-moderate-voices-dei-opinion.

Chapter 7

1. Mark C. Henderson, Charlene Green, and Candice Chen, "What Does It Mean for Medical School Admissions to Be Socially Accountable?," *AMA Journal of Ethics*, December 2021, https://journalofethics.ama-assn.org/article/what-does-it-mean-medical-school-admissions-be-socially-accountable/2021-12.
2. Kimberly West-Faulcon, "Affirmative Action After *SFFA v. Harvard*: The Other Defenses," *Syracuse Law Review* 74 (2024): 1101–78.
3. Most seats at TJ are assigned by taking the top 1.5% of eligible applicants from the county's middle schools. Liebert, Cassidy, and Whitmore, "High School Admissions Process Deemed Non-Discriminatory," LCW Legal, June 22, 2023, https://www.lcwlegal.com/news/high-schools-admissions-process-deemed-non-discriminatory/.
4. The *SFFA* ruling overlapped with the debacle of the FAFSA roll out, and it will be challenging to understand what changes in enrollment can be tied to one versus the other.
5. "Yale's New Flexible Testing Policy," Yale University Admissions, February 2024, https://admissions.yale.edu/test-flexible.

6. Michael N. Bastedo, Mark Umbricht, Emma Bausch, Bo-Kyung Byun, and Yiping Bai, "Contextualized High School Performance: Evidence to Inform Equitable Holistic, Test-Optional, and Test-Free Admissions Policies," *AERA Open* 9 (2023): 23328584231197413; Michael N. Bastedo, Mark Umbricht, Emma Bausch, Bo-Kyung Byun, and Yiping Bai, "How Well Do Contextualized Admissions Measures Predict Success for Low-Income Students, Women, and Underrepresented Students of Color?," *Journal of Diversity in Higher Education* (2023): 1–16.
7. See for example Zachary Mabel, Michael D. Hurwitz, Jessica Howell, and Greg Perfetto, "Can Standardizing Applicant High School and Neighborhood Information Help to Diversify Selective Colleges?," *Educational Evaluation and Policy Analysis* 44, no. 3 (2022): 505–31; Christopher Bennett, Brent Evans, and Christopher Marsicano, "Taken for Granted? Effects of Loan-Reduction Initiatives on Student Borrowing, Admission Metrics, and Campus Diversity," *Research in Higher Education* 62 (2021): 569–99.
8. For benefits to moderately selective institutions see: Kelly Rosinger, Dominique J. Baker, Joseph Sturm, Wan Yu, Julie J. Park, OiYan Poon, Brian Heseung Kim, and Stephanie Breen, "Exploring the Relationship Between Test-Optional Admissions and Selectivity and Enrollment Outcomes During the Pandemic," EdWorkingPaper 24-982 (Annenberg Institute for School Reform at Brown University, 2024); Christopher Bennett, "Untested Admissions: Examining Changes in Application Behaviors and Student Demographics Under Test-Optional Policies," *American Educational Research Journal* 59, no. 1 (2022): 180–216.
9. Shout-out to all of the tired parents who are constantly trying to remind their kids the difference between *needs* and *wants*.
10. In our research, in some (but not all) models, test-free policies, when compared to test-required policies, were linked with increased enrollment among Black, Latinx, and low-income students. See Rosinger et al., "Exploring the Relationship."
11. I'll blame my own Midwestern naivete and desire to see the best in everyone, or what my more cynical East Coast friends will call a tendency to be easily impressed.
12. I am tempted to list the elite schools where I've been less impressed by alumni, but that seems unnecessary.
13. Julie Renee Posselt, Ozan Jaquette, Rob Bielby, and Michael N. Bastedo, "Access Without Equity: Longitudinal Analyses of Institutional Stratification by Race and Ethnicity, 1972–2004," *American Educational Research Journal* 49, no. 6 (2012): 1074–1111.
14. Nabeel Gillani, Eric Chu, Doug Beeferman, Rebecca Eynon, and Deb Ro, "Parents' Online School Reviews Reflect Several Racial and Socioeconomic Disparities in K–12 Education," *AERA Open* 7 (2021): 2332858421992344.
15. When our team at CAF Co-LAB analyzed Common App applicant data, we found that among selective college applicants (those applying to at least one school with an admit rate of 40% or lower), about 20–25% receive fee waivers, and 60% come from the top 20% of high-income communities.
16. Ozan Jaquette, Crystal Han, and Irma Castañeda, "The Private School Network: Recruiting Visits to Private High Schools by Public and Private Universities," *Research in Higher Education* (2024): 1–47.
17. Jeffrey Selingo, *Who Gets In and Why: A Year Inside College Admissions* (Scribner, 2020).

18. Brian Heseung Kim, Julie J. Park, Pearl Lo, Dominique J. Baker, Nancy Wong, Stephanie Breen, Huong Truong, Jia Zheng, Kelly Ochs Rosinger, and OiYan Poon, "Inequity and College Applications: Assessing Differences and Disparities in Letters of Recommendation from School Counselors with Natural Language Processing," EdWorkingPaper 24-953 (Annenberg Institute at Brown University, 2024), https://doi.org/10.26300/pmv2-r349. See *Research in Higher Education* for the final version.
19. Natasha Warikoo, *Is Affirmative Action Fair?: The Myth of Equity in College Admissions* (Polity Press, 2022), 10, 20.
20. Isabella Glassman, "Careerism Is Ruining College," *New York Times*, September 24, 2024, https://www.nytimes.com/2024/09/24/opinion/college-linkedin-finance-consulting.html.
21. Warikoo, "Is Affirmative Action Fair?"; Lani Guinier, *The Tyranny of the Meritocracy: Democratizing Higher Education in America* (Beacon Press, 2016).
22. A dystopian image pops into my head of a prep center for boosting your community service game, and something like that probably already exists. Being Korean American, I have to envision a "community service *hagwan*." *Sky Castle*, anybody?
23. West-Faulcon, "Affirmative Action."
24. Or at least before it decided to weaken some of its strongest core offerings.
25. Centerville High School, represent!
26. "Admitted Student Stats," Miami University, https://miamioh.edu/admission-aid/apply/first-year-students/admitted-student-statistics.html.
27. "Rose-Hulman Once Again Tops US News' Engineering Rankings," Techpoint, September 25, 2024, https://techpoint.org/digital-innovation/rose-hulman-once-again-tops-u-s-news-engineering-rankings/.
28. For more, see the website of Colleges that Change Lives, https://ctcl.org/.
29. Elizabeth Redden, "A Fairy Godmother for Once-Overlooked Colleges," *Inside Higher Ed*, January 3, 2021, https://www.insidehighered.com/news/2021/01/04/mackenzie-scott-surprises-hbcus-tribal-colleges-and-community-colleges-multimillion.
30. David Mickey-Pabello, "The Anti-Affirmative Action Avalanche: The Rise of Underrepresented Minority Enrollment at For-Profit Institutions," *Sociology of Education* 97, no. 1 (2024): 37.
31. Dyvonne Body, "Worse Off Than When They Enrolled: The Consequence of For-Profit Colleges for People of Color," *Aspen Institute*, March 19, 2019, https://www.aspeninstitute.org/blog-posts/worse-off-than-when-they-enrolled-the-consequence-of-for-profit-colleges-for-people-of-color/.
32. Body, "Worse Off."
33. Bastedo et al., "Contextualized High School," 8, 12. When I was in high school, no one took AP courses until junior year; now students take APs during sophomore and even freshman year—a byproduct of both relentless optimization and the College Board being eager to make more money on exams. Back then, I muddled through AP Calculus AB during senior year with my much brighter classmates, but now students are expected to take AP Calculus BC junior year, and a real STEM superstar would take it earlier. A family friend actually got a 5 on the Calculus BC AP exam in the eighth grade, which I didn't even know was possible.

34. The audacity of hope, indeed. Thanks to President Barack Obama for bringing those powerful words to the public. That phrase may seem like it's from another planet, a lifetime ago, but it's as urgent and inspiring as ever.
35. Charles Lawrence III and Mari Matsuda, *We Won't Go Back: Making the Case for Affirmative Action* (Houghton Mifflin Harcourt, 1997).

Acknowledgments

As always, there are too many people to thank. My biggest thanks goes to my family: my partner, for being a constant source of support, and my two kids, who motivate me to work for a better world, or at least a saner and more equitable admissions process. I love you all so much, and thanks for supporting my book even if it isn't as exciting as Ramona or the BFG. Lifelong thanks go to my parents for always supporting me and praying for me. Thanks, Mom, for shuttling me to every activity growing up, and to both of you for showing your love in so many ways. Thanks, Dad, for enduring your long commute in the pre-work-from-home era, so we could get a great education. Thanks to my siblings, who paved the way for me by being mediocre at piano, sports, and Korean school, but really great at (non-Korean) school, Odyssey of the Mind, and speech and debate. Thanks to all the teachers and parent volunteers at Centerville High School; I still think fondly of you and appreciate you way more now that I am a parent.

Special thanks to all the academic moms who provide endless support, especially AM2017 and the one and only Ji Son Kitani. I greatly appreciate Michelle Espino, Candace Moore, Bridget Turner Kelly, and Chris Travers for holding down our academic fort while I was on sabbatical. Thanks to the University of Maryland, College Park and Will Liu for giving me the time that I needed to write this book, and Kimberly Griffin for being a great dean and friend. Thanks, Nick Bowman and Zach Bleemer for letting me pick your brains on standardized testing. Special thanks to Liliana Garces for writing a wonderful forward and of course, the awesome team at the College Admissions Futures Co-Laborative: OiYan Poon, Kelly Rosinger, Dominique Baker, and Brian Kim. Our wonderful graduate students, past and present, include Nancy Wong, Pearl Lo, Joseph Strum, Jia Zheng, and Stephanie Breen. Thank you to the Bill & Melinda Gates Foundation for making much of our work possible. Thanks to Molly Cerrone for being a helpful and supportive editor, and the team at Harvard Education Press for making this book possible.

About the Author

Julie J. Park is Professor of Education at the University of Maryland, College Park. Her research addresses racial equity in higher education, addressing the campus racial climate and college admissions. She also studies the complex ways that Asian Americans experience structural advantage and/or disadvantage in the realm of education. She served as a consulting expert in the landmark lawsuit *Students for Fair Admissions* (SFFA) *v. Harvard* on the side of Harvard, and also codirects the College Admissions Futures Co-Laborative (www.cafcolab.org). She is the author of several books examining the interplay between college admissions and the campus racial climate. In *Race on Campus: Debunking Myths with Data* (Harvard Education Press, 2018), she tackled misconceptions about how race and diversity work in college admissions and campus life. She also wrote *When Diversity Drops: Race, Religion, and Affirmative Action in Higher Education* (Rutgers University Press, 2013), an examination of how everyday student lives in California were affected by the 1996 statewide ban on race-conscious admissions. A second generation Korean American, she earned her PhD in Education from UCLA and BA from Vanderbilt University.

Index